HELLENISTIC WAYS OF DELIVERANCE AND THE MAKING OF THE CHRISTIAN SYNTHESIS

DOVE OF THE HOLY SPIRIT ADAPTED FROM THE MOSAIC
OF THE BAPTISM OF CHRIST IN THE DOME OF THE
BAPTISTRY OF THE ORTHODOX IN RAVENNA PROBABLY CA.
450 A.D.

DRAWN BY *F. J. Woodbridge*

JOHN HERMAN RANDALL Jr.

FREDERICK J. E. WOODBRIDGE PROFESSOR EMERITUS
OF PHILOSOPHY, COLUMBIA UNIVERSITY

HELLENISTIC WAYS OF DELIVERANCE AND THE MAKING OF THE CHRISTIAN SYNTHESIS

COLUMBIA UNIVERSITY PRESS

New York and London

1 9 7 0

BR 128
G 8
R 395
cp 2

COPYRIGHT © 1970 COLUMBIA UNIVERSITY PRESS
ISBN: 0-231-03327-3
LIBRARY OF CONGRESS CATALOG CARD NUMBER: 74-137339
PRINTED IN THE UNITED STATES OF AMERICA

To

FOREWORD

This volume would have been quite impossible without the stimulus, the incentive, and the wise interpretations of Arthur Cushman McGiffert, persuasive analyst and expositor of Christian thought. During my student days McGiffert had the reputation of being the best lecturer on the Columbia campus, and many from the University crossed to Union Theological Seminary to learn from his beautifully organized lectures. He inspired me with a lasting interest in the history of Christian thought, which he carried down to the Ritschlians and Schleiermacherians of those days. He taught me most of what I have ever learned and little I have ever had to unlearn about that fascinating subject.

McGiffert enabled me to understand and appreciate the Pauline version of the Christian message, which my upbringing under the tutelage of my father, a liberal minister from the Chicago Divinity School of the 1890s, had led me to underestimate. McGiffert also emphasized the great importance of Irenaeus in uniting the two early strains of Christian sensibility, the mystical and the moral. He made clear to me what the intellectual and experiential issues involved in the controversy over the Trinity and Nicaea actually were, and conveyed something of the greatness of Origen. To the volume *The Continuity of Christian Thought* (1884), by A. G. V. Allen, the biographer of Phillips Brooks, which I found in my father's library, I owe my understanding, such as it may be, of the Trinity as a philosophical solution to intellectual problems.

My views on the distinctive message of the Prophet of Nazareth, as my friend Nathaniel Schmidt—also my father's teacher—calls him, were initially colored by Felix Adler, founder of the Society for Ethical Culture, whom I first met personally in his office when a college friend introduced me to him. I still remember his counsel to the young student: "Study Kant, not Hegel, as so many do today." My views on the noncognitive nature of religious beliefs have in fact ever since followed Kant rather than Hegel. Adler, with due humility, regarded Jesus as one of his greatest forerunners as a moral teacher; though he was incisive about the liberal Christians of those days who took the moral teachings of Jesus as final ethical truth. Many others, from my father to Tolstoi and Gandhi, and by no means least my wife, Mercedes, have influenced my interpretation of the Christian ethical teaching.

But this little volume as a whole bears the imprint, as does so much of what I have thought and written, of my teacher Frederick J. E. Woodbridge. He has colored my ideas on the Hellenistic Schools; he made central what I here call "the fortunes of Greek philosophy in Rome": his appreciation of the importance of Cicero for subsequent philosophizing in the West, later buttressed by the studies of his pupil Richard McKeon, was a revelation. The title of this book—the first half is from Henry Osborn Taylor—comes from Woodbridge: he gave yearly a notable series of talks on "The Making of Christendom." The very notion of that process as not a corruption but an enrichment—new to my Protestant soul—derives from him. I should like to think that what appreciation I may have of the Hellenistic ways of deliverance was first stimulated by him—though I owe my enthusiasm for Epicurus and Lucretius to my teacher Nelson Glenn McCrea—and that Woodbridge would view without disfavor my general approach to Patristic thinking. On Augustine, my analysis derives mainly from that of his enthusiastic admirer, McGiffert.

In my student days, we all had to choose four different

philosophers for an oral examination before the Department. One of my own four, after Plato—whom everyone selected— was Plotinos. The view of Plotinos here set forth, as the Greek Spinoza, as a pure rationalist whose thought culminates in a kind of rational mysticism, dates from the intensive study of those days. The suggestion came to me originally from my teacher Wendell T. Bush.

The dedication tries to indicate those pervasive traits of my first-born son that make it seem appropriate to inscribe to him a book dealing with ways of deliverance and salvation that can be rationally supported. Like the ancient thinkers here dealt with, he has learned from reflection on the experience of living the importance of those ways of life which religion consecrates, clarifies, and criticizes.

John Herman Randall, Jr.

Peacham, Vermont, July, 1970

ACKNOWLEDGMENTS

My debts are great to those who have carefully read the first draft of this little book and corrected its errors of fact and infelicities of expression. Foremost is my colleague and friend Paul Oskar Kristeller, who for years has conducted a course in Hellenistic philosophy, one of his major fields of specialization. Here too belongs my son, Francis B. Randall of Sarah Lawrence, who has rectified my faulty historical emphases. The chapters on Christian thought have benefited from the knowledge and the Calvinistic insights of the Reverend Mr. J. Paul Wilson of West Barnet, Vermont, who is now teaching in Cyprus. They have also been improved by two Methodist thinkers, the Reverend Dr. Paul W. Hoon of Union Theological Seminary and Dr. Edwin C. Kemble, Professor Emeritus of Physics at Harvard.

The volume owes its consistency, as usual, to Joan McQuary of the Columbia University Press. And my wife, Mercedes, has given it her usual careful and critical attention.

Once more I am indebted to Frederick J. Woodbridge, the architect, for the medallion of the Holy Spirit, adapted from the dome of the Baptistry of the Orthodox in Ravenna. The Dove thus joins the Owl of Athene and the Swan of Apollo as symbols of ancient philosophy.

CONTENTS

FOREWORD   *vii*

I. THE HELLENISTIC WORLD   *1*

II. FIRST OR GREEK HELLENISM   *13*

III. THE EPICUREAN RETREAT INTO THE GARDEN   22

IV. STOIC PEACE IN THE MIDST OF BATTLE   *37*

V. THE SKEPTICAL DEFENSE AGAINST THINKING   *56*

VI. THE FORTUNES OF GREEK PHILOSOPHY IN ROME   *80*

VII. THE REVIVAL OF RELIGIOUS PHILOSOPHIES   *100*

VIII. THE INTELLIGIBLE UNIVERSE OF PLOTINOS   *117*

IX. THE MAKING OF THE CHRISTIAN SYNTHESIS   *135*

X. THE GOSPEL OF JESUS AND THE MYSTERY CULT OF PAUL   *145*

XI. GNOSTICS, MORAL CHRISTIANS, AND APOLOGISTS   *158*

XII. THE CHRISTIAN PHILOSOPHY OF THE GREEK FATHERS: CLEMENT, ORIGEN, AND ATHANASIUS   *165*

XIII. THE LATIN CHURCH: TERTULLIAN AND ARNOBIUS   *184*

XIV. THE MANIFOLD EXPERIENCE OF AUGUSTINE   *188*

XV. THE AUGUSTINIAN THEORY OF BEING AND KNOWLEDGE *204*

XVI. THE AUGUSTINIAN DOCTRINE OF SIN AND SALVATION *214*

XVII. THE AUGUSTINIAN DOCTRINE OF THE CHURCH *224*

XVIII. THE AUGUSTINIAN DOCTRINE OF THE CITY OF GOD:
CHRISTIAN SOCIETY AND THE PHILOSOPHY OF HISTORY *228*

XIX. EPILOGUE: THE HERITAGE OF ANCIENT PHILOSOPHY *232*

INDEX *237*

HELLENISTIC WAYS OF DELIVERANCE
AND THE MAKING OF THE
CHRISTIAN SYNTHESIS

I THE HELLENISTIC WORLD

The deaths of Alexander in 323 B.C. and of Aristotle in 322 B.C. mark the end of one phase of civilization and culture, and the beginning of another. "Greece" is gone; what we call "the Hellenistic world" has now taken its place. We encounter, of course, much that has persisted, much historical continuity. But in a genuine sense there is a new form of society, with a new background, new problems, and above all new intellectual interests. It is a world we moderns can understand: it is so much like our own. The citizen of New York, were he set down in ancient Athens of the classical fifth or fourth century, would be bewildered: he would feel at home in Alexandria. Moderns admire and may even worship classical Athens; they would probably hate to have to live in such a tightly structured community. But they can understand and sympathize with the life of Alexandria, Rhodes, or Pergamum. Then, too, Hellenistic civilization and culture endured for a thousand years, whereas "Greece" in the classic sense lasted a mere century and a half—from the battle of Marathon, in 490 B.C., to the death of Aristotle in 322 B.C.

In this Hellenistic culture, there were intellectually two primary factors. First was the heritage of classic Greek thought. For a millennium this heritage was reworked and reconstructed, with very little in the way of fundamentally new ideas acquired. The rest of ancient philosophizing is largely a rearrangement of ideas that had been worked out in the earlier Hellenic or Greek period. But on the other hand, men certainly confronted new intellectual problems; and they encountered them with new feelings, new emotions, and hence with new values. In consequence, the absence of major new ideas did not mean an absence of thinking: there was in fact an intense intellectual activity.

This whole process of reconstruction of the Greek heritage we conventionally speak of as a gradual Orientalization[1] of men's attitudes and thinking. In a sense, it was a final victory for Persia, a victory that had for a brief interval been staved off at Marathon and Salamis. The Hellenistic and the later universal Roman empires were fundamentally Oriental monarchies, complex commercial societies, quite alien to the simple life of the older Greek *poleis* or city-states. What we conventionally designate as the triumph of Christianity in that Hellenistic world means a conquest of Greek values by those of the Oriental cultures, of Persia, Palestine, Mesopotamia, and Egypt.[2]

Hellenistic intellectual life, finally organized and brought to a synthesis in the Christian system that transmitted it to posterity, is the story of the rationalization, as we call it, of the non-Greek values, attitudes, and problems of the diverse Mediterranean world, in terms of concepts found in earlier Greek thought. It is the first great raid, the first great act of what Scott Buchanan has called "intellectual piracy," made on Greek thought by societies with a quite different kind of social and cultural experience, the first great remaking of Greek thought to fit an alien texture of human experience.

[1] For Hellenistic civilization, "Oriental" means the cultures of the great Near Eastern civilizations of the Mediterranean world.

[2] In the West, the Middle Ages were at first thoroughly Oriental in this sense. The immediate heir of Greece and Greek culture was not medieval Europe, but the rich civilization of the Arabs. Not until they began to learn of and from Greece from the Arabs they encountered in Sicily and in Spain did the Western Europeans begin to abandon their originally Oriental culture inherited directly from closing ancient times. The Byzantine Empire, wth a few renaissances of Greece, remained until its demise Oriental, and Russia inherited much of this culture.

In the development of Hellenistic civilization, we can distinguish three main stages. First was the age of Greek empires, from 323 to 146 B.C., the date of the final conquest of the Greek East by the legions of Rome. The second stage is the period of rapid decline that ensued, which lasted from 146 B.C. to the establishment of the Roman Principate of Augustus in 30 B.C. The third stage is the gradual revival of Hellenism under the Roman Empire, after it managed to achieve a working form of government for the Mediterranean world, and the synthesis of that Hellenism with Oriental values. This third stage lasted on to whenever we choose to terminate ancient intellectual life—traditionally, this occurred with the closing of the philosophic schools in Athens by Justinian in 529 A.D. A thousand years of intellectual activity had by then ended. But there was no real change in 529 A.D. The basic change had already taken place, when men turned from the Greek search after truth to the pursuit of deliverance and "salvation" as their central goal. By 529 A.D. the way of salvation had been perfected.

The first of these three stages, the age of Greek empires, presents us with an international world, uncomfortably like our own. The Peloponnesian War had left the Greek city-states exhausted. The age of independent, sovereign, and warring city-states, with more or less democratic polities, had been followed by an age of great military empires, ruled by autocratic dictators. All the Greek mainland had fallen into the hands of Philip of Macedon, and had then been swallowed up in the empire of Alexander. The Greek cities had managed to achieve what they called "liberty," but they had failed miserably to effect political unification and organization[3]—as we have so far failed in our own world. That is, the city-states had failed to effect unification and organization through rational

---

[3] See Herbert J. Muller, *Freedom in the Ancient World* (New York, 1961), especially ch. 7, "The Failure of Classical Greece."

cooperation. The union and organization they so desperately needed was in the end forced on them by military power. Even that union, as we might expect, was not intelligently administered till centuries of experience had been won.

At Alexander's death, his empire was divided again by his generals. There were left three great powers: Egypt under the Ptolemies, with its capital at Alexandria, which speedily became the greatest city in the whole Mediterranean world; Syria and its neighbors under the Seleucids, with its capital at Syrian Antioch; and Macedonia under the Antigonids, which lacked a fixed capital, but possessed a commercial center at Corinth, and an intellectual center at Athens. In this international world, there were also a number of lesser powers, which from time to time rose and fell again. There were smaller Greek states and leagues of states, like Pergamum on the coast of Asia Minor. There was the island of Rhodes, dominating a commercial league of free city-states. This whole Eastern Mediterranean was much like what we used to call euphemistically "Christendom," or what with equal euphemism we today call the "Free World." There was a unity of civilization and culture, with a basic unity of economic and commercial relations, combined politically with international struggles and competition.

The second stage, the period of decline, from 146 B.C. to the assumption of power by Augustus in 30 B.C., was the period of the Roman conquest and consolidation of the Eastern Mediterranean. Since the Greek world had not exhibited the political intelligence or sense to work out an organization in any other way, in the end political unity was forced upon it by universal military conquest. Economically, this was a period of the emergence of great social problems: the rise of capitalism, of economic imperialism, of class conflicts, of international and civil wars.

The Roman conquest of the Eastern Mediterranean was at first, according to our modern historians, an almost unmitigated disaster. The Romans of the last century of the Republic seemed not capable of ruling their new Empire intelligently. They almost ruined Greece economically, and they well-nigh ruined Italy itself in the process. The Eastern provinces were at first given over to economic exploitation; the population of the Greek mainland itself even declined. Commerce with the East was seriously impaired. Piracy began to flourish, preying on the traders. The Romans themselves at home were demoralized and corrupted: they began to fall, with their newly gotten wealth, into all the typical ruling class excesses. The Roman proletariat was corrupted, and made servile. All this was the first wages of empire. For Rome this disintegration lasted from around 202 B.C., when Carthage was finally conquered at Zama and the Western Mediterranean absorbed, until the appearance of Augustus.[4]

During this period also the rebellious Oriental nationalisms began to submerge the thin veneer of Hellenism Alexander had spread throughout the East. India, Bactria, Parthia, broke away from the political sway of the Greek world. Egypt, which had enjoyed an imposed upper layer of Greeks and Greek culture, began to reassert its native traits; the Jewish colony in Alexandria began to take over the leadership in both commerce and culture. Asia Minor at this time became largely Judaized.

With the establishing of the Roman Principate in 30 B.C., conditions slowly improved. Hellenism began gradually to re-

[4] See M. Rostovtseff, *History of the Ancient World,* Vol. II, *Rome* (Oxford, 1927); see also his *Social and Economic History of the Roman Empire* (Oxford, 1926), and his *Social and Economic History of the Greek Empires* (Oxford, 1941). The best general account is still Paul Wendland, *Die hellenistisch-römische Kultur,* 3d ed. (Tübingen, 1912).

vive. Augustus and his successors instituted a workable administrative system for their huge Empire. But Rome did not start as an organizing power: recent ancient historians tell us that for long it was far from being the best-governed empire of antiquity. It took, in fact, some four centuries for the Romans to perfect the rudiments of imperial administration. It was not until the later days of Diocletian and Justinian that the Romans acquired enough experience to justify their subsequent reputation as able administrators.

Rome, in fact, contributed one thing preeminently to that ancient world. It was not its own culture that appealed to other peoples. Rome had no science to offer, its art was monumental but hardly distinctive, its literature—*pace* the Renaissance scholars—remained silver rather than the gold of Greece. Rome gave the Mediterranean world one thing—peace. And for long it gave peace, not by wise government, but by sheer force and power. The early Roman Empire is thus a cardinal illustration of the value of sheer peace—of peace even without freedom. And that peace soon came to outweigh every other shortcoming of Roman rule. For it eventually made possible the development of the richest, the most enduring, the most enlightened and humane civilization the Western world has ever enjoyed, the only one the West can offer to compare with that of China, which was likewise made possible by one thing, and by one thing alone, the establishment of peace. The lesson of the Roman Empire is that if you can secure and maintain peace, nothing else fundamentally matters. For with peace, and with time and patience and great effort, everything else can in the end be achieved.

Peace—the *Pax Romana*—gave scope to commerce, which was carried on not primarily by Romans but mainly by Greeks, Jews, and Syrians. It gave scope to the spread of Enlightenment, which was diffused not by the Roman administrators but chiefly by the Greeks. The Romans themselves remained about as enlightened and intelligent as the old British civil servants administering the British Empire, after training in Oxford and Cambridge.

The *Pax Romana* enabled the whole Mediterranean world to share, to assimilate, to digest, what any part of it, any cultural tradition, had to offer. Claudius was the first really Hellenistic emperor; he was followed by the Flavians and the Antonines, with Hadrian and Marcus Aurelius as outstanding. Under Rome, the Orient did, to be sure, ultimately win out; but Greek ideas were there, as an essential ingredient, to be incorporated into the final synthesis, there to be handed on to those who came later.

Intellectually, the Hellenistic period furnishes a great contrast with the classical Athenian times. In the Athenian age, we find a time of original thinkers, of pioneer discoverers. Athenian culture was founded on the life of the city-states. It exhibited "freedom," it was politically minded. Life still seemed to be a social achievement, a work of intelligence.

Secondly, men's attitude was what we call today "naturalistic." The world and life were taken in their own terms, for what they were found to be. Problems were treated in their own domain, as something to be solved by skill and intelligence, by what Aristotle called "practical reason." Such a "naturalistic" attitude seems about the hardest perspective of all for the human mind to attain.

Thirdly, Athenian thought was fresh and original. Men felt no weight of past tradition, of an imposing cultural heritage to which submission must be made. The Greeks did not even have to study the Greek language. They could hence look at

man and the world directly; there is in them the constant
appeal to everyday observation and experience, as in Socrates'
continual citation of the arts and crafts.

Finally, the Athenians exhibited, in Aristotle, a universal
intellectual interest, justifying his famous observation, "All
men by nature desire to know." Aristotle, we are told, left only
botany unexplored. His pupil Theophrastos supplied the lack
in his *History of Plants*.

In marked contrast, the Hellenistic Age is a period of
teachers and prophets, rather than of thinkers. There was for
it always a Greek culture there to be studied and pored over—
this was the overwhelming intellecttual fact in Hellenistic
experience. Men could no longer begin with Nature and man's
experience of it; they had first to study the teachings of the
earlier Greeks. To be sure, as contrasted with the later Scholas-
tics, personal experience remained fundamental, as in Augustine himself, perhaps the most consummate experiencer of
all time. But that experience when won had to be construed
in terms of traditional Greek concepts and categories. Men
could no longer approach their world with a freshness and
originality. And even the great Hellenistic systems of thought,
except those of the Neo-Platonists, came at the beginning of
the long Hellenistic period. The later Hellenistic Age looked
back at that first creative century with a reverence equal to
what they bestowed on the classic Greeks—but they still looked
back. Toward the end, there were only reconstructions, eclectic and syncretistic.

The Greek city-state was gone, with its political life of par-
ticipation. There was now instead a Great Society. The change
was almost as momentous as that effected in the later Western
world by our Industrial Revolution. The naturalistic attitude
and approach have disappeared. Sir Gilbert Murray gave this
change the classic designation, "the failure of nerve." Men's

confidence, their sense of skill and intelligence and achievement, as sources of power, were gone.

The moral problems of the individual were now made
central; other intellectual concerns faded into the background.
Thinkers concentrated on a way of life, a way of deliverance,
of salvation. There was a turning to religious escape from a
society and a world from which men were now, in our
Hegelian phrase, "alienated." At first, deliverance was sought
in the world. Then, as this longing grew, salvation was looked
for *from* the world.

It was, in the phrase of Graham Wallas, a Great Society.[5]
Horizons were broadened, but the problems now seemed too
hard, too insoluble. The issues of class and national adjustment
proved too much for men. It is not that the world was actually
going to pieces; in fact, much of it was economically far
richer, with far more material accomplishment. But—it seemed
too big, too complicated. What could even an emperor, a
philosopher-king, like Marcus Aurelius, hope to do with the
problems? Confidence was lost, as in many quarters it has
been lost by the more alienated in mid-twentieth century.

The ancient world lacked the one great asset on which we
can rely: the power of applied science and technology. Hence
they developed no philosophy of "social control." That was
clearly, to our modern prejudices, their greatest need. But they
had really little to control. There was no instrument of technology to be guided and directed. The first Hellenistic centuries did indeed see some significant technological advance—
larger ships, water wheels, the introduction of cement. But on
the whole, the Romans were too practical to bother; the
Greeks, we say, were too aesthetic, too contemplative. For both,
slaves were too cheap to encourage the Alexandrian impulses

[5] See Graham Wallas, *The Great Society* (New York, 1916).

toward technology. Ludwig Edelstein[6] has added, the failure
to build science into a cumulative tradition; new "schools"
were always being started, with little sustained continuity. In
any event, whatever the underlying reasons, there was a
failure of Greek science and Roman practicality to join hands.
And when the power came, it was what Henry Adams has
called the power of the Virgin, not the power of the dynamo.[7]

Two fundamental cultural currents became dominant.[8] On
the one hand, there is the widespread individualism. For the
average man, all sense of social responsibility was lost; that
is to be found only in the Roman ruling class. The individual
man was submerged. Stoicism alone had a social philosophy,
foreshadowing the later Christian ideal of "catholicity." It became the philosophy of Empire, of administrators bearing the
Roman's burden, an idealistic philosophy of Empire. But it
was able to give even faithful administrators no sense of joy
in social life, no real motive for performing their necessary
function. They were carrying on from a sheer sense of duty.

As the counterpart to this ruling-class social philosophy of
Stoicism, there was only individualism for the now dis-
franchised Greeks, which went side by side with a growing
sense of cosmopolitanism. The ideal of freedom from sur-

----

[6] Ludwig Edelstein, "Recent Trends in the Interpretation of Ancient Science," *Journal of the History of Ideas,* XIII (1952), 573-604.

[7] Henry Adams, *Mont-Saint-Michel and Chartres* (Boston, 1913; privately
printed, 1904).

[8] On Hellenistic culture, see W. W. Tarn, *Hellenistic Civilization* (London,
1930); Moses Hadas, *Hellenistic Culture* (New York, 1959). For more detailed
studies, consult: J. P. Mahaffy, *Greek Life and Thought to the Roman Conquest* (2d ed.; London, 1896), and *The Silver Age of the Greek World*
(Chicago, 1906); Henry Osborn Taylor, *Ancient Ideals,* 2 vols. (2d ed.; New
York, 1913), and *Deliverance* (New York, 1915); Samuel Dill, *Roman Society
from Nero to Marcus Aurelius* (2d ed.; London, 1905), and *Roman Society
in the Last Century of the Western Empire* (2d ed.; London, 1899). P.
Wendland still stimulating.

rounding life became the aim of all the Schools, "self-sufficiency," *autarkeia*. The Epicureans called it "tranquillity,"
the Stoic "integrity," the Skeptics, "indifference." The Platonic
faiths and mysticisms had their own names, primarily
"ecstasy." Political ties and associations gave way to the social
bond of friendship, and to the brotherhood of schools and
sects.

Literature now exhibits this individualism. There emerges a
vogue for biography, and the analysis of character. History begins to emphasize persons: compare Polybius with Thucyd-
ides. There are now written love poems and love stories,
short stories or idylls, lyrics expressing personal emotion.
There appear for the first time prose novels of character and
adventure. Comedy becomes realistic: Menander and the New
Comedy emerge. Sculpture and painting become realistic, as
in the Pergamum frieze and the Laöcoon.

Above all, there is now expressed an emphasis on the worth
of the individual, in himself. This is a new element, formulated in the Stoic gospel of the equality of men. We encounter condemnations of slavery, which earlier only Antisthenes the Cynic had protested against. There is emphasized
the inviolability of the individual soul. This emphasis on the
equality of all men, which in the Christians represented a
fusion of Stoicism with the Hebraic tradition, played a large
part in making the Christian gospel the core around which
all these other ideas were organized. Most moderns would
regard this new emphasis on the worth of the individual man,
a precious, perhaps the most precious, part of our entire
heritage from the Hellenistic Age.

In this new age, philosophy became definitely the guide to
a satisfying way of life. Ethics was now supreme—and not a
mere analysis of the language of ethics. Theoretical thought
largely disappears: theory exists only for the sake of such prac-

tical ends. Philosophy becomes primarily a source of moral strength: it gives the power to endure. Philosophy becomes a kind of personal religion, offering men peace, sustaining power, freedom, independence of fortune, deliverance: indeed, offering all those satisfactions and personal integrations men have called "salvation." Philosophers now became professionals, a kind of popular clergy, offering men spiritual comfort. Alexander, after the murder of Clitus, called in some "philosophers" to give him consolation. Philosophers now began to enjoy tremendous respect, and achieved perhaps the highest status they have ever enjoyed in the West. They were now sent on diplomatic missions, as in the famous mission of Carneades to Rome. The profession was democratized: it drew on the lower classes, even on slaves, like Epictetus. It gave such lowly men the chance to ascend in the social scale, as did the later Church. But it offered training, rather than reasoned wisdom.

At first, the philosophers taught a religion founded on reason, not on revelation. This is the great glory of the Hellenistic Schools, that they taught a rational religion, a liberal religion. But men looking for peace, for sustaining power, and deliverance, and not truth, could not stay with such a rational religion. Faith was bound to win out: it offered a surer peace, a stronger power. Just so, we have found out today, when the supreme need becomes the need for salvation, for certainty, in spite of all our boasted scientific spirit, it is faith, the unquestioned revelation of some Truth, that wins out—the revelation to Hitler, or to Marx and Lenin, or to the prophets of some other Church.

To the practical, ethical spirit of Rome succeeded the religious spirit of the Orient, and it conquered. Men had lost confidence in reason, and pushed on into a kind of universal eclecticism and skepticism. All views are true—all or none.

Is it gods or atoms? In that atmosphere, faith proved inevitable. Neo-Platonism was the end, and it passed into the Christian synthesis, the counterpart of the Byzantine Oriental monarchy that now ruled the world of practice.

II FIRST OR GREEK HELLENISM

During the period of first or Greek Hellenism, during the age of Greek empires, two quite different types of intellectual interest emerged. On the one hand was the development of specialized scholarship and science, which was carried on chiefly at Alexandria and in a few other centers. Here we find the most intense scientific activity in the ancient world. The Alexandrian scientists were the true heirs of Aristotle's concern with research, and also the direct ancestors of our own modern science, which was resumed from the fourteenth century on in Western Europe.[1] The second and very different type of intellectual interest was carried on primarily in Athens,

[1] The authority in English on Alexandrian science is now George Sarton, *History of Science*, Vol. II, *Hellenistic Science and Culture in the Last Three Centuries B.C.* (Cambridge, Mass., 1959). See also the older T. L. Heath, *History of Greek Mathematics* (Oxford, 1921), *Archimedes* (Cambridge, 1897), and ed. of *Euclid's Elements*, 3 vols. (2d ed.; Cambridge, 1925); M. Cantor, *Vorlesungen über die Geschichte der Mathematik* (Leipzig, 1880-1908); Benjamin Farrington, *Greek Science*, 2 vols. (Penguin, 1944-49), a very Marxian interpretation, to be used with great caution.

Texts: Ivor Thomas, ed., *Greek Mathematics*, 2 vols. (Loeb, 1939, 1941); Morris R. Cohen and I. E. Drabkin, eds., *Source Book in Greek Science* (New York, 1948).

See also the older study, M. Matter, *Histoire de l'École d'Alexandrie* (Paris, 1840); Pierre Duhem, *Le Système du Monde* (Paris, 1913ff.); W. A. Heidel, *The Heroic Age of Greek Science* (Baltimore, 1933); I. L. Heiberg, *Geschichte der Mathematik und Naturwissenschaften im Altertum* (Munich, 1925).

in the philosophical schools there set up, the concern with philosophy as a way of life and deliverance.

Specialized research was conducted at Alexandria. Alexandria was the major city in the Mediterranean world, the chief port, the melting-pot of races, the most cosmopolitan and richest city: in a word, the most modern of ancient cities. It had been founded by Alexander himself on a sand bar near one of the mouths of the Nile. It was seized by Alexander's general Ptolemy Soter, the wisest of the generals, who did not waste time fighting like the others, but instead fostered commerce and learning, and was himself tolerant and moderate. His son, Ptolemy Philadelphus, was especially interested in science and culture. The Egyptians in Alexandria did the hard work; but the city had little cultural connection with the rest of tradition-ridden Egypt. It had originally been a Greek colony, though it never was a city-state.

The Macedonians were the ruling class, and there was a large settlement of Greeks, who formed the upper class and the craftsmen. There soon followed a large colony of Jews from Palestine. The Jews speedily took the lead in both commerce and thought. But they were soon assimilated to Greek or Hellenic culture, and became thoroughly Hellenized, more Greek than many of the Greeks themselves, who began to "go native" and Egyptian.

Two great cultural institutions were set up in Alexandria, the Library and the Museum. Under Ptolemy Philadelphus the Library possessed some 400,000 scrolls, or 110,000 original works of Greek authors, a figure later increased to 700,000. It secured the library of Aristotle, and also the library that had been built up at Pergamum. On conquering that intellectual center, Mark Antony presented its library to Cleopatra: think of giving her a library! The position of Librarian was a post of honor, held by poets, scholars, and scientists, as when Archibald McLeish headed the American Library of Congress.

The Museum was literally a temple consecrated to the Muses. It had thirty to fifty Fellows, presided over by a priest; so naturally British scholars say, "It was just like an Oxford college." But it was a government institution, unlike the Schools of Athens, which were private corporations. It was devoted primarily to research and erudition. It edited the texts of Greek authors, but spent more and more time on teaching. Its most original work was done in the sciences, in mathematics, medicine, and natural history. To it were attached large zoological gardens; and it sent out geographical exploring expeditions all over northern Africa. At Alexandria also other colleges were later set up. The Jews early had a Yeshiva from which came the Septuagint, the seventy scholars who translated the Hebrew Scriptures into Greek in the third century B.C., and which Philo of Alexandria attended. A Christian college was set up under the Antonine emperors, the Didaskeleion, reputed to have been founded by St. Mark the Evangelist. Of this college, Clement of Alexandria and Origen were heads.

There were other Hellenistic intellectual centers: above all Rhodes, where Poseidonios the Stoic taught the last century B.C.; Antioch in Syria, which became a Christian teaching center, conservative and strongly under Oriental or Persian influence. For a time Pergamum flourished. There were also many other lesser teaching centers, like Tarsus, where St. Paul learned to become a Hellenized Jew. Under Ptolemy VII, who was a good bit of a tyrant, Alexandria itself declined, between 146 and 48 B.C. Syracuse flourished for a time under Archimedes.

The investigation carried on in Alexandria was both in literary scholarship and in science. In connection with the first, the science of grammar was worked out for the Greek language, dictionaries were compiled, rhetoric fostered, and philological study carried on. The greatest editors of older texts were Callimachus and Aristarchus of Samathrace, who served as Librarians. The Alexandrian scholars also spent time on what were literally *belles lettres*. These writings were academic and not popular; the best known of them are the *Idylls* of Theocritus.

The sciences were fostered by independent and specialized study, till about 200 A.D., when a religious interest replaced the earlier scientific concern. In natural history, great collections were made, following the lead of Aristotle's biological interest. Geography was made critical and mathematical. Large expeditions were sent out, and exact maps and measurements prepared. Eratosthenes (276-195 B.C.) was the greatest geographer, both mathematical and critical. Maps were drawn by Hipparchus, and, best known of all to posterity, by Claudius Ptolemy (c.150 A.D.), the last great Alexandrian scientist except for the mathematicians. Strabo was a more popular and descriptive geographer: he wrote the Baedeker of the ancient world, still quoted for the Mediterranean tourist in the *Guides Bleus*.

In medicine, the Greek school of Hippocrates of Cos (d. 372 B.C.), was fused with the Egyptian school (who appear in Herodotus as the first medical specialists). Hierophilus (c.300 B.C.) taught; Erasistratus (30 B.C.) was the first great dissector, and an accurate anatomist. Celsus (50 A.D.) gave his name to the later Renaissance physician Paracelsus ("equal to Celsus"). Galen (120-200 A.D.) wrote a textbook on medicine, his *Canon* or *Ars Medica*, the text used by the later medieval Italian medical faculties, from Salerno on to Padua and Bologna; he was essentially a systematizer.

In mathematics, the *Elements of Euclid* were compiled, systematizing earlier Greek geometry; they were collected under Ptolemy Philadelphus. Archimedes of Syracuse (287-212) wrote a book on conic sections. Apollonios of Perga (247-205) wrote eight books on *Conic Sections*. In the late fourth century A.D. Diophantos developed a kind of algebra. Pappus, and Hypatia, familiar through Charles Kingsley, were the very last Alexandrian scientists and mathematicians.

In astronomy, then essentially a branch of mathematics, Aristarchus of Samos, teaching in Alexandria from 280 to 264 B.C., developed the heliocentric hypothesis. He also calculated the sizes and the distances from the earth of the sun and the moon, using a method today regarded as correct. By general repute, Aristarchus was the best Greek astronomer. Eratosthenes was an indefatigable measurer and calculator. Hipparchus, first at Rhodes and then from 146 to 126 B.C. at Alexandria, was the greatest astronomical observer. He had extensive tables, and possessed spherical geometry; he measured the precession of the equinoxes, and the exact length of the solar year. Finally, Claudius Ptolemy (150 A.D.) wrote his *Megalē Syntaxis*, known in Arabic later as "Al Megisti," the standard medieval textbook on astronomy. He made many geometrical calculations, though he was essentially a systematizer of the tradition: he was not interested in novel hypotheses like Aristarchus' heliocentric theory. He was content with a machinery of calculations that would "save the appearances" or observations.

The names in mechanics are those of Archimedes of Syracuse, who worked out statics and especially hydrostatics, and made many practical inventions: the screw for raising water, still in use on the Nile; burning mirrors for focusing the sun on enemy ships and destroying them; cranes, etc.; and Hero of Alexandria, who had a primitive steam turbine. Indeed, many "Yankee" inventions are reported from Alexandria, like devices for automatically opening temple doors when the worshiper approached. But slaves were too cheap to apply this inventive genius to manufacturing.

By the time of Hadrian, the religious schools of the Jews, the Christians, and the Platonists had come to overshadow the scientific Museum. In Athens, philosophy as a way of life and of deliverance, not as scientific inquiry, had long been carried on. But it is well to remember that this new interest was accompanied at the same time by the vigorous scientific activity at Alexandria and Rhodes, just recounted. This need not surprise those accustomed to see our immense energy in scientific research carried on side by side with the human and anthropocentric concerns of the Phenomenologists and the Existentialists. The one major philosophical current familiar to us the Hellenistic Age refused to develop and support was a scientific experimentalism that would be both scientific and humanistic in its concerns at the same time. There was no Hellenistic John Dewey, and no scientific naturalism directed to human welfare.

As the British scholars like to say, Athens was the Oxford of the Hellenistic world, while Alexandria was its Cambridge. Athens came to have a conservative, humanistic university; and it remained a quiet college town, till the rise of Neo-Platonism around 200 A.D. Then the intellectual center of this humanistic interest also shifted to Alexandria. It was Corinth that had become the commercial center of the Greek mainland, as is familiar during the travels of St. Paul.

Athens contained four philosophical Schools: the Academy, the Lyceum, and the newer Garden and Porch. They were all four founded before 300 B.C., that is, at the very beginning of the long Hellenistic period. They all became more and more teaching colleges, what has been called by moderns the

"University of Athens." They offered an upper-class education such as Oxford—or Princeton—used to do, in the not too distant past. The aristocracy of the entire Mediterranean world sent its sons to study at Athens, especially, after about 100 B.C., the Roman upper class. Cicero's son and his nephew attended, and some of Cicero's best letters are addressed to them as students in Athens. Cicero himself studied in Athens, as a graduate student, for a term of six months, hearing lectures and discussing eagerly with the Greek thinkers. He gives a vivid account of this experience at the beginning of Book V of the *De Finibus.* These were actually the great men his Roman teachers had told him of with awe. The Romans were, in fact, much like modern Fulbright scholars in England. This was really Athens! One could visit the Academy, where Plato and Carneades had taught. One could see the very house of Sophocles. This was the beach where Demosthenes rolled pebbles under his tongue, practicing oratory. Here was the tomb of Pericles. Why, this was historic ground!

The Schools were private foundations; they were finally given endowments by the cultivated emperors, especially by Hadrian and Marcus Aurelius. They continued in existence under their "Scholarchs" till finally all the philosophers were expelled from the Empire under Justinian in 529 A.D. and fled to Persia.[2]

At first, the Lyceum, under Aristotle and his successor, Theophrastos, was the most important. Under the latter we are told it enjoyed some two thousand students. The Lyceum grew more and more devoted to positive science, especially with Dicaearchos and Aristoxenos,[3] following Aristotle's own developing interests. But science went to the larger cities, especial-

---

[2] Since this historic date rests on the evidence of a single manuscript, it has never been questioned until quite recently.

[3] Best known as author of the only surviving Greek treatise on music.

ly to Alexandria. Even Aristotle's own library, including the manuscripts of his scientific lectures—our Aristotle—is rather dubiously reported to have been lost completely by the Lyceum. At this time only Aristotle's Platonizing early dialogues were known and published. Aristotle himself was taken as a faithful disciple of Plato, as one of the Platonists. In any event, the Lyceum after several generations became negligible, and served as a mere undergraduate college. In Cicero's day, before the manuscripts of the lectures were rediscovered, it could be disregarded. Cicero could hold seriously that Aristotle agreed in everything save his terminology with the Stoics. Then in 70 B.C., Andronikos of Rhodes, the Scholarch of the Lyceum, edited and issued the newly found manuscripts. This step initiated in the Lyceum the study, not of the world, but of the text of Aristotle. Thereafter, among the scholars in the Lyceum, we encounter the names only of editors and commentators, most famous of whom was perhaps Alexander of Aphrodisias, Scholarch from 198 to 211 A.D., a commentator with a rather Platonic interpretation of the more Platonistic passages in the Aristotelian text, like the one about the "*Nous* that makes all things"—the so-called "Active Intellect."

After 529, Peripateticism went to the East, where the Arabs found it in Bagdad when they came upon the larger scene. It was carried on in the East until the eleventh century, when a combination of fanaticism and mysticism among the Eastern Moslems drove it to take refuge in Moorish Spain. Here it was found by the medieval Latin Christians, when the Spanish conquered Toledo in 1085 A.D.

After Plato's death the Academy also became primarily a college of liberal arts under Speusippos and Xenocrates. They had a marked mathematical interest, and practically lapsed into Pythagoreanism, as Aristotle complained. This situation lasted until 240 B.C., when the Academy was definitely losing out to the aggressive Stoics. Then Arkesilaos brought philosophic Skepticism into the Academy's teaching. Thereafter, for over two centuries, till the shift to Middle Platonism, and then to what we call Neo-Platonism, the "Academic" philosophy was synonymous with the position of Skepticism. It thus appears in the writings of David Hume, who was steeped in Cicero.

But the Schools of Athens were not merely teaching colleges. They became the headquarters of the four great philosophic sects of the Hellenistic world, the four philosophical denominations or liberal religions.

This later function is mainly known to us through Roman writings, set down when the four philosophies had become established ways of deliverance or religions, and had come to accept the world. Of the founders of the two new Schools, the Garden and the Porch, Epicurus and Zeno, we possess only "fragments," with three letters of the former, together with what Diogenes Laertios tells us. We do have the writings of three later Roman Stoic moralists, Epictetus, Seneca, and Marcus Aurelius, and those of Cicero, whose most original thinking, on social philosophy, was Stoic; and we have the poem of Lucretius the Epicurean.

Otherwise, what these Schools had come to stand for in the later Hellenistic world is known to us largely through the popular manuals of Cicero. Therefore it is well to read Cicero about them; the scholars, in fact, get much of their materials from him. If one wants to contrast the Epicureans with the Stoics, and to find out about Academic Skepticism, one can read Cicero's *De Finibus,* his *De Natura Deorum,* and his *Academica* and *Tusculan Disputations.* In each of the first two, an Epicurean begins by expounding his doctrine; he is then refuted by a Stoic, who goes on with his own gospel. Finally both are demolished by an Academic Skeptic, who concludes with the last word. The Academy was Cicero's own old school tie.[4] These popular manuals of Cicero, largely paraphrases of standard texts of the Schools, are very revealing as to what the Schools and their teaching had come to mean by Roman times—by the last century of the Republic.

[4] See below, chapter 6.

III THE EPICUREAN RETREAT INTO THE GARDEN

The Epicureans were the first to feel the spirit of the new age. They offered a way of life, a way of deliverance—what was in fact a secular religion. They had no interest whatever in knowing, in *nous,* in *theōria.* They were almost completely individualistic and socially irresponsible. Yet during their long history they never changed; and so in Roman times they remained the most Greek of the philosophic schools. That fact largely explains why they lost out. For them life is still, as for the Greeks, a work of art, though now a very modest one, an art ordered by intelligence, an individual masterpiece. Civilization still appears, in Lucretius, as the human use of natural materials. In this sense, Epicureanism remained the most naturalistic of the religions of the Hellenistic Age. It tried to found itself on a purely secular theory of the world. Epicurus appears as a sort of Herbert Spencer, offering an encyclopedia of second-hand information to support a preconceived gospel. Of course, to later antiquity Epicurus did not seem to be founding his religion on science, as he has seemed during the modern period. Science at that time meant either the mathematical tra-

dition associated with Platonism, or the inquiry and investigation of the medical tradition and of Aristotle. Epicurus was
not consciously trying to capture the prestige of science for his
way of deliverance, for atomism had in that time no scientific
prestige.

Indeed, the chief criticism directed against the Epicureans
in antiquity, by the Academics down to Cicero, is not that their
view is irreligious, or even morally inadequate, but that it is so
unscientific. It completely fails to make the world intelligible,
it fails to explain the world man encounters. Cicero is quite
prepared to admit that the Epicurean ideal of the Wise Man
very much resembles the ideal of the Stoic Sage. But, he goes
on, "Epicurus committed the capital offense in natural philosophy," by "admitting something without any cause"—the
"declination" or "swerve" of his atoms.[1] He denies infinite
divisibility, in his very conception of an ultimate "atom" or
"indivisible." He should really have studied mathematics,
which would have taught him the impossibility of an "indivisible." He thinks the sun is only so large as it appears, some
"one foot" across. Why did nobody teach him any astronomy?
He has no conception of force, of efficient cause. He knows no
logic, he has no test of scientific verification. He accepts sense
observation, the immediate appearance of phenomena, uncriti-
cally.

The standing reproach brought against the Epicureans is
that they are so uneducated, so ignorant of scientific knowledge. Epicurus himself not only wrote in a barbarous Greek,
with no style; his followers were forbidden to read any writings
but his own. And, significantly, the only answer Cicero makes
his Epicurean spokesman, Torquatus, give to these charges in
the *De Finibus,* is, Why should we study literature, which is

---

[1] Cicero, *De Finibus*, Bk. I, vi, vii.

a mere childish amusement, all right for schoolboys, but not for grown men with serious concerns? Or why should we study the sciences, which not only set out from false premises, but which, even if they were true, would make our lives no pleasanter? Clearly, to the ancients the Epicureans were not so much like Herbert Spencer, with his scientific knowledge, genuine if secondhand and incomplete, as like the Christian "Scientists"; that is, they based their distressing gospel of salvation on a very loose and weird conception of what science is.[2]

What was central for Epicurus was not disinterested inquiry, but a gospel of salvation. And that gospel is simple: it is freedom from pain, *ataraxia*, "imperturbability," tranquillity of soul, peace of mind.[3] This is not the freedom to *enjoy* anything

[2] For the charges of Cicero and the answers of Torquatus, see *De Finibus*, Bk. I, vi, vii, xxi. Good summary in A. E. Taylor, *Epicurus* (New York, 1910).

[3] Epicureanism, Texts: in Diogenes Laertius, Bk. X; H. Usener, *Epicurea* (Leipzig, 1887), basic collection of texts. C. Bailey, *Epicurus, the Extant Remains* (Oxford, 1926), Greek texts wth English trs.; complete Bailey tr. in W. J. Oates, *The Stoic and Epicurean Philosophers* (New York, 1957). Carlo Diano, *Epicuri Ethica* (Florence, 1946). G. Arrighetti, *Epicuro, Opere* (Turin, 1960), includes fragments from papyri; Eng. tr. in Jason L. Saunders, *Greek and Roman Philosophy after Aristotle* (New York, 1966), pp. 47-57.

Lucretius, *De Rerum Natura*, many texts and Eng. versions. Text: C. Bailey (Oxford, 1913). Text and tr., W. H. D. Rouse (Loeb, 1924; 3d ed., 1937). Eng. trs.: H. A. J. Munro (London, 1864); W. E. Leonard (Everyman, 1921).

Studies: W. Wallace, *Epicureanism* (London, 1880); A. E. Taylor, *Epicurus;* G. Santayana, *Three Philosophical Poets* (Cambridge, Mass., 1910), ch. 2; G. E. Woodberry, *The Inspiration of Poetry* (New York, 1910), pp. 172-202.

Fuller Studies: C. Bailey, *The Greek Atomists and Epicurus* (Oxford, 1928); F. M. Cornford, *Principium Sapientiae* (Cambridge, 1952), pp. 12-30; E. Bignone, *L'Aristotele Perduto e la Formazione Filosofica di Epicuro*, 2 vols. (Florence, 1936); N. W. De Witt, *Epicurus and His Philosophy* (Minneapolis, 1954); R. D. Hicks, *Stoic and Epicurean* (New York, 1910); G. K. Strodach, *The Philosophy of Epicurus* (Evanston, 1963). J. Masson, *Lucretius, Epicurean and Poet* (London, 1909); J. M. Guyau, *La Morale d'Épicure* (Paris, 1878); C. Martha, *Le Poème de Lucrèce* (Paris, 1869); A. J. Festugière, *Epicurus*

at all. Democritus the atomist was known to antiquity as "the Laughing Philosopher"; his was an ethic of joy. Not Epicurus: he took no joy in anything. His gospel is hedonistic only in the very negative sense that pleasure, *hēdonē*, is the absence of pain, and the ensuing peace of mind. As against those earlier positive hedonists, the Cyrenaics, Epicurus held that the highest pleasure is not enjoyment, but rather the blessed relief from pain, especially from mental uneasiness or pain, relief from what we today call dread, *Angst*, anxiety. His is a gospel of quietism; pleasure is purely incidental to it. It is a philosophy of liberation, of renunciation of the world: it counsels, Watch, do not act!

> Sleepe after Toyle, port after stormy seas,
> Ease after warre, death after life does greatly please.[4]
>> The crown of olive let another wear;
>> It is my crown to mock the runner's heat,
>> With gentle wonder, and with laughter sweet.[5]
>>> Sweet is it, when the breakers roar,
>>> To watch the waves in wild commotion;
>>> And from the safety of the shore,
>>> See others struggling in the ocean.[6]

Epicurus was seeking a refuge, he was seeking safety. The Stoics were seeking one also, but they had to find one in their own souls—they were not granted even a garden into which to retreat. Nietzsche called Epicurus "the first decadent"; and we are told he was a lifelong dyspeptic. But whatever its psy-

---

and His Gods (Paris, 1946; Eng. tr., Oxford, 1955). W. Schmid, "Epikur," *Reallexikon für Antike und Christentum*, Vol. V (1961), pp. 681-819.

Philodemus: Herculaneum fragments, especially "On Methods of Inference"; see R. Philippson, "Philodemos," in Pauly-Wissowa, Vol. XIX, cols. 2444-2482.

[4] Edmund Spenser, *The Faerie Queene*. Bk. I, canto 9, st. 40.

[5] George Santayana, Sonnet XIII, in *Sonnets and Other Verses* (New York, 1906).

[6] Lucretius, *De Rerum Natura*, Bk. II, lines 1-2; tr. by Irwin Edman.

chological motivation and causes, the gospel of Epicurus found a ready welcome: the generation after Aristotle was ready for such teaching. Real force came into that Hellenistic world again only with the new religions, and especially with Christianity. One is impressed after reading Epicurus, or Marcus Aurelius, who shared much the same temperament, with the strength and power of the great Fathers of the Church, and of their missionary effort. Whatever else St. Augustine was, he was a Holy Terror. Hence Christianity seems to have been not a failure of nerve, as Sir Gilbert Murray has it, but rather a regaining of confidence. It did indeed save the world; but not by intelligence and reason alone.

This negative, quietistic flavor of early Epicureanism comes partly from Epicurus' own temperament. The other and later Epicureans we know about are much more robust, especially the Romans, Lucretius, and the Torquatus of the *De Finibus*. Torquatus makes Epicureanism a kind of sober Utilitarianism, a rational calculation of pleasures and pains. The passions are all to be controlled by reason, and the pleasures secured by practicing all the virtues.

The Wise Man is always happy; his desires are kept within bounds; death he disregards; he has a true conception, untainted by fear, of the Divine Nature; he does not hesitate to depart from life, if that would better his condition; the things that matter, the great concerns of life, are controlled by his own wisdom and reason.[7]

The answer of Torquatus to the charge that it is obviously un-Roman and subversive to try to get any pleasure out of life—how could one be a hedonist in a language whose only term for "pleasure" is *voluptas*?—is: the Epicurean would

[7] Cicero, *De Finibus*, Bk. I, xviii.

find his pleasure in being a perfect Roman hero, and observing good form throughout.

Lucretius, too, is not negative, like Epicurus. He is a poet, and a little mad, a chaos of passions seeking peace of mind through the vision of *Naturae species ratioque*, of "Nature's aspect and her law." He is seeking peace of mind through impersonality, through the vision of the sweep of Nature. He finds relief from his own tensions and conflicts in the joy he manifestly takes in Nature's sweep, in her "face."

Epicurus (341-270 B.C.) was a native of the island of Samos, of Athenian parentage. He early studied philosophy on the coast of Asia Minor, under followers of Democritus as well as of Plato. He began teaching at Mytilene, on the island of Lesbos, around 311 B.C. He went on to teach at Lampsacus near the Hellespont, where he began to acquire disciples. Finally, in 307-306 B.C., he set up the school called the Garden in Athens.

The school of Epicurus included women as well as men, and accepted even slaves and hetaerae. Friendship, the one natural good Epicurus recognized, became merged in the bond of the brotherhood of the Epicurean community. Later, it seems that the Apostle Paul often in his missionary efforts found the widely scattered communities of Epicureans a fruitful field for his efforts. Epicurus' major disciple, Metrodorus (330-277 B.C.), wrote extensively, attacking both Plato and Democritus.

The final editor of the compilation known as "Diogenes Laertios" seems to have been much interested in the Epicureans, for the entire last or tenth book is devoted to Epicurus. There are to be found the three Letters of Epicurus, our only writings from his hand; and also the collection of *Kyriai Doxai* or Cardinal Opinions. Fragments of an Epicurean library have been unearthed at Herculaneum, including portions of his large *Peri Physeōs* in thirty-seven books, which are published in the *Epicuro* of Arrighetti. This Herculaneum library belonged to the group of Epicureans set up at Naples toward the beginning of the first century B.C. by Philodemos of Gadara, in Syria. The writing of Philodemos *On Methods of Inference* is the only Epicurean document we possess, aside from Lucretius, and is the only one treating the Epicurean Canonic or logic.[8]

Epicureanism is the classic example of that ethical theory known as Hedonism, in which the chief good is taken to be pleasure. There are and have been in the Western tradition many varieties of hedonism, which need to be carefully distinguished. First, there is the strong, robust hedonism, the taking of a fierce joy in experience. This is the hedonism of the Renaissance, of Benvenuto Cellini. It is often magnificent and admirable, though it is hardly wise; but it is, we may say, life itself. One cannot, of course, secure all the experiences of life, as Faust, another Renaissance figure, discovered; and so such Romantic hedonists normally end as idealists, convinced they can secure it all in imagination at least. That is, like Cellini, they end as liars.

Secondly, there is the hedonism of the voluptuary, who finds sharp limits to the pleasures that prove intrinsically satisfying. He hence has to shut out and exclude much of experience. This is the hedonism of the morning after, when pleasure has turned to dust and ashes. Such voluptuary hedonists normally end as cynics: they are the Don Juans, the Casanovas. Voluptuous pleasure is impermanent, and soon passes, leaving only disillusionment. This is the wisdom of the ages: as Oscar Wilde put it, "The wages of sin is cynicism."

---

[8] See I. M. Bochenski, *Ancient Formal Logic* (Amsterdam, 1951).

Thirdly, there is the hedonism of the aesthete. He finds, the only pleasure with no morning after is aesthetic pleasure, a passive sipping of beauty. So, he counsels, eschew all else! This is the hedonism of Walter Pater, with his single rose petal in the bowl in his Oxford chambers. Such a hedonism withdraws from life, and also from art: the artist normally has a burning faith in something other than mere pleasure.

Again, there is the hedonism of the pessimists: eat, drink, and be merry, for tomorrow we die. This is about the saddest philosophy in the world, a philosophy of sheer desperation. "We are all *condemnés* to death, with an indefinite reprieve."[9] The only wise course is to drown one's sorrows, in complete disillusionment; for all faith in anything is gone.

Then, there is the hedonism of the reformer, who feels deep sympathy for the pains of others, and exclaims, "We must pass new laws against what is making men unhappy." These are the Utilitarians. Lucretius was just such a reformer, and a liberator of mankind; but he proposed to free men from superstitious fears, not from harsh laws.

Now, Epicurus himself was not robust or Romantic, he was no voluptuary, he was not an aesthete, he was not disillusioned, he was not a reformer—he was just tired. He stood for the gospel of the simple life: reduce to the barest minimum your wants and desires, and you may then be able to satisfy them.[10] "Let us eat—a crust of bread; let us drink—a cup of water; for tomorrow, thank the gods! we die." Marcus Aurelius ex-

[9] Walter Pater, *The Renaissance* (5d ed.; London, 1901), "Conclusion."
[10] Nelson Glenn McCrea, an outstanding authority on Epicureanism and on Lucretius—he taught me what Roman poetry I know—used to put it persuasively, as the essence of Epicureanism:

> The cow is in the garden,
> The cat is in the lake,
> The baby's in the coal scuttle—
> What difference does it make?

hibits the same temperament: he too was tired. Though formally a Stoic, he expresses the same philosophy, when he says, "Depart from life satisfied, for He who releases thee is satisfied." For Marcus, too, life was too much for him. Death is a hoped-for release, a deliverance from life. And the best life is a deliverance from life.

The Epicurean way is thus an anticipation of mortality, the closest possible approach on earth to the peace of death. Avoid entanglement with any vital concern, with any desire! That way lies only pain. "He who least craves for the morrow will go to meet it most happily." Reduce our wants to the barest minimum. "We must release ourselves from the prison-house of business and politics." "Live unnoticed by others"; shun all reporters and publicity. "Those desires which do not lead to pain if they are not satisfied, are not necessary": all such desires are to be stifled. "Cheerfulness on a couch of straw, is better than a golden couch, and a sumptuous table, and disquiet of mind therewithal."

Above all, flee marriage and its responsibilities, its squalling children, for: "If one once has a child, it is no longer in us to refrain from loving or caring for it." So be careful. The passion of love, even without the responsibilities of marriage and parenthood, is wholly a curse. "Sexual intercourse has never done any man any good; and he is lucky if it has not harmed him." According to the stories, it drove Lucretius to madness and suicide; and there is Lucretius' unforgettable tirade against sexual love, in Book IV of *De Rerum Natura*.

The desire to know is equally tyrannous. "Set sail on your bark, and flee every form of culture or learning!" "If we were not troubled by suspicions of the phenomena of the sky, and not concerned with the terrors of death, we should need no knowledge of Nature." Such knowledge has a wholly negative and liberating function.

"Men do not see that the draught of birth poured out for each is a deadly poison."[11] Epicurus relents, in his fear of all life and desire, on only one point: "Friendship is really pleasant." Such friendship, above all the brotherhood of the philosophic school, is the only social relationship Epicurus will tolerate.

The Epicurean way of life is thus a search for deliverance from life, a release from the concerns of living. The atomistic system Epicurus takes over because it alone promises a sure release: When you are dead, thank the gods! you will stay dead. Epicurus is afraid, not of Hell, but of just living on. He is afraid, not of death, but of life. He is afraid of fear. For mental pain, anxiety, dread, is the most intense of all, the fear of the future. Epicurus removed the fear of a future life, and of the gods, by making the world and the soul matter. The gods cannot get you; they have nothing to do with running the world, they will not even notice you. There is no Providence. Epicurus emphasizes the psychological fact that belief in Providence is a great source of anxiety.

Lucretius, of course, is more social: the priests cannot get you. He was an anticlerical because he was not a Greek but a Roman. In Greece the priests had almost no power; but in Rome, especially toward the close of the Republic, religion was made pretty consciously the "opiate of the people." By the last century B.C., Lucretius could say with much justification: *Tantum religio potuit suadere malorum.*[12]

Lucretius has of course a case in his anticlericalism. Despite its manifold services, the Church, or "organized religion," has

---

[11] These *kyriai doxai,* Cardinal Opinions or Golden sayings, are all to be found in Diogenes Laertius, Bk. X. They are also given in Jason L. Saunders, pp. 53-57.

[12] Lucretius, *De Rerum Natura,* Bk. I, line 101. "Such are the crimes to which religion leads," W. E. Leonard, (Everyman, 1921).

undoubtedly also produced more evils than any other indispensable social institution, even the family, as a Freudian might admit. This is clear to the candid today. But it is also worthwhile to suggest, what is not always so generally recognized, that there is keen insight in Epicurus' more psychological critique of religion—the role of religion itself in producing fear and anxiety. For it is a universal technique of religion to arouse fear, so that men will be impelled to do what that religion takes to be good.[13] And this does not mean merely hell-fire religions: the same holds true of our best and most enlightened forms of religion. We set out by giving men a "conviction of sin": we emphasize the "nausea" of "alienated" modern life, we reiterate that "modern man finds life meaningless."

We know today that such an overemphasis on men's guilt, which is the natural and inevitable result of this widespread religious technique, is the cause of anxiety and of assorted neuroses. Hence Epicurus possessed genuine insight in insisting that religion produces more fear and anxiety than it is able to cure. This seems to be as true of our most liberal religion as of the typical evangelist. The only catch in the argument of Epicurus is, as any psychiatrist will tell us, that unfortunately we do not eliminate anxiety and fear by just getting rid of religious beliefs. And it is obvious that both Epicurus and Lucretius would today be considered as very gifted neurotics.[14]

It is noteworthy about Epicureanism, that there is in it no trace of what has been the great motive for materialism in modern times, the possibility of the control of natural forces and of man through scientific knowledge. The Epicureans had

[13] Felix Adler, founder of the Society for Ethical Culture, used to counsel, "First make them feel a great pain, and then show them the way out."

[14] This is hardly the final word about religion, but it is worth reflecting upon. We can say, it may well be far better to be a pleasant and earnest neurotic than to enjoy the "peace of mind" preached by some fashionable preachers.

no interest in any such enterprise. Throughout modern times, materialism has been the great vision of man's control, of technology. For it, the world is a great machine, to be controlled through the manipulation of its parts. Materialism has served as the philosophy for the applied scientist, the engineer. It has enjoyed its greatest vogue among the Baconians, among those committed to Bacon's aim of "extending the bounds of human empire over Nature, to the effecting of all things possible."[15] Materialism has never been a philosophy for the pure scientists, for the "knowers," for whom knowledge is more important than control, and who hence always emphasize the intelligible structure of the universe, mind, idea, intelligible order, like Aristotle, Spinoza, Newton, or Hegel.

The Epicureans, far from being either engineers or scientists, far from being the scientific school of Hellas, as they have sometimes appeared from the perspective of modern times, were in fact the narrowest, most conservative, most intolerant, and most sterile school of all. They preached a dogmatic religion, without the slightest interest in scientific inquiry. They worshiped their founder, and would not tolerate a new idea, nor read any works but his. They formed a narrow orthodoxy, insisting on a single-minded acceptance of their creed, their negative theology, an orthodoxy which makes our own Protestant theologies seem wildly liberal in contrast. They were noted for their narrow dogmatism, their air of self-assurance: "Never doubt anything," commanded Epicurus. In five hundred years, after the first disciple, Metrodorus, who died before the founder, they produced only one follower of

[15] See my *Career of Philosophy in Modern Times:* Vol. I, *From the Middle Ages to the Enlightenment*, Bk. II, ch. 8, "The New Aim of Knowledge as Power," and Ch. 9, "The Search for a Fruitful Method," 239-55. See also John Dewey, *Reconstruction in Philosophy* (New York, 1920; rev. ed., Boston, 1948); and Fulton Anderson, *Francis Bacon: His Career and His Thought* (Los Angeles, 1962).

any note, Lucretius the poet, who was himself rigidly orthodox in creed. We have from the school only one other document of significance, the logical fragment on induction of Philodemos, dug up at Herculaneum.[16] And all this happened during an age of vigorous scientific activity.

There is hence no need to trouble ourselves greatly with explanation of the atomistic system as Epicurus adapted and reconstructed it, and of the curious jumble that was the outcome of his modifications. Epicurus furnishes a classic illustration of trying to build a philosophy on a particular scientific theory, rather than on the scientific method and spirit. He is a beautiful example, also, of what happens when religious philosophers turn to science to rationalize their religious commitments and ideals. Like all such apologists for religion who turn to scientific theories for confirmation, Epicurus completely misses the point of his selected theory, the atomistic hypothesis, as a scientific explanation of anything. He held, in his letters to Pythocles and to Herodotus, that any theory of natural phenomena is all right, so long as it dispenses with the intervention of the gods and their supposed Providence. The more alternative theories you can devise the better, for if you try to find the one true explanation, you will be trying to "know," to pursue scientific inquiry; and that will be an end to your peace of mind. Epicurus' desire for a plurality of hypotheses springs from no scientific concern, but from his fear of any involvement in scientific discovery.

Epicurus consequently takes theories that are quite contradictory, like atomism and sensationalism, and tries to combine them, because they both serve to bolster up his faith. It is significant that the only problems Epicurus is interested in explaining—he makes this quite explicit in his Cardinal Opinions

[16] See above, chapter 1, note 8.

—[17] are those that lie at the basis of men's superstitious fears. He attempts to account for the phenomena of the sky, what the ancients called *meteora,* which were taken as signs, omens, and portents, and made the basis of the auguries, and hence of priestly power. The gods might be watching and trying to influence you. Secondly, Epicurus tried to account for dreams, ghosts, visions, which must be explained through his theory of sense-perception, by means of *idola.* This theory he adopted, not as an adequate construing of knowledge—he had no interest in epistemology—but as a naturalistic and materialistic theory of ghosts and dreams. His sensationalism and *idola* theory saved his central tenet of the mortality of the soul—the dead do *not* return.

There are good accounts of the materialistic system of Epicurus in the manuals.[18] Epicurus took over atomism at second-hand from Democritus (though incidentally Epicurus is reported to have denied he had ever read Democritus; he was quite as self-assertive about his insights as Descartes, and insisted all his ideas were original with him). Where he tried to change and improve upon his Democritean sources, he succeeded only in making the theory more confused. And he mixed up atomism with certain Aristotelian theories with which it is logically inconsistent.

He added sensationalism to Democritus, not as a sound theory of knowledge, but as a useful theory of ghosts. Democritus had been no sensationalist and no empiricist: he saw clearly that the atomic theory had to be founded on reason, not on sense observation. Atoms are hardly given in immediate experience, as phenomena.

---

[17] See p. 31, note II.

[18] Especially in the little book of A. E. Taylor; though as a Platonist, Taylor is hardly too sympathetic to Epicurus, and all his criticisms are drawn from the Academic Cicero's *De Finibus.*

Epicurus added "weight" to the atoms: they all move "down." This is intelligible in the universe of Aristotle, where "down" means a definite direction: toward the center of the earth and of the universe. But it is meaningless in Democritus' infinite worlds, which have no center.

Epicurus added his most famous original idea, the "swerves" or "declination" of the atoms falling downward, to avoid determinism. "Fatalism," he insisted, "is worse than belief in the gods and their Providence." He was even afraid some necessity lurked in the disjunctive logical propositions: "To-morrow Epicurus will either be alive, or not alive." So he denied the Law of Excluded Middle—and not from any concern with a multi-valued logic.

Men, especially modern anticlericals, have often wondered why Epicurus refrained from denying the existence of the gods, in his concern to deprive them of all interest or control in human affairs. Instead of such a denial—atheism had already been maintained by Euhemerus—Epicurus assigned to the gods an eternal and happy existence in the *intermundia,* the regions between the different "worlds" or universes.

One can only surmise that Epicurus needed existent gods to account, on his principal of Idola, for the fact that so many men had beheld them in vision. But it has also often been pointed out, that they serve as concrete embodiments of the Epicurean ideal of the perfect Wise Man. They are a further indication that the Epicurean way of deliverance needed, like so many religions, an imaginative symbol for its ideal.[19]

Epicureanism is the classic illustration that materialism has served primarily as an ethical philosophy, and not as a scien-

[19] See A. J. Festugière; also Knut Kleve, "Gnosis Theon: Die Lehre von der natürlichen Gotteserkenntnis in der epikureischen Theologie," in *Symbolae Osloenses,* fasc. supp. XIX (Oslo, 1963).

tists' philosophy at all. Thus during the nineteenth century, in its heyday, materialism was advocated by Herbert Spencer, who erected a materialistic edifice to bolster up his social individualism; by Karl Marx, who used materialism as a weapon with which to attack capitalism and its bourgeois superstructure; by Santayana, the poet and aesthete, who employed materialism to inculcate "respect for Nature" as a moral principle; by Bertrand Russell, who as a young man preached materialism as an ethical gospel in his early—and since repudiated—*Free Man's Worship*. And materialism has been the philosophy of the anticlericals through all the ages, who have been driven to it, not by science and scientific considerations, but by the Established Church or the Holy Synod.

During the nineteenth century, philosophically-minded scientists were either Neo-Kantians, or phenomenalists. More recently, they have been functional experimentalists, or logical positivists. But they have rarely been materialists. Even where Dialectical Materialism reigns, the scientists have been driven to emphasize and reinterpret the "Dialectic" rather than the "Materialism" of Diamat.

IV STOIC PEACE IN THE MIDST OF BATTLE

In this chapter the emphasis will be placed upon the Greek Stoics and the Stoic system they worked out, although there have come down to us the works only of later Stoics of Roman times, who wrote when the system had been largely abandoned in the face of the penetrating criticisms of Carneades and the other Skeptics. Greek Stoicism, like Early Greek philosophy, is for us today an affair of "fragments" diligently collected from all possible sources.[1]

[1] Texts: J. H. von Arnim, *Stoicorum Veterum Fragmenta,* 4 vols. (Leipzig, 1905-1924), mostly taken from Diogenes Laertius; Eng. tr. in Jason L. Saunders, *Greek and Roman Philosophy after Aristotle* (New York, 1966), pp., 60-132; and in Gordon H. Clark, *Selections from Hellenistic Philosophy* (New York, 1940), pp. 62-105.

Zeno: A. C. Pearson, *Fragments of Zeno and Cleanthes,* with introduction (London, 1891). See Diogenes Laertius, ed. and tr. by R. D. Hicks, 2 vols. (Loeb, 1925), Vol. II, Bk. 7, "Zeno."

Cleanthes: see Pearson; also G. Verbeke, *Kleanthes von Assos* (Brussels, 1949); G. Zuntz, "Zum Hymnus des Kleanthes," *Rheinisches Museum für Philologie* (1951), pp. 337-41.

Chrysippus: see Von Arnim; also É. Bréhier, *Chrysippe et l'Ancien Stoicisme* (Paris, 1910; rev., 1951); B. Mates, *Stoic Logic* (Berkeley, 1953); M. Pohlenz, *Die Stoa* (Göttingen, 1948).

Epictetus: W. A. Oldfather, 2 vols. (Loeb, 1926-28), text and Eng. tr. Older trs.: Elizabeth Carter (1768); George Long (1877); P. E. Matheson (1916). See also E. V. Arnold, *Roman Stoicism* (Cambridge, 1911); see his article in *Hastings Encyclopedia of Religion and Ethics* (New York, 1937). A. F. Bonhöffer, *Epiktet und die Stoa* (Stuttgart, 1890).

Cicero: exposition of Stoic ethics in *De Finibus, Bk. III;* in *De Officiis* (Bks. I and II follow Panaeios); of Stoic natural theology in *De Natura Deorum,* Bk. III. *De Re Publica* and *De Legibus,* Cicero's most Stoic writings, and best accessible exposition of Stoic social philosophy, see ch. 6. All in Loeb Classics. See P. Milton Valente, *L'Ethique Stoicienne chez Cicéron* (Paris, 1956), and Alexander Litman, *Cicero's Doctrine of Nature and Man* (New York, 1930).

Seneca: *Moral Essays,* J. W. Basore, ed., 3 vols. (Loeb, 1928-1935); *Moral Letters,* R. M. Grummere, ed., 3 vols. (Loeb, 1918-1925). Eng tr. in Moses Hadas, *The Stoic Philosophy of Seneca* (New York, 1958). *Questiones Naturales,* tr. in J. Clarke, *Physical Science in the Time of Nero* (London, 1910). See Samuel Dill, *Roman Society from Nero to Marcus Aurelius* (2d ed.; London, 1905); P. Grimal, *Senèque* (Paris, 1957).

Marcus Aurelius: *Meditations,* C. R. Haines ed. (Loeb, 1916). M. Casaubon (1634), in Everyman; George Long (1862); G. H. Rendall (1898); John Jackson (Oxford, 1906); A.S.L. Farquharson (1944); collation of Long and Jackson, James Gutmann, ed. (New York, 1963). Epictetus and Marcus Aurelius tr. complete in W. J. Oates, ed., *Stoic and Epicurean Philosophers* (New York, 1957). See F. W. Bussell, *Marcus Aurelius and the Later Stoics*

Zeno of Citium in Cyprus (336-264 B.C.), the founder of the Stoic School, came to Athens at the age of twenty-two, as an Oriental businessman, to sell goods (the story runs, he was shipwrecked off the Piraeus). He came from a Phoenician community in Cyprus, and was thus "Semitic," not Greek, in background. But his merchant-father had taught him about Socrates, and in Athens he learned more. He was especially fascinated by the Cynics. One of them, Krates, seemed to him a *Socrates redivivus*. Zeno left business to study philosophy under Krates, and under every other great teacher he could find: Xenocrates and Polemon, the Academics; Stilpo and Diodorus Kronos, the Megarians. The latter taught him dialectic: Stoic logic has a Megarian background.

Zeno opened a school of his own in 294, at first called the Zenonians, but later the "Stoics," since he gave his lectures in

(Edinburgh, 1910); H. D. Sedgwick, *Marcus Aurelius* (Cambridge, Mass., 1920); Matthew Arnold, *Essays Literary and Critical*, Essay 9, "Marcus Aurelius."

Studies: Sir Gilbert Murray, *The Stoic Philosophy* (London, 1915); F. W. Bussell; E. R. Bevan, *Stoics and Sceptics* (Oxford, 1913).

Fuller Accounts: Eduard Zeller, *The Stoics, Epicureans, and Sceptics* (Eng. tr., London, 1870; rev. ed., 1962); R. D. Hicks, *Stoic and Epicurean* (N.Y., 1910), chs. 1-4; E. V. Arnold; É. Bréhier, *Études de Philosophie Antique* (Paris, 1955), chs. 11-13. See ch. 3 of Walter Pater, *Marius the Epicurean*; E. Renan, *Marcus Aurelius*, Vol. VII of his *History of the Origins of Christianity*; A. Schmekel, *Die Philosophie der Mittleren Stoa* (Berlin, 1892); A. Bonhöffer, *Epiktet und die Stoa* (Stuttgart, 1890), *Die Ethik des Stoikers Epiktet* (Stuttgart, 1894); Paul Barth, *Die Stoa* (Stuttgart, 1902); M. Pohlenz; T. R. Glover, *Conflict of Religions in the Early Roman Empire* (London, 1909), ch. 2.

Stoic Physics: S. Sambursky, *Physics of the Stoics* (London, 1959). See tr. (Loeb, 1935). See Benson Mates; and I. M. Bochenski, *Ancient Formal Logic* (Amsterdam, 1951).

Stoic Physics: S. Sambursky, *Physics of the Stoics* (London, 1959). See also Ludwig Edelstein, "The Philosophical System of Posidonios," in *American Journal of Philology*, 57 (1936), 286 ff.; K. Reinhardt, *Poseidonios* (Munich, 1921).

the *Stoa Poikilē,* the Painted Porch, the portico on the north side of the Agora, facing the Acropolis, in which were located the paintings of Polygnotus.[2] Zeno possessed a righteousness and a moral earnestness the scholars like to call "Semitic" or Oriental: he was blunt, dogmatic, an Oriental prophet rather than a Greek lover of wisdom. He affirmed, "Thus saith Reason." His message is Hellenic and Greek; but his manner and his prophetic temper and spirit seem Asiatic. He exhibits a blend of Greek and Oriental values, just suited to the Hellenistic Age and its peoples. With Zeno philosophy began to be Orientalized.

In the face of the breakdown of the older Greek tradition, of the moral code based on the city-state, now gone, and confronted by intellectual and practical skepticism, Zeno thought what Athens most needed was a message. So he proclaimed the old Greek practical wisdom and self-control as a gospel: "The Good Life is not living well. You cannot actually do that. It is being good. Every man can be good. If he is good, then he will be free. He will have no further fears or desires. He will be happy, for he will want nothing more. The way to be happy and free is to want only what you can get. You can always get what you want, if you are careful to want only what you can get."

Thus Zeno preached peace through submission, the acceptance of one's lot, adjustment to one's circumstances. This is one of the few philosophical doctrines that is absolutely true; for it is a tautology. Do you want a million dollars? Then you will never be happy, for if you get them you will then want another million. Do you want only your own income? Then you can be happy. But you will not get a million; and you

---

[2] Since the modern subway to the Piraeus runs in an open cut aross its site, it has not yet been excavated. The supposed site of Plato's Academy is the present railroad yards.

may well lose what you have now. We can thus choose between Stoicism and Romanticism. But the Romanticist is never
happy, he is always suffering from *Weltschmerz;* till he can
persuade himself he really has got everything he wants and cannot actually get—till, that is, he becomes an idealist. Epictetus
put this gospel of Zeno: "Do you want to lie with that woman?
Good Lord, man, you will never be happy! Do not want to lie
with her: want not to want to lie with her."

The second head of the Porch, Cleanthes (331-232), was a
prize-fighter from Assos in the Troad, who studied under
Krates, and then took Zeno's lectures for nineteen years by
night, working by day as a water-carrier. In the school he was
known as the "Donkey," he was so patient and plodding. He is
the most "Christian" of the Stoics: he wrote a noble *Hymn to
Zeus,* which displays all the moral strength and much of the
intellectual weakness of popular Christianity.

After thirty-two years of the leadership of Cleanthes, the
Stoics needed brains. They turned to another Phoenician,
Chrysippus (ca. 279-206) from Cilicia, the system-builder and
scholastic of Stoicism. Chrysippus was the real founder of the
Stoic system: it was said, "If there had been no Chrysippus,
there would have been no Stoa." Later scholars have called
him the "Saint Paul of the Porch." He is reported to have
said, "You give me the doctrines, and I will invent the proofs."
And he did it in some seven hundred books. After Cleanthes,
Chrysippus was a godsend.

The system was needed to show why you *ought* to submit.
Submit, because the world is a Providence, the course of the
world is good. Hence it is not only expedient to submit, but
also right. The world is a rational order. There was need for a
philosophy of Nature, a "physics," to prove it. And how can
we be sure? How can we be certain, the Good Life is just

being good? There was need for a "logic" to prove it, and to refute other views.

So the Stoic held that philosophy, which he defined as "the science of divine and human affairs," is like an orchard: logic forms the walls, physics the trees, and ethics the fruit. Or it is like an animal: logic is the bones, physics the soul, ethics the flesh. Or it is an egg: logic is the shell. Somewhere along the line the yolk and the white got scrambled. The Greeks held that physics is the yolk, and ethics the white; the Romans, that physics is the white, ethics the yolk. These three sciences were made into a dogmatic faith for the ordinary man. Stoicism became a liberal, rational religion. In Rome it emerged as practically an established religion for the upper class.

The Stoic logic is thus a support for faith. The Stoics needed to argue, especially against the Skeptics. Like every dogmatic faith, they were always getting into disputations. The Greek Stoics in particular felt this need. The Romans could hardly see why you needed to argue logically: for them it was enough just to believe. But the Romans did like to debate; so they reduced Logic largely to rhetoric.

The Greek Stoics had a real intellectual and scientific interest in logic.[3] Chrysippus developed a rounded theory, nominalistic, anti-Platonic, much like that of Antisthenes the Cynic. He invented the term "logic," which Aristotle of course did not know. Since the Stoics were staking their lives upon their faith, they needed a criterion of certainty. Some things must be absolutely certain: the mind grasps them directly, just as a fist grasps objects. The only alternative is complete skepticism, no faith at all. There must be some certain truth if we can know anything to be error. Knowledge must begin with such a *phantasia kataleptikē,* such a "grasping impression," in which

3 See Mates, and I. M. Bochenski.

the mind "grasps" or "comprehends" its object. The use of "comprehension" for a mental process is a Stoic term.

There are three kinds of judgment: assent, rejection, and "suspension of judgment," *epochē*. The mind is free to choose which attitude it will take. This is the only real freedom to be found in the Stoic system. The Stoic Wise Man or Sage will give his assent to "grasping impressions," to certainties, and only to them. Error comes from giving too hasty an assent. So the Wise Man will suspend judgment, maintain *epochē,* till he finds grasping impressions. At first, Zeno claimed that assent to grasping impressions is necessary: one cannot fail to recognize them. But he was confronted by the refusal of the unregenerate to agree with him, and was hence compelled to recognize the presence of "hindrances." When Alcestis returned to Admetus, he had indeed a grasping impression that it was his wife come back. But he did not assent, because he knew she was dead, and so he must be just seeing things. Hence to grasping impressions Zeno added freedom from such subjective hindrances. This is what *nous* had become at the hands of the Stoics. This Stoic dogmatism was an easy target for the Skeptics: they denied that man possesses any such "criterion."

All knowledge comes from such sense perception, which writes characters on the blank tablet of the soul, in a purely material way. Perception produces concepts, *ennoiai,* of two different sorts: first, those "natural" and common to all men, for which Chrysippus borrowed from Epicurus the term *prolēpseis,* "preconceptions"; and secondly, those artificially constructed in the sciences, and capable of being taught. "Reason" or *logos* is a store of preconceptions and notions; it develops by the age of fourteen. It can generate its own preconceptions. Thus the cosmos is known only through logos. These spontaneous preconceptions, like those of God, of Good, of Evil, of the Just and the Beautiful, are the same in all men. They are the same, not because they are "innate"—the Stoics were very anti-Platonic—but because they are generated by the same human experience of a world common to all men. It is these empirically learned preconceptions that are appealed to in all the Stoic arguments from universal assent, from what they called *sensus communis*, i.e., common opinion universally accepted. This is the theoretical basis of the universality of Law and Right, of the equality of all men in reason, of the whole universal and cosmopolitan social philosophy of the Stoics. This is the conception of experience at the foundation of their tremendous practical achievements. This is what the reason or logos in every man meant concretely.

These natural preconceptions are vague and inarticulate; they need development and clarification through reason to become a standard of judging. Such development is the intellectual task of philosophy. The artificial concepts are gained by abstraction from particulars, which alone exist; and the Stoics directed a nominalistic attack against Plato and Aristotle. They also systematized Aristotle's *Analytics*, and gave to them the form in which traditional formal logic was handed on. They also ruined it by destroying its purely formal character, say the moderns. They added a fourth figure of the syllogism, and hypothetical reasoning. They substituted the four *Summa Genera* for the Aristotelian categories.[4]

This whole theory of knowledge is an interesting and consistent empiricism, with provisions for the values of rationalism. As such, it is more adequate than the eighteenth-century empiricism. For it had a theory of meaning, *lekton*, as the subject matter of all judgments, inference, and reasoning. "Meaning" is to be distinguished from things, from mere

[4] Benson Mates has well analyzed these achievements of the early Stoics in logic.

words, and from mental or psychological processes, as "what
is expressed" or said: *"Lekton est id quod dicitur."* The three
others, things, words, and mental processes, are all bodily and
material; but the meaning expressed in our words is incorporeal. Along with Time and Space, it is the only incorporeal
and immaterial reality admitted into the otherwise thoroughgoing Stoic materialism.

In their second science, physics, the Stoics held that Nature
is rational: the world process is Reason, *Logos.* They sought
support for this doctrine in the ancient Ionian tradition, and
specifically in Heraclitus and his "logos," for he was congenial to them, being also a prophet. Nature is body, God is
body, the soul is body, and hence they are all as real as real can
be. Zeno's materialism came from his desire for certainty, not
from any scientific interest: its motive was like that of the
Christian doctrine of the Resurrection of the Flesh, or like
the motives that determine popular religion in general.

The cosmos is a living body: "Nature," *Physis,* is its life, or
world process. "Nature" is therefore for the Stoics not equiv-
alent to the universe as a whole, but is rather an ordering
principle: it is the "nature" of the cosmos, the "nature" of all
things. The Stoics, in worshiping Nature, were hence not
pantheists: no moral teachers are ever literally pantheists, for
they always make a distinction. The Stoics use pantheistic language when their religious feeling and piety are strong, as in
the *Hymn* of Cleanthes. But their whole faith in the rationality
of the cosmos, which justifies submission and gives practical
guidance, insists on the distinction between the world as it
seems to be, and the great rational process that really controls
it and is divine.

This Reason or Logos that is "the nature" or life of the
cosmos is, like everything else for the Stoic, corporeal and

material: they agreed with Heraclitus, it is "Fire." The human soul or reason is a part of this world reason or fire. In every man's breast there is a spark of the cosmic divine fire, which it is his duty to keep alive and burning, and at his death to bear back unsullied and pure to the great cosmic ocean of fire. In the end, the entire cosmos will return to pure fire in a final conflagration. Then the world process will begin all over again, in endless recurrence. This is a cyclical theory of history on a cosmic scale. It was revived again by Nietzsche in his doctrine of *die Ewige Wiederkunft*, in moral terms: man must be prepared to say to life, "Da capo!"

This striking Stoic materialism is utterly unlike the Epicurean materialism; it is a religious materialism. Its primary emphasis is on the providence and purpose in the world, viewed as the great process of Reason. Nothing takes place by chance; it is all the will of God or Nature. This is made material to emphasize its reality, as the popular religious imagination so often does.

The so-called Middle Stoa later developed, especially in Poseidonios of Rhodes, in the last century B.C., a physical theory with a genuine scientific interest. Poseidonios' theory differed from Epicurean atomism on two essential points, which are just those on which our own contemporary physical theory breaks most sharply with Greek atomism. Matter is not an inert stuff, but is essentially "force"; and organization controls its action throughout. The world is a system or field of forces, not a mere congeries of discrete atoms. The Stoic determinism is not the determination of events by specific and isolable chains of causation—not by chains in which the variables are limited—but determination by the whole system.

The cosmos has two *Archai* or principles, the Active and the Passive, *Causa* and *Materia*. They are inseparable: they are found together in all things, and in the cosmos as a whole. Both are body, corporeal and material. The Passive is matter without quality; the Active is a finer substance, or force, called "reason," *logos*. It is divine. It is "fire," or *pneuma*, "breath" or "Spirit"—a conception that figures in all Hellenistic religious thought. This force or Logos permeates everything, and holds all things together in a tension of opposites, an organized system of forces—the appeal is again to Heraclitus. Out of it arise the things of ordinary experience, and into it they fall back again. The Active in particular things is called their *logoi spermatiokoi,* their "seminal reasons." They give form to all that arises; they are the dynamic and formative element in all processes. These seminal reasons were taken over by the Neo-Platonists; they appear in St. Augustine and in the Augustinian tradition. These seminal reasons form the Active in the world as a whole, as the universal cosmic Logos, which appears equally as force and as providence: it is cosmic force or energy acting in determinate ways.

The chief doctrine of this Stoic physics runs, the cosmos as a whole is a rational process. What does this mean? It means that the universe has one great purpose, a good purpose, a purpose in which man can and must acquiesce. All is controlled by providence, nothing occurs by chance. What is this purpose? What is the goal of the world process? To this question, the Stoic has no answer: he is not interested. It is not mere chance, there is some reason for it all. That is enough for him. It is enough to know, there is some meaning, some direction in all events. However unsatisfying such an answer may be intellectually, it does have a tremendous sustaining power. It is all the Will of God. This is much like saying, "Father knows best, Father knows why." Parents unfortunately cannot get away with such an answer today. It is like saying, "It is all part of a process of Evolution." We may have no idea where we are going, but it does help to have the conviction that we are on the way somewhere. That seems at least better than going nowhere. And it is an immense satisfaction to know even that we are going to the Devil—especially if the other fellow does not know even that. The Stoic myth of the Eternal Recurrence makes it in the end all meaningless and irrational; but it also makes it all the more exciting.

This brings us to the Stoic ethics. For it all points to the main problem, "how shall a man find freedom and deliverance from the ills of life?" Marcus Aurelius puts it:

To say all in a word, everything which belongs to the body is a stream, and what belongs to the soul is a dream and vapor, and life is a warfare and a stranger's sojourn, and after-fame is oblivion. What then is that which is able to conduct a man? One thing, and only one, philosophy. But this consists in keeping the spirit within a man free from violence and unharmed, superior to pains and pleasures, doing nothing without a purpose nor yet falsely and with hypocrisy, not feeling the need of another man's doing or not doing anything; and besides accepting all that happens, and all that is allotted, as coming from thence, wherever it is, from whence he himself came; and finally, waiting for death with a cheerful mind, as being nothing else than a dissolution of the elements of which every living being is compounded.[5]

And the core of the answer runs:

Unhappy am I, because this has happened to me? Not so, but happy am I, though this has happened to me, because I continue free from pain, neither crushed by the present nor fearing the future. For such a thing as this might have happened to every man; but every man would not have continued free from pain on such an occasion. Why then is the former circumstance rather a misfortune than the latter a good fortune? . . . Remember too

[5] Marcus Aurelius, *Meditations*, II, 17; George Long tr., p. 112.

on every occasion which leads thee to vexation to apply this principle: Not that this is a misfortune, but that to bear it nobly is
good fortune.[6]

And Marcus concludes:

Wherever a man can live, there he can also live well. But he must
live in a palace; well, then, he can live well even in a palace.[7]

With this self-consolation of Marcus we may compare the
passages in Aristotle: "It is one thing to live, but another thing
to live well . . ." "Any man can get angry, and give away
money; but to do it at the right time and the right place and
in the right manner, this not every man can do: it takes
brains."[8] What has happened in the interval? It is the same
gospel, but the world has changed—or, for the Stoic, has
seemed to. The problem faced is no longer how to live well,
but rather how to bear misfortune nobly. Marcus makes clear
how the world looks to him:

Things are in such a kind of envelopment that they have seemed
to philosophers, not a few, nor those common philosophers, altogether unintelligible; nay even to the Stoics themselves they
seem difficult to understand. Carry thy thoughts to the objects
themselves, for which men strive, and consider how short-lived
they are and worthless, and that they may be in the possession of
a filthy wretch or a whore or a robber. Then turn to the morals
of those who live with thee, and it is hardly possible to endure
even the most agreeable of them, to say nothing of a man being
hardly able to endure himself. In such darkness then and dirt,
and in so constant a flux both of substance and of time, and of
motion and of things moved, what there is worth being highly
prized, or even an object of serious pursuit, I cannot imagine.
But in such a world, it is a man's duty to comfort himself, and
to wait for the natural dissolution, and not to be vexed at the

6 *Ibid.*, IV, 49; Long tr., p. 142.
7 *Ibid.*, V, 16; Long tr., p. 155.
8 *Nicomachean Ethics*, Bk. II, ch. ix.

delay, but to rest in these principles only: the one, that nothing will happen to me which is not conformable to the nature of the universe; and the other, that it is in my power never to act contrary to my God and my spirit: for there is no man who will compel me to this.[9]

In such a world the Stoics were seeking primarily consolation; and they found it. "Do what is in thy power!" Want nothing else! This is an admirable defense against Fortune. Epictetus puts it:

Everything has two handles, the one by which it may be borne, the other by which it may not. If your brother acts unjustly, do not lay hold of the act by that handle wherein he acts unjustly, for this is the handle by which it cannot be borne; but lay hold of the other, that he is your brother, that he was nurtured with you, and you will lay hold of the thing by that handle by which it can be borne.[10]

Marcus Aurelius bases this maxim on the principle of the economy of effort: he did not have a superabundance of energy. Do not fret, do what you can! Your soul at least is your own: it is an impregnable fortress. "How can that make a man's life worse which does not make him a worse man? . . . Nothing is either bad or good, that can happen equally to a good or a bad man." Nothing but goodness is good, as Zeno taught. And goodness is in the power of every man. No matter what happens, you can always do what you ought to do.

Do what? We ask the question in the need to find guidance for action. Yet for the Stoic the craving for consolation is always winning out over any direction for control and achievement. The Stoic answer runs, "Follow Nature!" You will have to anyway, so do it willingly. Do not kick against the pricks. But we still ask, Do what? The answer now comes,

---

[9] *Meditations*, V, 10; Long tr., p. 151.
[10] Epictetus, *Encheiridion*, aphorism XLIII, tr. by George Long.

"Follow your own nature! Follow *human nature!*" And for the Stoic that means, "Follow reason!" For reason is the divine spark in human nature. Be a man, play a man's part, do the proper work of a man in the great whole. And this means, first, Let reason always rule your life; this is the only real good. All else is indifferent. Be rational! Anybody, any man, can be rational. The Stoic is still seeking consolation rather than guidance.

It means, secondly, Do what reason "prefers"—not because it is good in itself; the ends at which reason aims are not to be desired at all. Nobody cares whether there are good emperors, or good slaves. But, if you are an emperor, you ought to try to be a good one; and if you are a slave, you ought likewise to try to be a good slave. That is, you ought to want your "appropriate ends," *ta kathēkonta*, ends that are fitting and suitable to your station and to the occasion. You ought to want to perform what the Roman Stoic calls your *officia*, your duties. You are living well if you want to do the appropriate things. Whether you can succeed or not, is a matter of complete indifference to you. That is not in your power. And so the force and energy that come from devotion and commitment, Plato's *erōs*, are sacrificed by the Stoic to his fear of failure. Stoicism is thus the great philosophy of safety first. Make no commitment!

What ought you then to prefer? To function as a man: and the positive content of Stoic substantive ethics, when we finally get to it, is fairly Aristotelian. That is, it consists in the traditional Greek values, now adapted to the Hellenistic scene. You ought to want to secure friends, and fame, and riches, together with all the moral virtues.

But the motive has changed. You ought to want them, not because you care anything about them in themselves, or think they possess any value or good in their own right, but because reason "prefers" them, because you ought to want them, because it is your duty to be a complete man, and a complete man would have them.

Take friendship, the one good about which Epicurus, in his fear of life, relents. Why is friendship good? Why ought a man to possess friends? Epicurus says, "That there may be someone to sit by him when he is ill, to help him when he is in prison or in want."[11] Seneca the Stoic condemns these motives given by Epicurus: no, such interested friendship is unworthy of the Wise Man, and is, moreover, a broken reed. A man will want friends, says Seneca, "That he may have someone by whose sick-bed he himself may sit; someone a prisoner in hostile hands whom he himself may set free. . . . To have someone for whom I may die, whom I may follow into exile, against whose death I may stake my own life, and pay the pledge too." This sounds very fine and noble and unselfish. But why? Seneca states *his* motives: "That I may practice friendship, that my own noble qualities may not lie dormant."[12] And consolation wins out in the end again: the Wise Man can always endure the loss of any particular friend; he can always do without that one, and find a new friend to practice friendship upon. One gets more kick out of making a new friend, anyway, remarks Seneca, than having the same old one hanging around all the time. We begin to wonder whether Seneca's "friendship" is really more disinterested than Epicurus'.

Stoicism emphasizes the new note of work, the dignity of labor, the scorn of idleness—it is no leisure-class ideal. Is it a

[11] Seneca, *Moral Epistles,* Letter IX; Loeb Classics, ed. by R. M. Gummere, I, 47.
[12] *Ibid.,* I, 47, 49.

slave-morality? Yes—because Stoicism appealed to those who had to work and could not retire into the Epicurean Garden: to slaves, emperors, and prime ministers. Above all, man's supreme duty is to help and serve all mankind, without limits. Benevolence, altruism, these are the cardinal duties of man. The world is one great "City of Zeus," whose boundaries are worldwide. It is this social feeling that made Stoicism the idealistic philosophy of Empire, of administrators bearing the Roman's burden. It is quite literally "cosmopolitan": our City, our *Polis*, is the world itself. All men possess the same divine spark of reason, all alike. Hence our human duties go out to all equally. "We are made for cooperation, like the feet and the eyes." "We are all members of one body." "*Homo res sacra homini*": man is a sacred thing to his fellow-man. "*Deus est, mortali mortalem iuvare*": God is, for one mortal to help another mortal.

And so the Stoic preached the equality of all men—a new note, not present in previous Greek ethics before, save among the Cynics. This same emphasis is to be found among the Hebrews, and the Christians; and, we like to think, among the moderns. This is undoubtedly the greatest permanent deposit left by Stoicism. Its inclusion in the Christian synthesis, by Paul and the Latin Fathers, especially by Ambrose, kept Christianity from becoming a mere scurrying off to private safety at the Judgment trump.

So Stoicism became the foundation of later Roman law, at the hands of Cicero and of the great jurists of the Justinian Age, who were all in philosophy Stoics. The natural reason in things led the Stoics to natural equality, and natural rights, for all: for all races, for slaves, even for women. Wherever in later ages Roman law was felt as a force, it proved a strong egalitarian influence. Stoicism was anti-slavery, anti-cruel punish-

ments, anti-gladiatorial combats, anti-nationalistic, anti-war—
something utterly cosmopolitan and ecumenical.[13]

It is a man's duty to serve all mankind, impartially. But—
you must not *love* mankind, or *care* anything for them. That
commitment would be fatal—to the freedom of your soul. Pity
and sympathy are mortal vices. Do good, without love or
concern. It is your duty as a man: disinterested bene*faction*,
but not bene*volence*. Do not care a hang about anybody else,
just help them. Above all, do not put your soul into it. Do not
trust any of your soul to another; you yourself must stay free
and detached.

Epictetus puts this cardinal Stoic warning: "Kiss your wife
and child, show them every mark of affection. But—do not
love them! If you do, you will be upset if they die." "Show
sympathy to the unfortunate, lament with them; but take care
that somewhere in your soul there is a place where you do not
lament." Remember, they are earthen vessels; you will then
not be surprised if they break. And, most pathetic of all, is
the counsel of Marcus: "Some pray, O God, do not take from
me my little son. The Wise Man will pray, Let me not be
disturbed when he is taken."[14] The framework of Christian
love is there; but it is not hard to see why the motive of "love"
came rushing in. To the Stoic, such love was an ignoble weakness: for it spelled defeat—defeat for freedom.

Marcus Aurelius sums up:

If thou workest at that which is before thee, following right
reason seriously, vigorously, calmly, without allowing anything
else to distract thee, but keeping thy divine part pure, as if thou

---

[13] For the social philosophy of Stoicism, see below, chapter 6. Cicero's
De Republica and *De Legibus* are the great philosophical documents of Stoic
social and legal philosophy and jurisprudence, aside from the later Justinian
Codes.

[14] Epictetus, *Encheiridion,* aphorisms III, XVI; Marcus Aurelius, *Meditations,*
IX, 40; Long tr., p. 240.

shouldst be bound to give it back immediately; if thou holdest to this, expecting nothing, fearing nothing, but satisfied with thy present activity according to nature, and with heroic truth in every word and sound which thou utterest, thou wilt live happy. And there is no man who is able to prevent this. . . .

Man, thou hast been a citizen in this great state the world; what difference does it make to thee whether for five years or for three? For that which is conformable to the laws is just for all. Where is the hardship, then, if no tyrant nor yet an unjust judge sends thee away from the state, but nature, who brought thee into it? the same as if a praetor who has employed an actor dismisses him from the stage.—"But I have not finished the five acts, but only three of them."—Thou sayest well, but in life the three acts are the whole drama; for what shall be a complete drama is determined by him who was once the cause of its composition, and now of its dissolution; but thou art the cause of neither. Depart then satisfied, for he who releases thee is also satisfied.[15]

Both Epicureans and Stoics stood for freedom through acceptance and resignation. Epicurus counseled freedom through quietism, inactivity: do not stick your neck out! The Stoics urged freedom through activity, doing your duty: do not stick your soul out! Epicurus preached peace through retiring from the struggle, to the Garden. The Stoics preached peace in the midst of battle. It is hardly surprising it usually turned out to be a losing battle. But both taught release from worry and anxiety, peace of mind.

---

[15] *Meditations*, III, 12; Long tr., p. 123. XII, 36; Long tr., p. 295.

V THE SKEPTICAL DEFENSE AGAINST THINKING

Another characteristic modern philosophy made its appearance in the Hellenistic world. From the death of Aristotle on, philosophical Skepticism never lacked brilliant spokesmen. It grew along with the schools of positive doctrine, and gave way only to the new wave of religious faith, which indeed often used Skepticism as its own intellectual weapon. It was inevitable that men seeking personal peace and freedom by intellectual methods, by thinking, by finding the truth, should in the end try to find them by giving up the attempt. And there was the long Greek tradition, stemming from Parmenides' "way of error," the Eleatics, and the Sophists—including the Socrates of the method of "eristic" about whom Gilbert Ryle grows enthusiastic—who relied on subtle thinking to demonstrate that thinking alone could never find the Truth, but only better warranted hypotheses. Greek Skepticism, at its best, led in the sixteenth and seventeenth centuries into our own experimental method, which we reckon our intellectual glory. The first great statement of experimentalism was called by Joseph Glanvill a *Scepsis Scientifica*, in his volume reissued in 1665. And Robert Boyle called himself in 1661 *The Sceptical Chymist*.[1]

[1] See my *Career of Philosophy in Modern Times*, Vol. I, *From the Middle Ages to the Enlightenment* (New York, 1962), Bk. III, ch. 7, "British Experimentalism before Newton"; on Joseph Glanvill, pp. 500-7; on Robert Boyle, pp. 507-16.

On the continuity between ancient Skepticism and modern experimentalism, see the leading American historian and defender of Skepticism, Richard H. Popkin. Full bibliography in *Encyclopedia of Philosophy*, ed. Paul Edwards

The intellectual search for the one way of life, the Skeptic held, is the real cause for the soul's trouble, the agelong search for certainty. Abandon it! Find deliverance in the saving realization that there is no one way. There is no certain truth. Each way will take you, all roads lead to Rome—all, or none. Believe everything at once, or believe nothing. It comes to the same thing in the end. Skepticism and "eclecticism" or "syncretism" finally merged, and were overwhelmed by faith and commitment.

Hellenistic Skepticism began—and ended—in intellectual weariness, in relief from the trouble of thinking. In between, it flourished in vigorous intellectual activity, in the most acute and penetrating critical thought in the Hellenistic Age—possibly, in the entire ancient world.

But for most of its long history, philosophic Skepticism[2] meant, abandon the unhappy desire to know, with all its per-

---

(New York, 1967), VII, 460-61. See also D. W. Hamlyn, in *A Critical History of Western Philosophy*, D. J. O'Connor, ed. (New York, 1964), pp. 72-75; bibliography, p. 578.

[2] The one surviving ancient document is Sextus Empiricus, *Outlines of Pyrrhonism, Against the Logicians, Against the Physicists, Against the Ethicists*, by R. G. Bury, ed. and tr. (Loeb, 1933-53). See also Cicero's version of Greek Skepticism in his *Academica* and *De Natura Deorum* (Loeb, 1933). Selections in Philip P. Hallie, ed., *Scepticism, Man and God* (Middletown, Conn., 1964), with introduction.

Studies: E. Bevan, *Stoics and Sceptics* (Oxford, 1913), ch. 4; R. D. Hicks, *Stoic and Epicurean* (New York, 1910), chs. 8-10.

Fuller Studies: E. Zeller, *The Stoics, Epicureans, and Sceptics* (Eng. tr. London, 1870; rev. ed., 1962). N. MacColl, *The Greek Sceptics from Pyrrho to Sextus* (London, 1869). Mary M. Patrick, *The Greek Sceptics* (New York, 1929), *Sextus Empiricus and Greek Scepticism* (New York, 1899). Léon Robin, *Pyrrhon et le Scepticisme Grec* (Paris, 1944). Best study is V. Brochard, *Les Sceptiques Grecs* (Paris, 1887; rev. ed., 1923). J. Croissant, "La Morale de Carnéade," in *Revue Internationale de la Philosophie*, I (1938-39), 545-70. German scholarship gives A. Goedeckemeyer, *Die Geschichte des griechischen Skeptizismus* (Leipzig, 1905); emphasizes Pyrrho rather than Socrates as the source of Arkesilaos.

sistent doubts and futile dogmatisms. You can be happy without knowing. Do not bother! Do not even try to get tranquillity of soul and the absence of pain, like Epicurus, by a theory of the universe bound to clash with accepted views, and by a moral ideal bound to cause collision with the accustomed ways of men. The only wisdom is complete "indifference," *adiaphora,* floating with the current, "conformity without conviction," together with "suspension of judgment," *epochē,* as to the truth or value of what you are following the crowd in doing. It makes for less trouble: you do not then have to argue in support of your distinctive choice. There are no gods! so let us worship them. It saves trouble; and there may be gods after all—who really knows? At least we know that their worship is established, and that most men perform it.

Now, there are many varieties of skepticism, just as there are varieties of hedonism. First, there is this practical skepticism of indifference, and disillusionment. Follow the crowd! They are silly, of course, but what is any better? Thinking is terribly hard, and nonconformity is one long uphill fight. See through the folly of others, but go through the motions. Rationally considered, all political parties are probably crazy. So vote for the Republicans, not because you think they are any better than the others, but to avoid the trouble of explaining why you did not, especially if the polls all report this will be a Republican year. Or vote for the Democrats, if you live in a Democratic region, like a university campus. Or for the Socialists—if that is what your crowd does, and you can find them on the ballot.

Secondly, there is the skepticism of the intellectual, of excessive knowledge. You know too much to be taken in by any one argument. You see the strength of every position, and also its limitations, and can hence have a glorious time exploring every idea, defending it and refuting it in turn. This is the skepticism of the dialectician, of disputation. Know every idea, but believe none. It is the skepticism of Socrates, of Hegel, of F. H. Bradley, of Renan, of Anatole France, before the Dreyfus case woke him up, or of Aldous Huxley, before he got religion. In it the passion for ideas stills any desire for action, knowledge is more attractive than commitment, till something happens to jolt you out of your indifference.

Thirdly, there is the scientific skepticism of the experimental temper of mind. This is an interest in ideas, but a distrust of them: they are all hypotheses, postulates, assumptions, that must be continually checked and refined, by confronting them with experience and observation. Such skepticism forswears absolute truth for the best warranted hypothesis, and is always looking for one better warranted. It is the willingness to live by probabilities.

All three types of skepticism are developed only in an intellectually sophisticated environment, in a passionately intellectual society, like Greece, or India at times, or like our cosmopolitan centers today. The first type, the skepticism of indifference, when developed in reaction against the excessive intellectuality of others, can be taken over by nonintellectual men, who are suspicious of ideas, and bewildered by them. It was this type of skepticism that appealed to the Romans, as their only defense against Greek cleverness. The second type, the skepticism of the intellectual, is next to the most difficult achievement of the human mind, its most unnatural state. For the mind by nature seems inclined to rest in unquestioned belief. Hence this type is incomprehensible to the practical man of action, to the Babbitts, and to the committed. It has been the recourse of the intellectual when the Babbitts— Roman or American, or, can we now say, Russian?—are in control. To the intelligent it is congenial, and often proves a great temptation. But it is clearly an escape-philosophy, or a defense mechanism—what it is now the fashion to call a form of alienation.

When combined with the spirit of curiosity, of vigorous inquiry and investigation, in the third type of skepticism, scientific skepticism, it seems to be the most fruitful of all intellectual attitudes. It is the scientific temper of mind, as we know it at its best today. And this is the one intellectual attitude that seems to be more difficult to achieve than the skepticism of the intellectual. It is the willingness to live by probabilities, to act resolutely on what one knows to be logically an hypothesis. Should it ever become a really central element in our culture, it would revolutionize our whole life. But there seems little danger that any large number of men will ever share this scientific temper. Certainly, outside their own narrow fields, the vast majority of scientists do not.

Now, all three types of skepticism were present in the tradition of Greek Skepticism. In Carneades and his doctrine of probability, the Greeks were close to the third type, scientific skepticism; and again, on a much lower level, in the medical school of Sextus Empiricus. But this attitude was being continually vitiated by the general atmosphere of intellectual defeat and escape. And in the hands of the Romans, Skepticism ended its days as a conservative apologetic for tradition. Consider the final defense of irrationalism by the Latin Fathers of the Church, Arnobius and Tertullian, before Neo-Platonic rationalism was imported into the West. For skepticism of the non-scientific variety, when pushed, always ends in fideism, faith in some gospel or commitment. With the power of reason destroyed, there is no recourse but tradition or sheer faith.[3]

There are three main stages in the history of Greek Skepti-

---

[3] Under the Weimar Republic, the youth were taught that intelligence was not sufficient to tell them what to do, that they should make an "existential commitment." So many of the young did—to Hitler.

cism: Pyrrho, the fortunes of Skepticism when grasped by the Platonic Academy, and the later Roman Skepticism.

The first centers on the figure of Pyrrho (365-275 B.C.), a contemporary of Epicurus and Zeno. Pyrrho is the first great skeptic (or "inquirer") of indifference. Born in Elis, he went with the army of Alexander to India, and there, we are told, he was fascinated by the ascetic indifference of the Hindu sages, especially the Gymnosophists. In Alexander's court he met Anaxarchus, a follower of Democritus, of his distrust of the senses, and of his eudaemonistic ethics, who became Pyrrho's teacher in philosophy. Pyrrho returned to Elis, where his fellow-citizens made him a high priest; he exhibited personally a noble character.

What Pyrrho taught was not a body of doctrine or a dialectical method, but rather an *agōgē,* a way of living. Nobody has yet found the truth. So why should we distress ourselves about the search? One can be unmoved and tranquil without getting excited over atoms, like Epicurus, or over Providence, like Zeno. In fact, only if one doubts everything can one be genuinely indifferent to all that happens. Appearances, *ta phainomena,* are enough to live by. Why think, why desire, why strive? Riches seem good; but whether they really are, nobody knows. So, if you have them, do not worry about whether you ought to give them to the poor; and if you do not have them, do not kill yourself trying to get them. An unfaithful wife seems pretty bad; but nobody really knows. So do not worry about her goings-on.

Once on a voyage a storm threatened the ship of Pyrrho. He looked on at a pig tied on deck, contentedly munching the garbage through it all, and remarked enviously, "There is true peace."

Yet even Pyrrho needed a theory of skepticism to defend himself. He found one in Democritus: that all sensations are subjective and misleading; and in Protagoras: that every theory can be supported or denied with equal cogency. All argument is mere dialectic, a mere postulate system: it is either an infinite regress, or else a circle.

So Pyrrho worked out a theory of agnosticism: truth lies neither in experience nor in reason. "Only what we perceive is real. No knowledge goes beyond appearances." Honey seems sweet, and the sky seems to be blue; but nobody knows whether they really are. Some of these "seemings" seem to follow each other regularly, so that we are led to expect the remembered sequences. But this is misleading and often deceives us. Every inference beyond immediate appearances is really unjustified. Atomism? One cannot see atoms. Providence? One cannot see its workings. Science is as futile as the search for *the* way of life. Pyrrho exhibits no scientific skepticism, no faith in hypotheses.

Pyrrho had many followers, and one disciple, Timon of Phlius, and later of Athens, who set down and systematized Pyrrho's arguments in writing. But Pyrrho left no school. Timon tells us that Pyrrho held, a philosopher should ask himself three questions. First, How are things constituted? Since we know only phenomena, we do not know the answer— such things are *adēla,* hidden from us. Secondly, what is our relation to our world? Here we must practice *epochē,* suspend our judgment, and acknowledge our lack of comprehension, and hence practice *aphasia,* maintaining silence. Thirdly, What will happen if we maintain *epochē* and *aphasia?* we shall then secure *ataraxia,* tranquillity of mind. The fruit of Skeptic wisdom is, as Anaxarchus taught, *eudaemonia,* happiness.

The Platonic Academy found itself losing out to the aggressive Stoics, when the Scholarch Arkesilaos (315-241 B.C.) snatched at Pyrrho's arguments, and made the Academy the stronghold of philosophic Skepticism, which it remained till the return to a more dogmatic Platonism some two centuries later. The ease with which the professed followers of Plato adopted skepticism may seem surprising, especially if we follow the later tradition, and identify "Platonism" with the great religious philosophy of Neo-Platonism, in which Greek thought ended its days. But we must remember, as Diogenes Laertios points out, that "while some maintained that Plato 'dogmatizes,'" that is, teaches a positive doctrine of his own, others had always denied that Plato himself had any positive teaching. There was a strong tradition in ancient times that Plato had no philosophy of his own, that he put all opinions in the mouths of his characters, but himself just sat back and smiled. To take Plato as offering his *theōria* as primarily a vision of human life rather than as an explanation of the world makes credible the otherwise rather incredible fact that for two hundred years the followers of Plato in the Academy felt skepticism to be true to the spirit of the master.[4] They made the "Academic" or the "Platonic" philosophy synonymous with philosophic Skepticism. This view is familiar to modern readers in Hume, who was of course steeped in the writings of Cicero, the "Academic" in this sense.

Arkesilaos was not a skeptic of indifference and disillusionment, but an intellectual, a skeptic of excessive knowledge, a dialectician at heart. He loved arguing on both sides of every issue; he did not want to settle questions and reach conclusions. He was a brilliant teacher, who found popularity in showing up every idea. That is always the easiest way for a teacher to

---

[4] See my interpretation of Plato's philosophy in *Plato: Dramatist of the Life of Reason* (New York, 1970), in which a sharp distinction is drawn between the "Platonism" of Plato, which the tradition took up as what we call "Neo-Platonism," and Plato's own philosophy, in its much more inclusive vision.

win applause. The man who gets the laughs is always the debunker, not the sympathetic expositor and defender. Arkesilaos held that his method was that of Socrates himself, but a plausible case can be made that it actually derived more from Pyrrho. But Arkesilaos disgusted Timon, the disciple of Pyrrho, by his subtle dialectic.

Arkesilaos was interested primarily in showing up, not common opinions and customs, like Pyrrho, but rather philosophical theories, above all, those of his chief rivals, the earnest and solemn Stoics. He showed that there cannot be proven to be any absolute certainty, any "grasping impressions," any *phantasiai kataleptikai,* that are self-evident and uncriticizable, any axiomatic truths, such as had been made the foundation of the Stoic logic. There are, he put it, no such "criteria." So, why should we struggle to do our duty? We should suspend our judgment, and not attempt any course too difficult. Cicero tells us that it was Arkesilaos who first counseled such *epoche.* As for action, which the Stoics charged he was paralyzing, Arkesilaos admitted one must do something and choose some course. He urged men to follow "the reasonable," *to eulogon,* which is the course one can support by good reasons in harmony with each other. These good reasons are not conclusive, but they will help us to live well, and to defend our way of life with plausibility. These good reasons of Arkesilaos have been revived by the moderns skeptical of any strict moral knowledge.

The school under Arkesilaos was called the "Middle Academy," which had broken with the Pythagorean and mathematical interests of the earlier Academy, which had continued through the predecessor of Arkesilaos, Krates. Arkesilaos' attack on the Stoics produced the defense and working out of the Stoic system by Chrysippus. This in turn led to a new skeptical attack on all the dogmatic schools in what is called the "New Academy," under the greatest Greek philosopher during the four centuries between Chrysippus and Plotinos, the very acute and subtle Carneades of Cyrene (213-129 B.C.). Carneades was a brilliant and penetrating controversialist; his arguments proved unanswerable. He can well claim the title of the David Hume of antiquity, especially since he contributed much to the thought of Hume himself. His disciple, Clitomachus of Carthage (called Hasdrubal in Phoenician), put his ideas and arguments into four hundred books, which are all "lost"—that is, the medieval monks saw no value in copying them for posterity. Carneades is hence known to us only through Cicero and Sextus Empiricus, with some assistance from Diogenes Laertios.[5] From all we can gather, had he left writings of his own, he would today be regarded as the intellectual equal of Plato and Aristotle. Indeed, to our day he might seem even greater, since his thought is far more congenial to the present intellectual temper, especially of professional philosophers.

Carneades maintained, we can never know any certain truth, for we have no criterion of certainty such as the Stoics supposed, no criterion of absolute truth. Such a criterion would have to carry conviction in itself, it would have to possess an intrinsic mark of its validity, it would have to be self-evident and axiomatic. But there are no discoverable self-evident axioms, even in geometry. There are no certain and self-evident *archai,* no clear and distinct ideas, as Descartes and the rationalists were to hold, no "true idea, that reveals itself and error," as Spinoza put it. And there is no experience carrying validity in itself, no experience that is incorrigible and a hard datum, as empiricists were to maintain. All *archai* are postu-

_____

[5] E. Zeller has done an excellent job in collating the various remarks of Cicero concerning Carneades.

lates, hypothetical assumptions, in themselves indistinguishable from assumptions that are demonstrably false. The senses offer no such criterion of truth: they are relative, contradictory, and subject to many illusions, and so need constant correction by reason.

But reason itself is mere dialectic, in the Aristotelian sense: it argues from unproved assumptions. It refutes itself, as in the famous paradoxes of the Eleatics. Its first principles or *archai* are merely taken to be true: reason builds postulate systems, not indubitable conclusions. Even mathematics, geometry, is a postulate system based on logical consistency; it does not present us with conclusions that are certain. It rests on terms that must remain undefined, and on assumptions that cannot themselves be demonstrated. And hence, in the form familiar in Bertrand Russell's definition, "Mathematics is the science in which we do not know what we are talking about, nor whether what we are saying is true." It is interesting to find Russell's characterization in Carneades.

Carneades thus marshaled the arguments against every form of rationalism and empiricism, and he proved to be unanswerable. The only alternative is a functional and experimental theory of truth or warranted assertibility.

From this logical position, Carneades proceeded to criticize and to demolish all the Hellenistic systems, especially the Stoic faith in Providence. We cannot prove the existence of any God who cares for men. His arguments are to be found in Cicero's *De Natura Deorum* and *Academica,* though certain crucial parts have been "lost." Carneades developed all the arguments against religious faith in controlling cosmic moral laws, and presented a critique of what came to be called rational or natural theology. In the eighteenth century Hume did it again, as Pierre Bayle had done it before him. But Bayle and Hume are no more devastating than Carneades, and both Bayle and

Hume had read Cicero; Hume called himself an "Academic."

There is, reasoned Carneades, no evidence of design in the world, only of order; and order is a brute fact. There is nothing divine, for example, about the orderly laws of disease. The teleological argument for a cosmic designer is thus invalid. And any belief in God must rest, not on evidence, but on pure faith. Hume put it, "Our most holy religion rests on faith." Any conception of God is so shot through, inevitably, with self-contradiction—the theologians came to call it analogical and equivocal—that it is rationally meaningless and untenable. The Wise Man will hence refrain from religious belief. Carneades was thus the real freethinker of antiquity, the real agnostic. He makes Epicurus and his interstellar gods seem a cautious compromiser.

Since absolute truth and certainty is unattainable, all we can get is probability. For action, we must follow "the persuasive," *to pithanon*. This is not for him a mathematical or statistical but an experimental conception. Carneades was not merely tired, like Pyrrho: he had a genuine scientific sense. He counseled living by hypotheses. We should trust in practice what appears most probable, most persuasive to us. We should follow the evidence of the senses that seems clearest, that is not contradicted by contrary evidence, that is sustained by cumulative evidence, and that will withstand thorough analysis and experiment. He emphasized experiment and negative instances. In all these ways he developed a logic of a positivistic and experimental science, before such a science had itself come into being.

In morals, Carneades assailed the dogmatic Puritanism of the Stoics, and especially their ethics of consolation, that made striving rather than achievement the true good. It is a probable opinion, he held, that the natural goods of life are really good. And so he vindicated the old Greek conception. But—we should not deceive ourselves. We have only probability, not certainty, even when we think that pleasure and natural goods are really desirable.

After the critique of Carneades, the Stoics never really believed their system again. Like Marcus Aurelius, they had to adjust their gospel to the uncertainty, "Is it gods or atoms?" Skepticism came to permeate all the schools, save that of the insulated Epicureans. At the same time, the Academy came to admit a liberalized and watered-down Stoic way as most probable and persuasive. This ethical probabilism grew in the Academy more and more dogmatic: this stage is reflected in Cicero himself.

This Skepticism was brought to Rome by Philo of Larissa, and, through Cicero, by Antiochus, but the Romans were hardly intellectual enough to doubt. Philo of Larissa (160-80 B.C.) insisted that Carneades had been misunderstood: actually, he was just arguing. In reality, he continued to teach "Platonic doctrine" without change. He never meant to deny that we really possess genuine knowledge, *epistēmē*. And Philo went on to apply probability, not merely, with Carneades, to actions, but dogmatically to theoretical beliefs.

Antiochus of Ascalon (130-68 B.C.; head of Academy after 79 B.C.) practically surrendered to the Stoic ethics. He made a dramatic recantation: he admitted that the tradition of Plato had been lost, and he returned to the "Old Academy," to which Plato, Aristotle, and all their disciples, along with Zeno, really belonged. All that Zeno the Stoic invented was a new terminology. And so Antiochus proceeded to teach the Stoic logic, physics, and ethics as the true doctrine of Plato and Aristotle. Zeno was an Academic anyway; and there is general philosophic agreement between Plato, Aristotle, and Zeno. Antiochus was the teacher of Cicero in Athens: his views are paraphrased in *De Finibus,* Books IV and V.

There was a later revival of dialectical skepticism in Alexandria under Aenesidemus of Cnossus (first century B.C.), a contemporary of Cicero. His *Pyrrhonean Discourses* are a kind of Skeptic's handbook. Truth lies in the appearances, in the common sense of men. Beyond that, all men disagree. Men choose their philosophies because of nonrational, temperamental, psychological reasons. Aenesidemus presented a famous list of Ten Tropes, which became the stereotyped Skeptic's paradoxes, proving that there is no certainty. Included is a rather Humean critique of the notion of causality. Aenesidemus, whose name has become a symbol for Skepticism, was a complete relativist both in knowledge and in ethics. Agrippa (first century A.D.) added five more Tropes, showing that logically there can be no certainty.

The last figure in the tradition is Sextus Empiricus (c.200 A.D.), the only ancient Skeptic whose writings have come down to us: he is the editor of the compilation that goes under his name. Sextus is not a dialectician, but a positivist and a physician, in the group of medical thinkers called the empiricals, who combatted speculative medical theories with observation and experience. They held, we do not know the causes of diseases, or of anything else; but we can observe the succession of symptoms, make a prediction or prognosis, and thus build a medical art of healing, if not a theoretical science of medicine, on them.

Sextus Empiricus represents positivism and empiricism of a pretty crude sort. But by his time the new religious faiths were too strong. With reason undermined, and destroyed, faith was bound to fill its place. The Skeptical arguments were seized upon by the religious irrationalists. The Latin Fathers of the Church, Arnobius and Tertullian, proclaimed, "*Credo quia absurdum.*" Nonscientific skepticism has always proved impotent in the face of the most irrational and dogmatic faiths.

The greatest and most interesting literary Skeptic of antiquity is Lucian of Samosata, on the Euphrates (c.115-c.200 A.D.),[6] who was a contemporary of Marcus Aurelius. He is the most brilliant and clever Greek writer, and the Greeks were a clever people. He belongs to the tribe of Erasmus, Rabelais, Voltaire, and Anatole France, and was their inspiration. He is master of witty dialogue: he undresses all the heroes in the approved modern manner. Lucian did it for the Greeks in the Roman Empire, not for the Romans. Like most Greeks, he had only amused contempt for the unclever Romans. Though a complete master of Greek literature, and full of allusions to it, he never mentions a single Latin writer.

Lucian's mockery is aimed at all types of mankind, even at himself; but it is directed especially toward the three forms of religion current in the second century: the official religious mythology of the Olympic pantheon; the new, weird Oriental

6 Texts: Complete works in *Luciani Samosatiensis Opera,* C. Jacobitz, ed. (Leipzig, 1887-88). Texts and Eng. tr., *Lucian,* A. M. Harmon, ed., M. D. Macleod, and K. Kilburn (Loeb, 7 vols. published, 1913-61). Complete Eng. tr. by H. W. and F. G. Fowler, *Works of Lucian of Samosata* (Oxford, 1905). Selections in *Satirical Sketches,* tr. with introduction by Paul Turner (Penguin, 1961). See especially *Hermotimus* (abridgment in Walter Pater, *Marius the Epicurean,* as "A Dialogue Not Imaginary.")

Studies, Standard: M. Croiset, *La Vie et les Oeuvres de Lucien* (Paris, 1882); J. Bernays, *Lukian und die Kyniker* (Berlin, 1880). See also suggestive interpretation in J. J. Chapman, *Lucian, Plato and Greek Morals* (New York, 1931). See W. H. Tackaberry, *Lucian's Relation to the Post-Aristotelian Philosophers* (Toronto, 1930); M. Caster, *Lucien et la Pensée Religeuse de son Temps* (Paris, 1937); A. Peretti, *Luciano: Un Intelletuale Greco contro Roma* (Florence, 1946); J. Bompaire, *Lucien Écrivain: Imitation et Création* (Paris, 1958).

faiths, and their charlatanry; and the modernized liberal religion of the philosophical Schools of the intellectuals and the
upper classes, their smug complacency, their pretentiousness,
their hypocrisy.

With traditional mythology, Lucian's method is not to deny
its truth but to make the reader realize just what it means.
In his *Dialogues of the Gods,* he gives close-ups of the gods in
negligé, with a simple, direct adherence to the details of the
legends. The effect is devastating, and it is no longer possible
to hold the gods in awe. There is Zeus in the maternity ward,
about to give birth to Pallas Athene from his forehead. There
is Zeus trying to explain to the innocent boy, Ganymede, just
what his dishonorable intentions really are. There is Hermes,
confronted by his son Pan, the result of assuming the form of
a goat in one of his exploits. There is Zeus and his wife Hera,
arguing about his various affairs: Hera is a good competitor for
Wagner's Fricka. There are the gods in council, on Olympus,
worried by the immigration problem presented by the strange
new dog-faced foreigners, bulls, apes, who are appearing on
Olympus in Roman times. There is Zeus confronted by a
Cynic philosopher, who cross-examines him as to his weakness,
and as to the very faulty workings of his Providence.

With the new Oriental faiths, Lucian's method is the simple
narration of the charlatanry of impostors, and the stupidity of
their dupes. Peregrine the Cynic explains how he fooled the
simple Christians, and then double-crossed them; in the end
he sets himself on fire in the theater, as a supreme exhibition-
ist. There is Alexander the Oraclemonger, a kind of ancient
Elmer Gantry; Lucian tells the story of his knaveries.

With the professional philosophers, Lucian shows more personal feeling. Lucian had been trained as a lawyer. When he
came to realize that it was impossible for a lawyer to be an
honest man, he gave up his practice, and sought out the philos-

ophers, till he saw through them also. We must understand, the philosophical Schools had come to resemble our own religious denominations. The so-called philosophers were popular preachers, "prima donnas of the pulpit"; or else parasitic chaplains and confessors in great houses, hangers-on of rich men. They were a fashionable clergy, with churches on Park Avenue, attended by the best people.

All these philosophers claimed to teach, how to be happy, a practical way of life. Lucian takes them at their own word. He has no concern with intellectual problems, with science or understanding—such interests had vanished by the second century. He judges them by their fruits, and finds them a hollow pretense. Despite their claim to be very practical, they spend most of their time discussing foolish questions of no earthly moment: Platonic Ideas, Aristotelian forms, atoms and the void, futile logical puzzles, like those of Zeno the Eleatic. These concerns seem to have become as meaningless in Lucian's days as our traditional Reformation theologies have become in our own.

Still worse, these philosophers never themselves practiced what they preached; especially the Stoic Puritans, the most popular of all, with their impossible ideal of the perfect Wise Man. There is a sharp picture of these time-serving sycophants in *The Hireling Philosophers,* of their hypocrisy, jealousy, and greed. This is the immemorial complaint of mankind against a priesthood, a clergy, against all who set themselves up as moral teachers, and at the same time remain themselves very human.

There is the presumption of their claims to teach men how to be happy, when nobody really knows. In the *Sale of Lives,* the famous philosophers are put up for auction like slaves, and sold for their real cash-value. Socrates is the only one who commands a good price, though Aristotle's *Ethics* does not come off badly. Diogenes the Cynic goes for a drachma. In *The Fisherman,* Lucian is hailed to court on the Acropolis and tried before the judge Philosophy for assailing all philosophers. He makes the irrefutable defense: "A jest spoils no real beauty, but rather improves it; as gold is polished by hard rubs." And he goes on: "I hate pretension, and imposture, lying and pride, I love truth and beauty, and simplicity, and all that is akin to love." He distinguishes between the true philosopher, and all miserable pretenders. Acquitted by the judge Philosophy, Lucian takes a hook and line, baits it with gold, throws it over the wall of the Acropolis, and catches a great haul of rascally philosophers.

Lucian's most serious dialogue is the *Hermotimus,* which was translated by Walter Pater in *Marius the Epicurean,* in chapter 24, as "A Conversation not Imaginary." Lucian here encounters an earnest seeker after the true way of life, who has spent twenty years looking for it. Where is happiness to be found? There are so many ways offered! The seeker's generous enthusiasm for the Stoics is killed by Lucian's questions. Explore all the Schools? It is not worth it! It is very doubtful whether any of them have found the secret. Avoid all such vain hopes!

And believe me, if that blissful, that beautiful place, were set on a hill visible to all the world, I should long ago have journeyed thither. But, as you say, it is far off: and one must needs find out for oneself the road to it, and the best possible guide. And I find a multitude of guides, who press on me their services, and protest, all alike, that they have themselves come thence. Only, the roads they propose are many, and towards adverse quarters. And one of them is steep and stony, and through the beating sun; and the other is through green meadows, and under grateful shade, and by many a fountain of water. But howsoever the road may be, at each one of them stands a credible guide; he puts out his hand and would have you come his way. All other ways are wrong, all other guides false. Hence my difficulty!—The number and variety of the ways! For you know, *There is but one road that leads to Corinth.* . . . . .

Lucian replies:

We may go to all philosophers in turn and make trial of them. Still, I, for my part, hold it by no means certain that any one of them really possesses what we seek. The truth may be a thing that no one of them has yet found. You have twenty beans in your hand, and you bid ten persons guess how many: one says five, another fifteen; it is possible that one of them may tell the true number; but it is not impossible that all may be wrong. So it is with the philosophers. All alike are in search of Happiness—what kind of thing it is. One says one thing, one another: it is pleasure; it is virtue;—what not? And Happiness may indeed be one of those things. But it is possible also that it may be still something else, different and distinct from them all.

——What is this? There is something, I know not how, very sad and disheartening in what you say. We seem to have come round in a circle to the spot whence we started, and to our first incertitude. Ah! Lucian, what have you done to me? You have proved my priceless pearl to be but ashes, and all my past labour to have been in vain.

——Reflect, my friend, that you are not the first person who has thus failed of the good things he hoped for. All philosophers, so to speak, are but fighting about the "ass's shadow." To me you seem like one who should weep, and reproach fortune because he is not able to climb up into heaven, or go down into the sea by Sicily and come up at Cyprus, or sail on wings in one day from Greece to India. And the true cause of his trouble is that he has based his hope on what he has seen in a dream, or his own fancy has put together; without previous thought whether what he desires is in itself attainable and within the compass of human nature. Even so, methinks, has it happened with you. As you dreamed, so largely, of those wonderful things, came Reason, and woke you up from sleep, a little roughly; and then you are angry with Reason, your eyes being still but half open, and find it hard to shake off sleep for the pleasure of what you saw therein. Only, don't be angry with me, because, as a friend, I would not suffer you to pass your life in a dream, pleasant, perhaps, but still only a dream—because I wake you up and demand that you should busy yourself with the proper business of life, and send you to it possessed of common sense. What your soul was full of just now is not very different from those Gorgons and Chimaeras and the like, which the poets and the painters construct for us, fancy-free—things which never were, and never will be, though many believe in them, and all like to see and hear of them, just because they are so strange and odd.[7]

What then for Lucian is the way? Lucian learned it from the soothsayer Tiresias, on a voyage to Hades, whither he often journeyed to talk with the heroes of old:

The life of the ordinary man [Lucian agrees with the Odysseus of the Myth of Er in the *Republic*] is the best and most prudent choice; cease from the folly of metaphysical speculation and inquiry into origins and ends, utterly reject their clever logic, count all these things idle talk, and pursue one end alone—how you may do what your hand finds to do, and go your way, with ever a smile and never a passion.[8]

Skepticism, in its attack on dogmatic rationalism, is intellectually impregnable. Every candid thinker today must admit, we know no absolutely certain truth—no "Truth" with a capital "T." If we should happen to, it would be an accident: we could never be sure of knowing it. As the Skeptic puts it, there is no "criterion" of truth—no idea and no experience carrying any intrinsic mark of its validity in itself. The age-long quest for such certainty, though probably ineradicable, and despite its many incidental fruits, has unquestionably been productive of much intellectual futility.

It is important to insist on this core of the Skeptic teaching

[7] Walter Pater, *Marius the Epicurean* (London, 1911), pp. 154, 167-68; tr. of *Hermotimus*.

[8] Lucian, *Menippus*, I, 167.

today; it is the only way to preserve one's intellectual sanity amidst the temptations of the many persuasive and seductive— although conflicting—dogmatic faiths, both rational and irrational, so loudly calling for men's allegiance. On this point, it seems the part of wisdom to agree with those contemporary philosophies that put their faith in the experimental temper of mind.

But when the Skeptic goes on to take as his aim *ataraxia,* imperturbability, and as the means *epochē,* suspension of judgment, in all matters of belief, and conformity in action, the modern will part company. Such a conclusion, he will recognize, is unjustified intellectual defeatism, and a practical escape-philosophy—it is intellectual alienation from the intellectual resources we now command. It was natural enough in the Hellenistic Age, and under similar conditions later. But it is hardly tenable in the face of the practical demands of today, and with the intellectual methods and procedures now at the disposal of thinkers.

For Western culture has developed a method of criticizing and testing beliefs, unknown to the Greeks. In the light of these scientific methods of criticism and verification or warranting, it is no longer true that for the modern all beliefs are intellectually of equal standing. Logically considered, our whole complex procedure of verification is an assumption, an *archē.* But unlike other procedures for judging beliefs—unlike those developed in Greek thought, and critically analyzed by the Skeptics—it is a method that is self-verifying; and it cannot be disregarded with impunity.

Even the Skeptic admitted, men must act. Amidst our various postulate systems, we must choose that one which best guides action toward what our postulate-system of values assumes is better than the others. Logically analyzed, all our systems of beliefs are hypotheses: they rest on ultimate assumptions, on a logical faith, if we will. But they rest on assumptions whose power to organize our experience is perfectly objective— that power can be publicly tested and verified. That we must follow the best hypothesis available, and not one less good; the most probable, and not the less probable; that tested beliefs are better than those untested and that that belief is best that can pass the most rigorous tests better than all the others—this is the essence of what has here been called "scientific skepticism," the attitude of scientific intelligence. There is no evidence that the most vigorous action demands unquestioned belief, rather than tested beliefs; that it requires dogmatic faith, rather than the faith in testing; that even in time of crisis, intelligence must give way to force without intelligence, to sheer coercion.

If skepticism lacks such faith in testing, as superficial skepticism normally does—only Carneades among the ancient Skeptics really possessed it—what does following probabilities, being reasonable, really mean? It means, "Follow the crowd," do what everybody is doing, refrain from doing what is not done. In other words, Skepticism of the nonscientific variety is always a conservative attitude and force. If nothing can be known to be true or better, why should men bother to change? It is the part of wisdom to follow the custom of the country. Here we find Montaigne, Hume, A. J. Balfour—the great skeptical philosophers are all conformists—it is the easiest way.

The radical needs faith in reason or intelligence. He needs to be able to prove that what is, is wrong, and that something else is better.[9] Skepticism is often held to be a radical and dan-

[9] That is why the Communists, when in radical opposition, are normally such intellectualists, with such a minimum of passion and emotion, with such an emphasis on reason and logic and science—far too much for an irrational world. Of course, where Communism has become itself the Establishment, the situation is different. Emotion always comes to the support of the status quo.

gerous doctrine. In truth, the dangers come from commitment
—especially if it be irrational. The skeptic may smile; and he
is often irritating. But the nonscientific skeptic will never inter-
fere with any established racket, or any respectable stupidity
or injustice. Conservatives should welcome such a skepticism:
it is always their greatest ally. It paralyzes just those intelligent
enough to combat them.[10]

Such conservative acquiescence was what Greek Skepticism,
forgetting Carneades, led to:

We attend to the appearances of things and lead a human life,
observing the conditions of such a life, without holding any
opinion, since we cannot give up action altogether. This observation of the conditions of life seems to come under four heads:
firstly, there is the way marked out by Nature, by which we are
so constituted as to have certain sensations and thoughts; secondly,
there is the compulsion of our bodily feelings, the hunger that
drives us to food, the thirst that drives us to drink, and so on;
thirdly, there is the tradition, embodied in customs and laws, by
which we are taught as a matter of practical life that religion is
a good thing and that irreligion is a bad thing; and lastly, there
is technical skill, by which we can maintain our activity in the
various arts and crafts that have come down to us. But in saying
all this we imply no opinion as to truth. . . . We follow the ordinary ways of society without opinion, so that we may not give up
action. . . . We live following established laws and customs and
natural appetites, without opinion as to their validity.[11]

Hence, naturally enough, Skepticism was seized upon by
the religious traditionalists, the priests of the official Olympian
religion, as their best apologetic:

The Skeptic will be found acknowledging the gods according to
the customs of his country and the laws, and doing everything

10 That is why commitment, even though irrational, offers greater promise
than skepticism. For it can always lead on to analysis and even planning
for the future that may become, with painful learning, rational and intelligent.
11 Sextus Empiricus, *Outlines of Pyrrhonism*, pars. 23-24, 226, 231.

which tends to their proper worship and reverence, but in the region of philosophic inquiry he makes no rash assertion.[12]

In Cicero's *De Natura Deorum,* it is the Roman High Priest, the Pontifex Maximus, Cotta, who is the spokesman for Skepticism. He argues:

I have always defended, and will always defend the traditional ceremonies of religion, and no argument of anyone, learned or simple, will ever make me budge from the belief which I have received from our ancestors as to the worship of the immortal gods. . . . If you, as a philosopher, can justify my religion on rational grounds, good: but I am bound to follow our ancestors, even though they give no reason.[13]

Cotta then proceeds to demolish the Stoic rationalized religion by the arguments of Carneades.

The Christians in Rome followed suit. Caecilius, in the dialogue of Minucius Felix, *Octavius,* is a Skeptic defending paganism against Christianity. Just because Nature is dark and truth undiscoverable, "how much better to follow the religious practices handed down to you, to worship the gods whom your parents taught you to fear rather than to know with too close a familiarity, to advance no opinion as to the divine powers, but to follow the men of old."[14]

The conservatives could not take the old religious practices, beliefs, and mores seriously, but the new ones were no better. We know nothing about the Gods, so let us stay in the Established Church: at least we know it is established. This was the sole defense of paganism against the new Oriental faiths, like Christianity. It is a recurrent attitude. We have only to compare the long line of Christian skeptics: Pascal, Kierkegaard, Cardinal Newman, Karl Barth, and the Neo-Orthodox. Yet

---

[12] Sextus Empiricus, *Against the Mathematicians*, IX, 49.

[13] Cicero, *De Natura Deorum*, III, 5.

[14] Minucius Felix, *Octavius*, 6.

invariably skepticism without faith in scientific method is prone
to give way to some faith that promises more. Christian skeptics, and skeptics of the Christian tradition, are notoriously
liable to turn to Rome in the end, from Augustine to John
Henry Newman, and the followers of Anatole France.

Today, when traditional forms of religion have ceased to
mean much to the intellectual class, nonintelligent skepticism
means social conservatism. And the turning to the strongest
faith in sight has come to mean, for intellectuals in many
parts of the world—though not in the United States—turning to faith in the dogmatic rationalism of the Communists—
to Marxism–Leninism, or to Maoism.

VI   THE FORTUNES OF GREEK PHILOSOPHY IN ROME

Rome became mistress of the Mediterranean world in 146 B.C.
She was eager for culture, and ready to make it hum. Every
Greek philosopher who could secure passage sailed to Rome to
lecture: they nearly all came, sooner or later. Some secured
posts as tutors in the great senatorial houses: Lucian gives an
unforgettable picture in his dialogue *The Hireling Philosophers*. The Romans of the Republic had a passion, not so much
for knowledge as for education and culture; and they wanted
it without waste of time. Their children, of course, must have
the best education available.[1]

1 See Ueberweg-Praechter; E. Bréhier, *Études de Philosophie Antique* (Paris,
1955), and F. C. Copleston, *History of Philosophy*, 6 vols. (Westminster, Md.,
1946-1960), Vol. I, Part ii; E. V. Arnold, *Roman Stoicism* (Cambridge, 1911).
Samuel Dill's two volumes, *Roman Society from Nero to Marcus Aurelius*

The Epicureans got to Rome first, and so won a head start over the other Schools. Their doctrine proved popular and pleasing to the Roman *nouveaux riches.* They hence made and sustained a reputation in Rome they had never really achieved in Greece, and were there recognized by the Romans as a fourth School of philosophy. The Roman conservatives became alarmed. They expelled two Greek Epicureans in 173 B.C., and in 161 B.C. excluded all the dangerous Greek rhetoricians.

In 156 B.C., ten years before Rome finally swallowed up Greece, Athens sent her ablest philosophers and arguers on a mission to Rome to try to stave off what the Greeks saw coming. The heads of the Lyceum and the Porch were in the mission, which was led by the famous and brilliant Carneades, Scholarch of the Academy. In Rome, Carneades delivered "Lectures on Justice." The first day, he set forth what justice is, using the arguments of Socrates, Plato, Aristotle, and Chrysippus. The next day he argued, there is no such thing as justice, there is only power. Justice is a convention made by a people in its own interest. If there were any such thing as natural justice, superior to what the most powerful nation can get away with, the Romans would give up their conquests, and would not now be preparing to engulf Greece.

This was the first time the Romans had been treated to Greek dialectic. It was also a diplomatic hint. Cato, of course, was outraged. He declared that justice is eternal, and has nothing to do with power. And he concluded his reply, as usual, by declaring, *"Carthago delenda est."*

(2d ed., London, 1905), and *Roman Society in the Last Century of the Western Empire* (2d ed., London, 1899); J. P. Mahaffy, *Silver Age of the Greek World* (Chicago, 1906), chs. 5-7; A. W. Benn, *The Greek Philosophers* (2d ed.; London, 1914), ch. 12. For Latin philosophical terminology, see Cicero and also Quintilian. Walter Pater, *Marius the Epicurean*, a fine recreation of the Roman atmosphere in the second century of our era.

The Greek philosophers soon learned what the Romans wanted, and laid in a plentiful stock. Epicureanism and Stoicism proved the most popular: they could both be adopted without too much intellectual exertion, and they were both very practical. The Greek systems in each case were pushed into the background, and the ways of life brought forward. The lecturers retailed moral principles drawn from anywhere, with few technicalities, and no hard things to do; they also lectured on the story of philosophy.

A new Sophistic period followed in Rome. There were teachers of a vague enlightenment, and of a variety of doctrines, eclectically joined. The teachers were skeptical in their beliefs, and cynical in their practice. Here were all the phenomena of a newly rich people earnestly seeking higher things. The better Romans were very serious. Thus Lucretius made Epicureanism into something definitely anticlerical, an instrument of reform, not a mere promise of peace of mind. On the whole, Stoicism suited the Roman sensibility better, and by Cicero's day it had won out. It had a sound moral message, and was in fact an admirable rationalization of the traditional Roman ethic of duty. It had also just that vague religious feeling, that trust in Providence, left as a deposit by the fading of any particular and determinate religion. It was in Rome a time of religious disintegration. The old Roman religion had received no imaginative or intellectual development. Hence on first reflection, belief in it disappeared; yet it remained politically fundamental. The Stoic natural religion proved just the way to rationalize the ceremonies and rituals that had to be performed. Marcus Aurelius, for example, a Stoic in his philosophy, was always most punctilious in administering the official observances.

From the Romans' point of view, there was one great lack in Greek Stoicism: it had no clear conception of moral struggle

in the soul, or of the escape of the soul after death. The
Romans felt deeply the sense of sin. Hence to the Stoic ethics
and religion, the Romans added Platonic ideas about the divi-
sions of the soul, and about its eternal destiny. This fusion of
Stoic and Platonic teachings prevailed, until the rise of philosophies offering a more definitely otherworldly salvation. Such
uncritical eclecticism was the inevitable consequence of philosophy's becoming popular, a liberal religion for those who had
outgrown mere tradition.

Three Greeks were especially influential in the formation of
the Roman philosophy, Panaetius, Poseidonios, and Antiochus.
Panaetius (185-110 B.c.), lived in the house of Scipio Aemili-
anus, the final conqueror of Carthage, and head of the first
circle of Romans to introduce Greek culture into Rome. Panaetius stood for enlightenment through Greek thought, release
from the bondage to mere tradition: he was a religious rationalist. He also gave a rationalistic critique of the Stoic dogmas.
For him, there was no foolish idea of a succession of world
conflagrations, or of personal immortality, or of divination.
There are, he said, three kinds of theology: that of the poets,
that of the philosophers, and that of the statesmen. The first
kind is anthropomorphic and false; the second is rational and
true, for the educated. The third, maintaining the established
political religion, is indispensable to governing the State. Significantly, early Roman Epicureanism was also primarily a
rationalistic, anticlerical philosophy, rather than an ethic of
escape. Lucretius has a genuine interest in the cosmos, but
he also shares very little interest in Epicurus' own quietistic
way of life.

Panaetius was liberal also in his ethics: he counseled no
useless striving to become the perfect Wise Man. The Wise
Man would be serenely good; but for a cultured Senator, that

was scarcely expedient. It was enough for the Senator to be honest and respectable; and Panaetius was very broad-minded and tolerant about what honesty is. Panaetius was a great success.

Panaetius wrote a book on *The Double Standard,* one for the Sage, perfect virtue, and another for the ordinary man, the *proficiens,* the man "on the road" to virtue, for whom the standard is expediency in the choice of external things. Panaetius' book is paraphrased by Cicero in his *De Officiis.* Cicero goes on to discuss, in the spirit of casuistry, whether the merchant should reveal defects in his goods, or rely on the principle of *caveat emptor;* again, Cicero discusses whether in a storm worthless slaves or a valuable cargo should be jettisoned to lighten the ship, and so on. Cicero concludes against immediate expediency; but the reader is permitted to disagree.

Poseidonios (135-51 B.C.) was a teacher at Rhodes, where Cicero studied under him for a term. He had wide scientific interests; but by that time few people cared. In fact, he showed an interest and a learning in geography, in natural history, in mathematics, and in astronomy, that were considered quite indecent in a Stoic. He measured the sun, the earth, and the tides. He wrote a history of his times. He was the last ancient with universal intellectual interests. Strabo complained that his spirit of free inquiry was much more appropriate to the Peripatetic School, and altogether out of place in a Stoic.[2]

Poseidonios put together the most popular inclusive intellectual system till the rise of Neo-Platonism, a system that seems to have furnished central ideas to men as different as Cicero, Philo Judaeus, Seneca, and Plutarch.[3] In the Stoic physics he developed most fully the notion of tension, the harmony of opposites, the physics of force and "the field." In Stoic ethics

[2] See above, chapter 4.
[3] See the anticipated edition of Poseidonios begun by Ludwig Edelstein.

he abandoned the radical religious rationalism of Panaetius, and added Platonic conceptions of an irrational soul, to explain the Roman experience of moral struggle and of sin. He added also a definite theory of personal immortality, to suit the new temper of the times. The soul lives on after death as "breath" or *pneuma,* dwelling in the air among the stars, watching the stars go round and studying astronomy. That is, pure souls do; the souls weighted with the foulness of the body hover until they have been purified in the denser air below the moon. The heaviest souls of all drop so close to earth that they are pulled back into new bodies, with all their passions and pains. The only Hell, that is, is to be found on earth, in human life.

Poseidonios is a very influential figure. In Rhodes, the greatest scientific center after Alexandria itself, he drew all scientific interests together into a great synthetic system. He furnishes the most systematic expression of what we call "Alexandrian thought." He produced the last scientific system in Greek thinking. His combination of monism and dualism was an important step in the formation of the later Neo-Platonic systems.

But the Romans wanted no new doctrines. They felt it was better to be quite orthodox as to the Stoic system; it hardly mattered anyway. What they wanted was sound moral doctrine: it was good for the young. Now and then a Roman took Stoicism seriously, and the result was terribly upsetting. It was much as though one were to take Christianity seriously today. Marcus Aurelius was just such a misguided soul.

Antiochus (d. 68 B.C.) was the skeptical head of the "New Academy," who returned to the "Old Academy," and surrendered to the Stoics on most points. He stood for a skeptical and eclectic Platonism, with a dash of Stoic duty. He taught Cicero, who brought his ideas to Rome: free speculation about the things nobody cared for or understood, together with a

Stoic ethics modified for the man of the world, the Roman Senator. Men can lead the happy life, the *Vita Beata,* by virtue alone. But external goods, the perfection of the whole man, are really good. And they are needed for the happiest life, the *Vita Beatissima.*

Thereafter, the Academics adopted a watered-down Stoic ethics; the Stoics in turn dropped the hard parts of their system and teaching and found a Platonic soul. They became in Rome the philosophy of high society: all the best people professed Stoicism. One could hardly expect them to practice it, much of the time. Stoicism became a respectable liberal religion, like, we are told, Boston Unitarianism in the old days.

Out of such Greek ideas, and out of Roman feeling and experience, above all, out of the experience of an expanding empire, the Romans managed to develop a fairly original Roman philosophy. From Augustus to Hadrian, Roman literature and thought felt little fresh Greek influence. This philosophy was an original creation of the Romans, built around the idea of empire. There emerged a common philosophy, usually called Stoicism—more precisely, Roman Stoicism—enormously influential on Roman law and administration.

This philosophy emphasized the idea of Nature, as a simple, universal Order. It was very congenial to the Romans: to them it meant their Empire. It meant that Providence intended Rome to rule the world: it was the idea of what Americans have called manifest destiny.[4] It gave the Romans a comfortable feeling of high responsibility: it was the Romans' burden to act as agent for Nature and Providence.

Then there was the idea of a universal Reason, which meant

---

[4] This idea of empire is expressed in classic form in the familiar lines from Vergil's *Aeneid*:

       Tu regere imperio populos, Romane, memento:
       Hae tibi erunt artes; pacisque imponere morem,
       Parcere subiectis, et debellare superbos.

                           Aeneid, VI, lines 851-53

the dignity of the Roman citizen, and was applied by faithful Roman administrators to all the lesser breeds without the law. What was natural was identified with what was reasonable. And what was both was what was useful—to the Roman people. One is reminded of the role played in the eighteenth century by the Newtonian Order of Reason and Nature. Enlightenment thought and sensibility was of course steeped in Augustan literature.

On this philosophy the Romans lived from Cicero to the second century of our era; it fills Augustan literature. Vergil, for example, is just such a Stoic, with Platonic touches around the soul, like all the Roman Stoics. The philosophical passages in Vergil seem to have come mostly from Poseidonios.

Of this Roman philosophy, the best example is the figure, so influential then and in the whole later Humanistic tradition, of Cicero (106-43 B.C.).[5] Cicero is typical of the best of

[5] See chapter 4, note 1. Texts of all Cicero's philosophical and rhetorical writings (except the *Timaeus*) in Loeb Library (1914-1952). In addition to the works mentioned in the text, Cicero's extensive writings on rhetoric are also of philosophic interest, both for ethics and for intellectual method. They form the basis of the third great medieval intellectual tradition, the rhetorical or Ciceronian. See Richard McKeon, "Rhetoric in the Middle Ages," in *Speculum*, 17 (1942). Cicero's rhetorical writings include *Brutus* (Loeb, 1952), *De Inventione* (Loeb, 1949), *Orator* (Loeb, 1952), *De Oratore* (3 vols.; Loeb, 1942), *Topics* (Loeb 1949).

Brutus, On the Nature of the Gods, On Divination, and *On Duties,* tr. by H. M. Poteat, with introduction by R. McKeon (Chicago, 1950). *Academica,* J. S. Reid, ed. (London, 1884; tr. by Reid, 1880). *Tusculan Disputations,* J. E. King, ed. and tr. (Loeb, 1927). *De Finibus,* H. Rackham, ed. and tr. (Loeb, 1914). *De Re Publica, De Legibus,* C. W. Keyes, ed. and tr. (Loeb, 1928). *De Re Publica,* tr. as *On the Commonwealth* by G. H. Sabine and S. B. Smith (Columbus, 1929; reprinted, Liberal Arts).

Studies: Alexander Litman, *Cicero's Doctrine of Nature and Man* (New York, 1930); R. Philippson, "M. Tullius Cicero, die philosophische Schriften," in Pauly-Wissowa, Vol. VIIA, cols. 1104-1192; W. Kroll, *The Humanism of Cicero* (Melbourne, 1954); and P. Milton Valente, *L'Éthique Stoicienne chez Cicéron* (Paris, 1956), good bibliography.

the cultured Romans, and he is also the greatest mediator between Greek and Roman thought. He studied Greek philosophy at Rome under Phaedrus the Epicurean, Philo the Academic, and Diodotus the Stoic. He then went on to Athens, where he heard the lectures of Zeno the Epicurean, and Antiochus the Academic, and then to Rhodes, where he studied under Poseidonios the Stoic. At Athens he was interested in all the sights, which he took in as a typical earnest Roman tourist.

It was primarily Cicero who translated Greek philosophy into the Latin tongue. Together with Quintilian, he invented all the Latin philosophical terms, and made Latin the philosophical language it has remained in the West ever since. But in the process he invented mysterious Latin words to fit other Greek words, rather than to fit things, words that ring with such an abstract and unreal tone in comparison with the vivid concreteness of the Greek of Plato or of Aristotle.

Take *aition*, which in Greek meant originally "something asked for" or "responsible," the "answer" to a question. Incidentally it meant also the "response" or "respondent" in a court of law. Cicero understood law courts, and he made *aition* into *causa*, a "case" in court. In the Latin no sense was left of the original meaning of "answer to a question," or "reason why," "responsible factor."

Or take *kathēkon*, which in Greek means an "appropriate act," an act performed with foresight and intelligence, and one that is hence *kalon*, "adapted" to the situation, suitable and fine. The Greek word is an artist's or a craftsman's term. Cicero translated *kathēkon* as *officium*, "duty," which carries no sense of any relation to an end, of any functional character. Cicero, following Zeno, defines an *officium* as "an act for which a reasonable defense can be given," the omission of which is a crime. An *officium* is a *faciendum*; Cicero transformed the Greek craftsman's term into a lawyer's term.

Or take *ousia*, "being" or "thing." Cicero made it *substantia*, which is the literal translation of the different Greek term, *hypokeimenon*, the "underlying." Now, what on earth is *substantia*? No wonder Descartes was later greatly puzzled by the to him meaningless question.

Cicero had little interest in science. "The heavens are too remote," he says, "the interior of the earth is too dark, the body too complicated, for any fruitful investigation." The sole motive for studying philosophy is not knowledge, but the desire for happiness. "Wisdom," *Sapientia*, is a cardinal virtue. But its content is to be purely moral and political: true Wisdom is the knowledge that makes men useful to the Commonwealth. And one can easily possess an excess of "wisdom": we must not devote too much time and energy to matters obscure, difficult, and useless as well. Moral excellence Cicero rates as definitely higher than intellectual excellence. "To be drawn by study away from active life is contrary to duty. For the whole glory of virtues is in activity." "Community" or "sociability" ranks much higher than "wisdom": "Any man would drop the inquiry into Nature to serve his country or his friend." Cicero is continually apologizing for his philosophical writings, always a little suspect in Rome: he has turned to them, he insists, only because he is for the moment out of power, and excluded from political life. It is clear, the theoretical life was not in Rome a serious rival to the practical life.

Theoretical knowledge is in fact beyond man's ken. The only object of philosophy is ethics. Hence, since some knowledge of the universe is necessary for that self-knowledge that is indispensable for living well, the world is to be known primarily in moral terms. Things are to be understood, that is, not as what they are in themselves, not as what they can do and accomplish, not in the light of the function they perform—

that is, things are to be known, not as "intelligible," as they appear in Aristotle's thought; they are to be understood rather as good or bad for men, as serving Man's moral purpose. They are to be known not as working out their determinate possibilities, as reaching their own specific entelechies; they are to be known as better or worse for man's interests. For Aristotle, the end or *physis,* the "nature" of the eye, is seeing; for Cicero, the end or *natura* of the eye is to realize man's moral purpose. Where Aristotle is exploring an intelligible scheme of ends, Cicero is setting forth a moral one.

Cicero thus managed to transform the Greek notion of the world as a *kosmos,* an intelligible order, beautiful because intelligible, into the Roman notion of the world as a *mundus,* a moral spectacle, a thing with a moral government, beautiful because of its moral grandeur, and adapted to gods and men. For the Greeks, *physis* was a principle of intelligibility. For Cicero and the Romans, *Nature* is a principle of moral government, a moral and aesthetic ordering principle, that is, a Providence. Thus Cicero picked from the wealth of Greek philosophy what an intelligent Roman could understand, and translated it from the idiom of free and heaven-questioning Athens into the Roman tongue of the market place and the law court. He gave it a characteristic Roman stamp.

Cicero thus created the type of Roman culture, the *Studium Humanitatis ac Litterarum,* the study, concretely put, of great men and of effective pleading. The Romans were stuffed from the cradle with moral hero-worship. Roman education was based on history, of the Parson Weems cherry-tree variety. It was utterly nationalistic. Greek education was based on the study of the poets: the Greeks took their illustrations from Homer, Pindar, and Hesiod. The Romans always cite Cato, Regulus, Lucretia, the Decii, statesmen and generals. The second basis of Roman education was eloquence, the art of persuading, of debate and legal pleading. The Greeks were always discussing, the Romans debating. And the difference is profound. The Greeks were interested in dialectic, which deals with ideas; the Romans in rhetoric, which leads to action. The Greeks loved discussion for its own sake, the clarification and the insights it brings: they always hated to stop. Plato gives the inimitable picture. Out of such discussion could come, at the hands of Plato and Aristotle—who summarized rather than exhibited it—truth, with all its complexities and distinctions. The Romans loved to win: with their words they were seeking power, not truth. Debating, it seems, utterly kills the spirit of inquiry, of science, of philosophy—at most it can strengthen commitment. The greatest debater is the lawyer, and the Romans were great lawyers. Obviously, the best possible defense is of the indefensible. And the Roman mind is at its most acute, from Seneca to Tertullian and Augustine, in defending the ways of Providence towards Man—after a preliminary training in defending the ways of Rome to its subjects.

Even Lucretius displays this typically Roman emphasis on great men and on eloquent pleading. Consider the grandeur of Epicurus, *"Homo Graius,"* and the eloquence of Lucretius' pleading against the fear of death, and against the passion of love. Who has ever made a nobler defense of things as they are, *Naturae species ratioque,* "Nature's aspect and her law"?

Cicero is the very epitome of Roman culture: a culture founded on rhetoric, willing to sacrifice anything to an effective phrase—"what oft was thought but ne'er so well expressed"—; on practicality, not intellectual curiosity and inquiry; on traditional morality, devotion to the ancestral mores, not on *theōria,* and its attendant aesthetic delight; and directed not to the Good Life, to *to eu zēn,* but to the *honestum,* which meant, alas, not "honesty," but the respectable, the conventional, *decorum,* propriety, good form.

When he was not engaged in orating in the interest of the landed class, Cicero wrote urbane and facile dialogues. They are intensely interesting as an expression of the Roman mind, of what intelligent Romans thought and felt; and they form admirable textbooks on what the views of the three philosophic Schools had come to mean in Rome (the Lyceum at this time was negligible). These dialogues are philosophical, the *Academica* and the *De Natura Deorum*; moral, the *De Finibus* and the *De Officiis*; and political, the *De Re Publica* and the *De Legibus*. The political dialogues are by far the most original, and Roman; the others are free paraphrase and adaptations of popular Greek philosophical writings.

Cicero himself belonged to the "old Academy" of Antiochus, his teacher in Athens: he did not want to be too dogmatic, and he did like to arrange the best briefs for and against every position. But he was quite unable to carry his speculative skepticism into moral and political matters. He followed Antiochus in finding the popular Stoic morality reasonable. The real philosophic fight is between the *Honestum,* the "Honorable," as the Chief Good, and *Voluptas,* pleasure. Unless the latter is vanquished, all virtue, honor, and true merit must be abandoned. When pleasure has once been refuted, then there is an "honorable quarrel" between the defenders of the *honestum* as the sole Good, and those who, while admitting that it overshadows all else, still think some bodily and external goods, like health and friendship, are really good—a quarrel between the Stoics and the Academics. Cicero himself inclines to the Academy; but he insists that the differences are merely verbal. Everybody really agrees anyway, except the un-Roman Epicureans.

Cicero fell back on the Stoic common preconceptions, the *sensus communis,* "common opinion" or universal assent. This is for him as for the Stoics generated by a common experience of a common world. Cicero adhered to a sentimental liberal religion, the belief in the Stoic Providence, in an immanent God, and in the immortality of the soul. In the *De Natura Deorum,* he opposes the devastating arguments of Carneades to the Epicurean ideal gods, and to the Stoic Providence, and then concludes: "The Epicurean was convinced, the truth lay with the Skeptic; but I judged 'appearances' were for the Stoic Providence." Such is the extent of Cicero's skepticism.

On the other hand, Cicero is at his best in emphasizing the social nature of man, universal "sociability," the natural attraction that unites men by the common bonds of reason and language in a common life. The whole universe is one great state, one "city of gods and men," united by the possession of reason for the common advantage.

That animal which we call man, endowed with foresight and quick intelligence, complex, keen, possessing memory, full of reason and prudence, has been given a certain distinguished status by the supreme God who created him; for he is the only one among so many different kinds and varieties of living beings who has a share in reason and thought, while all the rest are deprived of it. But what is more divine, I will not say in man only, but in all heaven and earth, than reason? And reason, when it is full grown and perfected, is rightly called wisdom.

Therefore, since there is nothing better than reason, and since it exists both in man and in God, the first partnership (*societas*) between man and God is in reason. But those who have reason in common must also have right reason in common. And since right reason is Law, we must believe that men are partners with the gods in Law. Further, those who have Law in common also share in common Right and Justice (*Jus*); and those who share these are to be regarded as members of the same commonwealth. . . . Hence this whole universe forms a single commonwealth, common alike to gods and men. And just as in States distinctions in legal status are made on account of the blood relationships of families, . . . so in the nature of things the same holds true, but on a scale much vaster and more splendid, so that men are grouped with gods on the basis of blood relationship and descent.[6]

One outcome of the social nature of man is the *res publica,* literally "the public thing," the "commonwealth," what people possess in common. Not, to be sure, any chance groups of men, but "an assemblage of men, associated in an agreement with respect to common rights, and a partnership for the common good and the common safety"—a partnership destroyed, alas, by Caesar.

Another outcome of the social nature of man is *Lex,* Law, which Cicero makes prior to and the source of *Jus,* Right or Justice.

Law is the highest reason (*ratio summa*) implanted in Nature, which commands what ought to be done, and forbids the opposite. This reason, when firmly fixed and fully developed in the human mind, is Law. Law is intelligence (*prudentia*), whose function is to command right conduct and forbid wrongdoing. . . .
The origin of Right and Justice (*Jus*) is to be found in Law; for Law is a force of Nature, the mind and the reason of the intelligent man, the standard by which Justice and Injustice are measured. (I, 18, 19)

Law is the very mind of God, the "Reason" by which the universe is ruled.

Law is not a product of human thought, nor is it any enactment of peoples, but it is something eternal, which rules the whole universe by its wisdom, in command and prohibition. Law is the primal and ultimate mind of God, whose reason directs all things by compulsion and restraint. It is the reason and mind of a wise lawgiver. (II, 8)

This perfected reason, or Law, is thus shared by God and man: it is the divine element in man himself. It is shared equally by all men; all men are equally bound by the Law of

---

[6] Cicero, *De Legibus,* I, 22-24; Loeb Classics, C. W. Keyes, ed.

Reason, all are equally able to discern it—at least, all men have an equal capacity to learn it, provided the obstacles are removed.

The whole human race is thus bound together in a unity of Reason, Law, and Right.

We are born for Justice (*Justitia*), and Right (*Jus*) is established not on men's opinions, but on Nature. This will immediately be plain if you once get a clear idea of man's fellowship and union (*societatem conjunctionemque*) with his fellow-men. For no single thing is so like another, so exactly its equal, as all of us men are to one another. Nay, if bad habits and vain opinions did not twist the weaker minds and turn them in whatever direction they are inclined, no one would be so like his own self as all men would be like all others. And so, however we may define "Man," a single definition will apply to all men. This is a sufficient proof that there is no difference in kind or race (*in genere*) between man and man; for if there were, a single definition would not apply to all men. And indeed, Reason, which alone raises us above the level of the beasts, and enables us to draw inferences, to prove and disprove, to discuss and solve problems, and to come to conclusions, is certainly common to all us men; and though it varies in what it learns (*doctrina differens*), at least in the power of learning (*in discendi facultate*) it is invariable and equal (*par*). For the same things are perceived by the senses; . . . and those first rude beginnings of intelligence which are imprinted on our minds are imprinted on all minds alike; and speech, the interpreter of the mind, though it disagrees in the words it uses, agrees in the ideas it expresses. In fact, there is no human being of any race who, if he accepts Nature as his guide, cannot arrive at virtue.[7]

This Law of Reason and of Nature is the source of all positive enactments. If any should contravene it, they have no force whatever as Law. The Law of Nature is thus the standard for judging all positive law and legislation.

[7] *Ibid.*, I, 28-30.

But the most foolish notion of all is to think that everything is just, which is found in the customs or laws of different peoples. Would that be true, even if these laws had been enacted by tyrants? . . . For there is but one Right and Justice (*Jus*); it binds every human society, and is based on one single Law, which is right reason applied to command and prohibition. Whoever knows not this Law, whether it has been set down in writing anywhere or not, is himself unjust.[8]

This conception of Natural Law and Right, the product of the Divine Reason itself, embodied in the great jurists of the Age of Justinian and in the Codes of Civil Law, made Roman law, whenever men later turned to it in societies embodying what seemed the unjust customs and laws of peoples and of tyrants, an egalitarian and revolutionary force in the social life and quiet of men.

The Roman Seneca (4 B.C.-65 A.D.) lived a hundred years later than Cicero, in a Rome of very different times.[9] In him we no longer find the sturdy devotion to the ancestral virtues that marked the Republic, to the Commonwealth facing limitless vistas and horizons of empire. That world has now gone. For Seneca, the problem has become one of sheer endurance. Yet Seneca is compassionate and humanitarian—and this strikes a new note in the Roman tradition. The call now is not for Justice but for Mercy.

[8] *Ibid.*, I, 42.

[9] Seneca, *Moral Essays*, 3 vols.; *Epistulae Morales*, 3 vols.; both in Loeb, together with the *Tragedies* (2 vols.), so influential in Elizabethan England, and the *Apocolocynthosis*. Tr. of *Questiones Naturales* by J. Clarke and A. Geikie, in *Physical Science in the Time of Nero* (London, 1910). Moses Hadas, ed., *The Stoic Philosophy of Seneca* (New York, 1958).

See Copleston, Vol. I, Part ii, pp. 172-75; Samuel Dill, *Roman Society from Nero to Marcus Aurelius*; T. R. Glover, *Conflict of Religions in the Early Roman Empire* (London, 1909), ch. 2; P. Grimal, *Senèque* (Paris, 1957).

Seneca, a native of Cordoba in Spain,[10] is typical of the new Roman world under the early Empire. Philosophy has become definitely the cure of souls; philosophers are father confessors and chaplains, offering the consolations of religion and practical moral guidance to the upper class. Men now felt deeply the need of help from outside themselves. The later Catholic system was already taking form. The philosophers had become "priests of Reason."

Among these priests of Reason, Seneca is the outstanding figure. He is supplied with an unfailing fund of moral advice and consolation, in a balanced, "pointed" style. He has an interest also in science, of a sort, in knowing. His *Natural Questions* contain a supply of pseudo-scientific illustrations for moral points and themes. He discusses the Stoic cosmology; but he is keenly aware of the objection that he is wasting time. Such matters "relieve no emotions, rout no desires." Seneca no longer exhibits even Cicero's intellectual interest in discussing and debating rival ethical theories.

Seneca is a religious liberal and a Stoic modernist; he has no "hard sayings." Philosophy aims at fellow-feeling; hence the philosopher must not be too unlike other men. "The great soul uses silver dishes as if they were earthenware." "It is the sign of an unstable mind not to be able to endure riches."

The Stoic Sage is still the ideal, the man of perfect reason, *"quod honestum est."* But most men are merely *proficientes,* men "on the road." *Commoda,* external goods, are also good, because their use demands good judgment: it is good to choose them wisely. Not what is chosen, but the intelligent choice itself, is the good thing. Show grief, yes, at the misfortune of

---

[10] The Chamber of Commerce of Cordoba, Spain, lists as the three most famous men born in that ancient city Seneca, Averroes, and Moses Maimonides.

another; but not "to excess." "We may weep, but we must not wail." Feel pain, yes, in the body; but do not be overcome by it. Friendship, yes; but why? what should be the motive? To exercise our own noble qualities upon our friends. And if the friend should die, get a new one to practice and exercise one's gift for friendship upon.

Seneca was excellent at the sheer endurance of misfortune; he is constantly offering sage counsel for bearing the afflictions of old age, sickness, and death and bereavement. But in justifying Providence and its ways, and why the righteous suffer so, he seems the supreme example of the special pleader—even Job revolted.

Seneca is perhaps at his best as what the French call a *moraliste,* the analyst of the pathology of the human soul, especially of his own. He knew just what he ought to do, wrote gracefully about it, and rarely did it. He was a monk, an ascetic, a Stoic Sage, and the millionaire tool and apologist of Nero, the moral reformer and preacher who defended Nero's murders. Carlyle could hardly endure Seneca:

Notable Seneca, so wistfully desirous to stand well with Truth and yet not ill with Nero, is and remains only our perhaps niceliest proportioned half-and-half, the plausiblest Plausible on record; no great man, no true man, no man at all. . . . "The father of all such as wear shovel-hats". . . . He is the father of all that work in sentimentality, and, by fine speaking and decent behavior, study to serve God and Mammon, to stand well with philosophy and not ill with Nero. His *force* has mostly oozed out of him, or corrupted itself into benevolence, virtue, and sensibility. Oh! the everlasting clatter about virtue! In the Devil's name *be* virtuous and no more about it.[11]

Was Seneca hypocrite? No, he was a tragic figure. He saw the best clearly, but the world was too much for him. What

11 Thomas Carlyle, *Essay on Diderot,* 1833; also diary, August 10, 1832.

could he, a mere prime minister, hope to accomplish? We read Seneca, and begin to understand the appeal of Christianity and the other religions of salvation in those times. He saw his failure: for him life was a losing struggle. "The flesh lusted against the spirit." The body was the prison-house of the soul. Seneca yearned for release.

What Seneca needed was not knowledge of the Good, but Power—the power that came to that age with "faith" and "grace." Christianity was made for men like Seneca: it brought them the much-needed power, the power of Divine grace. Seneca had the highest ideals and personal standards. He defended Nero's murder of his mother, and then, in expiation, became a vegetarian for a year. He was Nero's tutor and prime minister. He was a preacher and not a saint. He was excellent on moral advice and counsel; he found it easy to shun luxury, and to abstain from wine, but very hard to do right. He saw what was wrong, he understood the folly of evil and vice, and also its necessity. He was completely disillusioned, pessimistic about human nature. He was no child of light, but definitely a child of this world, a tamed cynic.

Yet he had no intolerance, but rather a generous pity and compassion for his fellow-sinners. All men alike fall short of the glory of God; forgive them! Bear and forbear! We too are all miserable sinners. Let us be merciful, even as we hope God will grant to us mercy, and not mete out to us justice—for we should then be surely lost.

Seneca was formally a Stoic. But men have always judged, "He is so Christian." The legend grew up that he learned it from St. Paul. There is no evidence, and the relation is quite unnecessary. Seneca's own experience of moral struggle is sufficient, his experience of the inability not to sin. *Peccavi, peccavimus.*

Reason had failed. Men were ready to try faith.

VII THE REVIVAL OF RELIGIOUS PHILOSOPHIES

Any one who turns from the great writers of classical Athens, say Sophocles or Aristotle, to those of the Christian era must be conscious of a great difference in tone. There is a change in the whole relation of the writer to the world about him. The new quality is not specifically Christian: it is just as marked in the Gnostics or Mithras-worshippers as in the Gospels and the Apocalypse, in Julian and Plotinus as in Gregory and Jerome. It is hard to describe. It is a rise of asceticism, of mysticism, in a sense, of pessimism; a loss of self-confidence, of hope in this life and of faith in normal human effort; a despair of patient inquiry, a cry for infallible revelation; an indifference to the welfare of the state, a conversion of the soul to God. It is an atmosphere in which the aim of the good man is not so much to live justly, to help the society to which he belongs and enjoy the esteem of his fellow-creatures; but rather, by means of a burning faith, by contempt for the world and its standards, by ecstasy, suffering and martyrdom, to be granted pardon for his unspeakable unworthiness, his immeasurable sins. There is an intensifying of certain spiritual emotions; an increase of sensitiveness, a failure of nerve.[1]

The first century of our era saw a religious revival in the ancient world. There was, first, a rebirth of the old pagan polytheism, the official and civic religions of Greece and Rome. These had retreated under the attacks of the Skeptics, like Carneades and Panaetios, and of the "Romance" of Euhemeros the Cyrenaic. During the last century B.C. a wave of Greek religious rationalism was popular in the Roman Republic. This was the time of the highest influence of Epicureanism in

[1] Sir Gilbert Murray, *Four Stages of Greek Religion* (New York, 1912), p. 103. This work was later revised as *Five Stages of Greek Religion* (New York, 1925).

Rome. The old Roman religion of the farming countryside, with its agricultural rituals, had become outgrown in the metropolis, and survived there only as the instrument of political intrigue. This naturally bred the kind of anticlericalism typical of a pre-revolutionary era.

With the completion of the enduring Caesaristic revolution, and the establishment of a strong government under Augustus, a religious revival ensued. There spread in Italy a wave of religious fundamentalism, not shared by the Latin poets of the Augustan Age, who formed a kind of cosmopolitan intelligentsia—or wanted to. Rome somewhat resembled modern New York or London, with its literary circle comprised of young men from the provinces, anxious to live it down. These Augustan poets give the wrong impression of the Roman temper of the time.

The Italian countryside remained deeply attached to the religion of Numa. There is an unforgettable picture in Walter Pater's *Marius the Epicurean*, Chapter I, "The Religion of Numa." This rural population were *pagani*, literally "dwellers in the sticks."[2] Their traditional rites and feasts were ultimately incorporated into Latin Christianity: local gods became Christian patron saints.[3]

There took place, secondly, a conscious revival of the older Roman religion, as an instrument of nationalism and piety, and as a social bond. The parallel with the revival of the older Japanese religion of Shinto after 1868 is striking. This revived civic religion was an affair of state, a bond with the past, a matter of loyalty to the new Principate. It involved no theologi-

[2] Or, in the phrase of H. L. Mencken, "hicks from the Bible belt."
[3] See Norman Douglas, *South Wind* (London, 1921). Also Frederick C. Grant, *Ancient Roman Religion* (New York, 1954); H. J. Rose, *Ancient Roman Religion* (New York, 1948); J. B. Carter, *The Religious Life of Ancient Rome* (Boston, 1911).

cal belief: it left the educated free to join the philosophic Schools, even—or especially—the Skeptics. Marcus Aurelius, for instance, was always most punctilious in performing the official rites. The newly revived religion lent itself to theocracy, the holding of the person of the Emperor to be divine—an attitude very much like the traditional deification of the American Constitution among conservatives. This official religion persisted among the upper-class Senators until the fifth century, as the letters of Symmachus show.[4]

Similar attempts at fostering a political religion from on top had preceded this Roman effort, in the Hellenistic empires, notably Ptolemy's reconstruction of the ancient Egyptian religion, now focusing on Serapis. Ptolemy Philadelphus built a magnificent temple in Alexandria, the Serapeum; and by far the greater number of the hundred-odd Egyptian temples still surviving were erected under the Ptolemies. Under Roman sway, these political religions tended to become nationalistic religions of protest against Roman domination, performing a function similar to that of Catholicism in nineteenth-century Ireland or Poland. This is what happened to Judaism in Palestine under the party of the Zealots.

But besides this revival of the traditional ethnic or national religions, the era saw the growth and spread of many Oriental salvation religions. The political religions ultimately failed in their purpose; the nationalistic protests were crushed, as Titus crushed the Jews in Palestine in 70 A.D. The revival was unsuccessful in winning popular support, even in Rome itself. The average man in the cities wanted more personal spiritual help. The national or ethnic religions of the Eastern peoples, now carried all over the Empire, especially by the troops from the East, began to appeal to men in other provinces of the

[4] In Samuel Dill, *Roman Society in the Last Century of the Western Empire* (2d ed.; London, 1899).

Empire for quite different reasons from those of national loyalty. The city populations welcomed the gods, new to them, coming from the East, not as tribal or national deities, but as personal "Saviors." The situation was somewhat like that in eighteenth-century England, where the new city dwellers flocked to the evangelical chapels. They wanted, not the comfortable Church of England, but the blood of the Lamb—in Rome, it was the blood of the Bull, of Mithras.

Paganism proved itself imperialistic: it welcomed and fused all these new Gods, with the sole exception of the jealous and exclusive deities of the Jews and the Christians. The only way to assimilate Christianity was to allow it to assimilate all the rest, which it eventually did: this was the path actually followed. The new cults were strong in the cosmopolitan cities, like Rome, Alexandria, and Antioch. Their growth began among the slaves, the soldiers, and the women, and then seeped upward to the upper classes.

These new salvation religions all had certain elements in common. There was a Nature worship: the particular savior was seen against a vague, pantheistic background. The stars were taken as real divinities, especially, under Persian influence, the sun and the planets. This time saw the spread of the seven-day week, named after the planets. A part of this worship of the stars was astrology, divination, and prophecy.

There was, secondly, a rather shadowy, transcendent cosmic Deity, remote, unknowable, far-off, and above all, morally pure and unsullied. And thirdly, there was a longing for salvation, especially from sheer death. Immortality seems at this time to have been felt as a personal need; this longing received no support in Epicureanism, and little in Stoicism. There was a striking growth of faith in the future survival of the soul, especially among the Platonists. Thus in Plutarch, in the second century of our era, such immortality appears as man's deepest need and instinct. Little moral interest was connected with this longing for sheer survival after death: the concern was with mere future "life," with sheer survival.

This longing for immortality was served by the sacramental religions, the Mysteries.[5] The older Greek traditions of Eleusis and of Orpheus now appeared in new Oriental forms. By a rite of initiation or baptism, men can achieve freedom from the body, or ecstasy, and also union with the Savior-God, enthusiasm. This was achieved first by partaking of the sacrament or mystery, that is, by a magic rite—the Blood of the Bull, for example, by the Mithraists, and a sacred supper; and secondly, by personal purity—by renouncing the body.[6]

There now appeared many such incarnation religions. In them, God is so far-off and so pure that man needs to reach him a "Mediator," a "Savior," a "Lord" or *Kyrios*. The Great God of the universe hence sends his Son, or a Messenger, who becomes man, suffers and dies as a sacrifice to secure the salvation of man, then rises again to Heaven. By joining the Lord of the cult, in sacrament or magic rite, the initiate or convert can rise with him, and thus become himself immortal and divine. Such mystery religions included a secret revelation, a gospel offering salvation, proclaiming that God died for man so that man can rise with God.

[5] "Sacrament" in Greek is *mystērion*.

[6] F. Cumont, *Oriental Religions in Roman Paganism* (2d ed.; Eng. tr. Chicago, 1911), and *The Mysteries of Mithra* (2d ed.; Eng. tr. Chicago, 1903). S. Angus, *The Religious Quests of the Graeco-Roman World* (London, 1930) and *The Mystery Religions and Christianity* (London 1925). Chief authority is R. Reitzenstein, *Die hellenistischen Mysterienreligionen* (Leipzig, 1910; 3d ed. 1927). See also Frederick C. Grant, *Hellenistic Religions* (New York, 1953), texts. A. W. Benn, *The Greek Philosophers* (2d ed.; London, 1914), ch. 13, "The Religious Revival"; S. Dill, *Roman Society from Nero to Marcus Aurelius* (London, 1904; 2d ed.; 1905); T. R. Glover, *The Conflict of Religions in the Early Roman Empire* (London, 1909); C. H. Moore, *The Religious Thought of the Greeks* (Cambridge, Mass., 1916).

Christianity, in the hands of Saul of Tarsus, the real formulator of Christian theology, and of certain other early Christians, notably the author of the Fourth Gospel, became one such incarnation and mystery cult among many other competitors. It became the Jewish rival of the cults of Isis, of the Great Mother, of Mithras, and of many Gnostic sects. In the end, Christianity happened to win out.[7]

For a time Mithraism was the chief rival of Christianity.[8] It too offered a moral salvation, and it differed significantly from the other Hellenistic religious cults in just the ways Christianity did: it had a thoroughgoing emphasis on righteousness, and on a dramatic philosophy of history, rather than the eternal repetition and timelessness of most Greek thought. It was the closest too in its rites: it had a Eucharistic meal, which the Christian Fathers naturally dubbed "the work of the Devil!" Mithraism markedly influenced Christianity: it led to the adoption of Sun-day as the Holy Day, not the Jewish Sabbath; it introduced the festival of the winter solstice, Christmas; it had its myth of the Magi, the Shepherds, and the Divine Star.

Mithraism was essentially the creed of fighters, with a high moral standard: it appealed to the Roman soldiers. Temples of Mithras are to be found where the imperial troops were stationed, especially on the borders of the Empire: on Hadrian's Wall in North Britain, on the Eastern limits. But Mithraism remained dualistic, reflecting its Persian back-

---

[7] It is not easy to be convinced by the arguments of Christian scholars that there is an essential difference between Pauline Christianity and the other mystery religions. The obvious differences, especially the emphasis in Paul on the moral character of salvation, seem due to the Hebrew background of St. Paul's formulation of the Christian vision. That is, it appears to be the Jews, and not God—or at least, not God acting independently of His Chosen People—who are responsible for what is distinctive in Pauline Christianity.

[8] See Franz Cumont, R. Reitzenstein, and the texts in F. C. Grant.

ground, and unintellectual: it did not fit its practical ethical dualism into a religious and philosophical monism. It did not, as did Christianity, lend itself to intellectual rationalization and development in terms of Greek thought; it was especially unresponsive to Platonistic philosophy. With its Persian atmosphere it remained alien to the Greek mind. Hence it was unable, as were the Christian mysteries, to form a focus for organizing the whole of ancient thought into a comprehensive synthesis. So in the end it lost out, and we moderns live in Christendom, not in Mithradom.

Under these conditions, philosophy became the intellectual justification and interpretation of such a religious atmosphere. In the end it found the Christian mystery the most adaptable. By 100 A.D. there appears a revival of interest in philosophic systems, in speculation, and in cosmology, now as a religious apologetic. The temper is ascetic, but not yet sectarian and exclusive. The great problem is furnished by the attempt to reconcile a dualistic morality with a monistic view of the universe.

The Academy now forgot its earlier Skepticism and became, under what the scholars call Middle Platonism, a rationalization of pagan religion. The Academy now definitely superseded all the other Schools. Representative are Plutarch, Apuleius, Maximus of Tyre, and Celsus, the adversary of Origen. Celsus is the most intelligent of the anti-Christian Platonists: the only work in which Greek philosophy, in Platonism, really comes to grips with philosophic Christianity, is Origen's *Against Celsus*, in which the arguments of Celsus are given.

The Platonists of the Middle period now held that all religions, rightly understood, are true and useful. The one great God they all worship is so far away that man needs the help of symbols, graven idols, and daimons, to save him and to make him immortal and pure. So the Middle Platonists undertook an allegorical defense of all mythologies, rites, and religious beliefs, and of oracles and prophecies. They recognized hierarchies of daimons, good and bad, who became, under later Christian auspices, the good and the fallen angels. Maximus of Tyre puts this view:

God himself, the Father and Fashioner of all that is, older than the Sun or the Sky, greater than time and eternity and all the flow of Being, is unnameable by any Lawgiver, unutterable by any voice, not to be seen by any eye. But we, being unable to apprehend his essence, use the help of sounds and names and pictures, of beaten gold and ivory and silver, of plants and rivers, mountain peaks and torrents, yearning for the knowledge of Him, and in our weakness naming all that is beautiful in this world after His nature—just as happens to earthly lovers. To them the most beautiful sight will be the actual lineaments of the beloved, but for remembrance' sake they will be happy in the sight of a lyre, a little spear, a chair, perhaps, or a running-ground, or anything in the world that wakens the memory of the beloved. Why should I further examine and pass judgment about Images? Let men know what is Divine (*to theion genos*), let them know: that is all. If a Greek is stirred to the remembrance of God by the art of Pheidias, an Egyptian by paying worship to animals, another man by a river, another by fire—I have no anger for their divergences; only let them know, let them love, let them remember.[9]

Plutarch (46-120 A.D.)[10] was a Greek, and typical of Greek thought in the second century of our era, of the more con-

[9] Maximus of Tyre, Or. viii, in Wilamowitz, *Lesebuch*, ii, 338 ff.; quoted in Gilbert Murray, *Four Stages of Greek Religion*, pp. 98-99 n.

[10] Plutarch texts in Loeb Library: *Parallel Lives*, 11 vols. (1914-1926); *Moralia*, 15 vols. 1927—). Eng. tr.: *Lives*, Sir Thomas North, tr. (1575-1603), in Everyman. *Moralia*, Philemon Holland, tr. (1603), selection in Everyman. See J. Oakesmith, *The Religion of Plutarch as Expounded in his Ethics* (London, 1902); R. C. Trench, *A Popular Introduction to Plutarch*

servative type. He did not feel the need of the new Oriental religions; the old customs of the fathers, liberalized by reason, were for him enough. But they need to be reinterpreted to meet the needs of the new age. He lived in a small town, in Chaeronea in Boeotia, and was a good deal of a Main Street moralizer. He was a mixture of Stoic and Platonic ideas, with Platonism getting the upper hand, because of his controlling religious interest. He loved the ancient and ancestral faith, the faith of his fathers, and he needed faith. He lived in the past: the great men of old were his heroes; that is why he wrote his famous *Lives*.

Plutarch was an institutionalist, who loved the hallowed rites and ceremonies of old.

Our father, then, addressing Pemptides by name, said, "You seem to me, Pemptides, to be handling a very big matter and a very risky one—or rather, you are discussing what should not be discussed at all, when you question the opinion we hold about the gods, and ask reason and demonstration for everything. For the ancient and ancestral faith is enough, and no clearer proof could be found than itself—

Not though man's wisdom scale the heights of thought—but it is a common home and an established foundation for all piety; and if in one point its stable and traditional character be shaken and disturbed, it will be undermined and no one will trust it. . . . If you demand proof about each of the ancient gods, laying hands on everything sacred, and bringing your sophistry to play on every altar, you will leave nothing free from quibble and cross-examination. . . . Others will say that Aphrodite is desire and Hermes reason, the Muses crafts and Athene thought. Do you see,

(London, 1873); O. Gréard, *De la Morale de Plutarque* (Paris, 1866); R. Volkmann, *Leben, Schriften, und Philosophie des Plutarch* (Berlin, 1869); R. Hirzel, *Plutarch* (Leipzig, 1912); Roger Miller Jones, *The Platonism of Plutarch* (Menasha, Wis., 1916); K. Ziegler, *Plutarch von Chaironeia* (Stuttgart, 1949).

then, the abyss of atheism that lies at our feet, if we resolve each of the gods into a passion or a force or a virtue?"[11]

The old beliefs could not be literally true, of course: they have to be reinterpreted—Plutarch is also a modernist. He was priest of Apollo, and an initiate of the Dionysian mysteries. He retains much of the Greek sense of the Good Life as a human achievement, of reason controlling and directing natural impulses, and using external goods. He has no scorn for such natural goods—he is no ascetic. Man is his own master, he is free, for there is no controlling Fate. Plutarch is strongly opposed to Stoic determinism.

Yet Plutarch felt the need for external help, from the Divinities: man is not strong enough to lead the Good Life by his own powers. He needs religion. This is the novel and un-Greek note in Plutarch. And so he turned to philosophy as a support for religion. Yet throughout he is afraid of the consequences of a thought that is too free: he exhibits the Will to Believe to secure moral help.

So he resorts to interpretations and allegories. There is really only one God, and one Providence: all rational men believe that. It is attested by the poets, by the tradition, by oracles, by the mysteries.

There are not Greek gods and barbarian, southern or northern; but just as sun, moon, sky, earth and sea are common to all men and have many names, so likewise it is one Reason that makes all these things a cosmos; it is one Providence that cares for them, with helping powers appointed to all things; while in different peoples, different honors and names are given to them as customs vary. Some use hallowed symbols that are faint, others symbols more clear, as they guide their thought to the divine.[12]

[11] Plutarch, *Amatorius,* 13, 756 A, D; 757 B; quoted in T. R. Glover, p. 76. The quotation is from Euripides, *Bacchae,* 203.

[12] Plutarch, *De Iside,* 67, 377 F–378 A; quoted in Glover, p. 93.

But this single God must be perfect, a pure ideal, pure Good; he can not be responsible for the evil in the world. And such an unsullied God is so far away, that he is of himself of no help to mortals.

Here is expressed clearly the double need, lying back of all Hellenistic religious experience, for an inspiring ideal, and for personal help. This was the universal cry. And it is a profoundly true interpretation of such experience. Perfection must be real and pure, it must be the Highest; yet it must also be somehow attainable by man.

In the mystery religions, this problem was solved by the conception of an incarnation of the divine. For Plutarch, the problem is solved by the deputy gods worshiped in the temples, taken as "emanations" of the supreme God; and by daimons, guardian angels, close to men, and also responsible for evil. These deputy gods pass on men's prayers, and bring to men blessings. They later became the Christian intercessary saints, and the angels, good and bad.

Plutarch believed in divination, in sorcery, and the rest. Yet he did not believe in "superstition": superstition is fear of the gods, rather than love of them, terror before the rites. As for Plato, in Book X of *The Laws*, for Plutarch such fear is far worse than atheism—it is the utter perversion of all religion.

All myths have some meaning, Plutarch holds. Perhaps they are not quite true, literally speaking; but they are so satisfying! Anyway they are the faith of our fathers, and we need faith. Religion must be somehow true. You can always interpret away the unpleasant things: they must be symbols of something or other. Believe, and worship. Do not worry too much about what precisely it all means. Besides, religion is so beautiful! It is so poetic and imaginative. Plutarch concludes with the most insidious seduction of all: the beauty of religious ritual and myth.

In this same intellectual and moral atmosphere, Pytha-goreanism too was revived as a religious philosophy. Pythago-reanism had itself grown out of the older Greek mysteries, with perhaps some impulse from Hindu religion. It had already a dualistic conception of human nature. For it, soul, *psyche,* is spirit, *pneuma,* not body or matter; it is immortal and separable from the body. Pythagoreanism also had a way of purification, ascetic in temper; it possessed a sacrament of initiation, and a revelation, to be accepted on faith.[13]

Pythagoreanism, revived, was fused with Platonism, which was identified with Pythagoreanism.[14] Under some Jewish in-fluence, it assimilated monotheism, and also much Persian mythology and ethical dualism. In it the rational concepts of Greek thinking became identified with the poetic images of Eastern mythology. The mystical "numbers" of the Pythag-oreans became angelic hosts, intermediaries between the one Spirit or *Pneuma* and the world. Spirit rules the world through Number Daimons; Ideas or Numbers are both thoughts of God, principles of explanation (Greek), and "messengers" or angels of dominion (Oriental and Persian).

Such Neo-Pythagoreanism (the "Neo" comes from nine-teenth-century German scholars) had its divine prophets, in

---

[13] See Philostratus, *Life of Apollonios of Tyana,* an interesting parallel to the Christian gospels, F. C. Conybeare, ed. and tr., 2 vols. (Loeb, 1912). Cf. Zeller on the Neo-Pythagoreans. T. Whittaker, *Apollonios of Tyana* (Cambridge, 1906); also G. R. S. Mead, *Quests Old and New* (London, 1901) H. Thesleff, *An Introduction to the Pythagorean Writings of the Hellenistic Period* (Turku, Finland, 1961). Texts in Maria T. Cardini, *Pitagorici: Testimonianze e Frammenti,* 2 vols., (Florence, 1958, 1962).

[14] W. K. C. Guthrie puts it: "The Neo-Pythagorean movement, which started in the first century B.C., was an amalgam of early Pythagorean material with the teachings of Plato, the Peripatetics, and Stoicism. All of this material was credited to Pythagoras, who was revered as the revealer of esoteric religious truths." *Encyclopedia of Philosophy,* Paul Edwards, ed. (New York, 1967), VII, 39.

particular Apollonios of Tyana, whose career is set down in the sacred gospel of Philostratus, around 200 A.D. Apollonios went about preaching reform of the religious tradition: God is to be served only in spirit, by virtue and wisdom, not through burnt offerings. Like any self-respecting prophet of those days, Apollonios was able to perform many miracles on his travels.

Judaism proved in Hellenistic times to be a very vigorous and proselytizing religion: in those days the Jewish Sabbath was widely adopted throughout the Orient. The intellectual center of Judaism was located in the great Jewish colony in Alexandria. There worked the Seventy, the LXX, the Septuagint, scholars who made a Greek translation of the Hebrew Scriptures. This enterprise was being carried out from the third century B.C. on. Interestingly, it had been supposed that the Septuagint Greek translation was a rather free version of the familiar Babylonian Masoretic Hebrew text. But the Dead Sea Scrolls contain portions of a somewhat different Hebrew text, and the Septuagint is a quite literal translation of this different Hebrew text, which seems to have been the one used at Alexandria. The legend has it that Ptolemy Philadelphus convoked the seventy scholars to do the work.

The Alexandrian Hebrew school soon assimilated Greek philosophy. The legend, again, attributes this to a certain Aristobulus, supposed to have lived in the second century B.C. He sought to get rid of all the traditional anthropomorphism in the Hebrew Scriptures; and he maintained the position that Plato derived all his "ethical monotheism"—by which he meant the Demiurge of the *Timaeus*—from Moses, whose writings he is supposed to have read in Greek translation. Consequently Platonism is really a Hebrew philosophy, and hence is to be studied and used in interpreting the Scriptures. There is today much doubt as to whether "Aristobulus" ever lived. But the enterprise attributed to him was certainly common in the Alexandrian school of Hebrews.

The outstanding philosophical mind of this Alexandrian Jewish movement is Philo Judaeus, Philo of Alexandria. The only date we know in connection with his life is that he was sent by the Alexandrian Jewish community as head of a mission to Rome in the year 40 of our era. So we assume he flourished from about 20 B.C. to 40 A.D.

Philo is the great assimilator of Hellenism, of Greek thought, among the Jews. In this he is comparable to Moses Maimonides as the medieval assimilator of Aristotelianism, and to Spinoza as assimilator of Cartesian science. Philo remained an orthodox Jew: that is, he held to the observance of the Law. Yet he succeeded in transforming Judaism into a mystical doctrine of salvation, drawing on the common Stoic–Platonic ideas to rationalize it: he seems to have been especially influenced by the Stoic philosopher Poseidonios, of the Middle Stoa.[15] Philo has had little intellectual influence on subsequent Jewish thought: the destruction of the Temple in 70 A.D. by Titus caused a natural reaction among Jews against all Hellenizing. But, ironically enough, Philo can be claimed as the real founder of Christian theology:[16] he set its intellectual problems and formulated its methods; and he is certainly the father of Christian exegesis of the Scriptures. The Prologue to the Fourth Gospel draws heavily on Philo.

Philo's method is an allegorical commentary on the Law, interpreting away its anthropomorphism, and bringing in the emphasis on man's need of salvation. Hence Philo's works are

[15] See the forthcoming edition of Poseidonios by Ludwig Edelstein.
[16] And has been so claimed by Harry A. Wolfson, in his *Philo: Foundations of Religious Philosophy in Judaism, Christianity, and Islam*, 2 vols. (Cambridge, Mass., 1948; 3d ed., rev., 1962).

very difficult for the modern reader to understand, and without special training almost unreadable. Philo made a skeptical attack on human knowledge. Certainty is to be found only in revelation and in prophecy—that is, in the Scriptures. But then reason must be employed to interpret the Scriptures aright.

For Philo, God is utterly above the world, the highest genus, pure Being. He is better than virtue, than knowledge, than the Good itself. Philo rejects all human and logical attributes of God: God is above the intelligible world of the Platonists. He includes and transcends it. God is not like anything else: He is the One. Only negatives will apply to Him: He is the Eternal, the Unchanging. The least inadequate symbol for God is the human mind, *nous*, reason. Yet God is also very near to man, filling the universe, ruling it, and filling the hearts of men in ecstasy and prophecy. Philo is absorbed in the mystic experience of the Divine Presence. Philo is thus the first formulator of what has come to be called the tradition of "negative theology."[17]

[17] Philo, text and Eng. tr. in Loeb Library, 10 vols., F. H. Colson and G. H. Whitaker, trs., and two supplementary volumes, Ralph Marcus, tr. (1929-62). Older Eng. tr. by C. D. Yonge (London, 1854). *Selections from Philo,* edited with introduction by Hans Lewy, Alexander Altmann, and Isaak Heinemann (Oxford, 1946).

Standard Greek text: *Philonis Alexandrini Opera,* ed. Leopold Cohn and P. Wendland, eds., 7 vols. (Berlin, 1896-1930). Ger. tr., *Philo von Alexandria, Die Werke,* Leopold Cohn et al., eds., 7 vols. (Breslau, 1909-38; 2d ed., Berlin, 1962-64).

Studies: Eduard A. Zeller, *The Stoics, Epicureans, and Sceptics* (Eng. tr., London, 1870; rev. ed., 1962); Harry A. Wolfson; J. Drummond, *Philo Judaeus,* 2 vols. (London, 1888); N. Bentwich, *Philo Judaeus of Alexandria* (London, 1910); É. Bréhier, *Les Idées Phiosophiques et Religieuses de Philon d'Alexandrie* (Paris, 1908; 2d ed. rev., 1925); J. Martin, *Philon* (Paris, 1907); E. R. Goodenough, *By Light, Light: The Mystic Gospel of Hellenistic Judaism* (New Haven, 1935); Isaak Heinemann, *Philons griechische und jüdische Bildung* (Breslau, 1932); E. Herriot, *Philon le Juif* (Paris, 1898); W. Völker, *Fortschritt und Vollendung bei Philon von Alexandrien* (Leipzig, 1938).

How is God connected with the world? Through His "powers," which are operating everywhere, and are both rational laws and Platonic Ideas. The "realm of Ideas" is actually God's mind (a view that seems to appear first in Antiochus). These powers form both the pattern of the cosmos, and active rational principles. They are what Plato called "Ideas," what the Stoics called "seminal reasons," *logoi spermatikoi*; and what the Jews, under Persian influence, called God's "messengers" or "angels," *aggeloi*. In the Scriptures they are symbolized as persons; but they are really aspects of the Self-Existent. The highest of these powers, which appear in the Scriptures as archangels, or cherubim, are God's goodness and His sovereign power. Philo is here undertaking a fusion of the notions of the Platonists and Stoics (particularly of Poseidonios) with Jewish mythology.

God's powers, taken as a totality, form the Logos, the Word. This is both the supreme rationality, the intelligible structure of the cosmos, and the rational, ordering, dynamic Law of Nature, God's instrument of creation and of Providence. Philo seems to have been original in making the *Logos* an intermediary between God and the world. The Stoics considered the *Logos* or Reason to be God Himself. This is clearly a response to the new need felt for a mediator between a pure and remote God and the world.

The *Logos* is *theos*, Divine, the proper object of worship. But it is logically dependent on the still more inclusive Being, *ho Theos*, God Himself. The *Logos* is God's mind or thought, the Hebrew "word of God," or the "spirit of God," the "wisdom of God"; it is "begotten, not made," and is hence eternal, like God Himself. It is embodied as the Divine Word in the Scriptures, and in the High Priest. The observance of the Law is the worship of the *Logos*. But it is a little below the free worship of God the Eternal, which is by faith, *pistis*.

That is, God and the *Logos* are to be distinguished in their worship, which takes place by faith and by observance of the Law, respectively.

The soul of man is the image of the Divine *Logos*, now imprisoned in the body. Salvation is turning away from self-love, which is sin, to God Himself. Man needs revelation, vision, and grace. Trust and faith in God bring the help of the *Logos*, of God's wisdom and power: all salvation comes from God.

Philo distinguishes two lives for man: the life of aspiration, of faith, hope, discipline, and effort, which is not ascetic, but embraces the wise use of the body and of the world; together with the final ecstasy, of peace and vision. This Philo conceives as an act of humility before God, not as a final union with God—he remains Hebraic. Yet his whole emphasis on personal salvation as the essence of religion is Hellenistic and not Hebraic.

In Philo the outlines of the future Christian theology are clear, as they appear in the Prologue to the Fourth Gospel, for example. The one exception is the unique incarnation of the *Logos*. Even here, it is significant that neither the Greek Fathers, nor even St. Augustine, had any real intellectual need in their systems for a unique incarnation of the *Logos*.

It was the Neo-Pythagorean Numenios (c.150 A.D.) who fused Platonism and Neo-Pythagoreanism and certain of Philo's ideas into what has been called since the early nineteenth-century Neo-Platonism. For him, too, Plato is "Moses talking Greek." Numenios has a trinity: the First God, who is *Nous*, the Principle of Being; the Platonic Demiurge, who is Philo's *Logos*; and the World-Life or *Psyché*, the "World Soul." Numenios exhibits an ascetic temper, and an otherworldly and dualistic scheme of ethics. The atmosphere for him has changed since even the Middle Platonism of Plutarch.

There is in all these systems of religious philosophy a common emphasis on the transcendence of God, who is apart from the evil and corrupt world, a pure ideal: that is, on a strong moral dualism. Yet God must be accessible to man and his bitter needs: there is an ultimate philosophical monism. This demands a mystic revelation, of a mediator, an incarnation of the Divine in the world. Perfection must be so unsullied and pure and distant and so unattainable by man's own efforts, that only perfection itself can help man to find it.

The whole world was crying for the incarnation of God, for the Word to be made flesh, the Divine brought to man, so that man might be brought to God.

VIII THE INTELLIGIBLE UNIVERSE OF PLOTINOS*

Plotinos, who lived from 204 to 270 A.D., is the organizer of that system of ideas that is now called Neo-Platonism. His thought is to be understood, not in the context of Plato and Aristotle, not even in that of the naturalistic religious philosophies of Epicureanism and Stoicism. To be appreciated, the thinking of Plotinos has to be viewed against the background of the supernatural religions and religious philosophies of the first and second centuries of our era. In the face of these apologetic philosophies and theologies, Plotinos stands for a relatively pure rationalism. He represents the protest of reason against myth and magic and allegory, the refusal to take

* This chapter appeared in unrevised form in the *Journal of the History of Ideas*, XXX (January-March, 1969), 3-16.

seriously the myths of creation or special incarnation, or the magic of salvation by sacrament and ritual.[1]

Plotinos held steadfastly to the conviction, that it is reason and not faith that gives men knowledge of the universe, and it is reason and not faith that can alone bring them salvation. He would make no compromise with polytheism: he would not offer sacrifices to the gods. For Plotinos, reason alone was *theios*, divine. Plotinos believed in Platonic immortality, to be sure; but he did not hold literally to a future life, to personal survival. Plotinos' thought can even be called naturalistic, because he refused to see any gulf between man and the world, or between man and perfection, that demands a supernatural bridge or mediator: Plotinos felt the need of no savior save reason. In one sense, indeed, Plotinos is the most consistent naturalist in Greek thought; though of course he is not an

[1] Texts: *Plotini Opera,* 3 vols. Paul Henry and H. R. Schwyzer, eds. (Paris and Brussels, 1951-67), now by far the best Greek text; É. Bréhier, *Ennéades,* 7 vols. (Paris, 1924-38), Greek text and excellent Fr. tr.; German tr. with Greek text, Richard Harder (Hamburg, 1956-67); Ger. tr. also available separately. First Eng. tr., Stephen MacKenna, *Enneads* (London, 1917-30); available in one volume (Pantheon Press, New York); Arthur H. Armstrong, *Enneads of Plotinus* (Loeb, 1966—), four volumes published, most useful ed.

Selections: Joseph Katz, *The Philosophy of Plotinus* (New York, 1950), in excellent Eng. tr.; Thomas Taylor, *Select Works of Plotinus* (London, 1817), reprinted (London, 1912), G. R. S. Mead, ed.

Studies and Accounts: Thomas Whittaker, *The Neoplatonists* (2d ed.; Cambridge, 1918), chs. 4-6. É. Bréhier, *La Philosophie de Plotin* (Paris, 1928; Eng. tr. Chicago, 1958). Joseph Katz, *Plotinus' Search for the Good* (New York, 1950). Irwin Edman, "The Logic of Mysticism in Plotinus," in *Columbia Studies in the History of Ideas,* Vol. II (New York, 1925). W. R. Inge, *The Philosophy of Plotinus,* 2 vols. (New York, 1918; 3d ed., 1948), full but eccentric study. B. A. G. Fuller, *The Problem of Evil in Plotinus* (Cambridge, 1912). G. Mehlis, *Plotin* (Stuttgart, 1924); F. Heinemann, *Plotin* (Leipzig, 1921), two Ger. studies; in Heinemann, a genetic study, see especially 3rd Teil, "Das System Plotin." Older, A. Benn, *The Greek Philosophers* (2d ed.; London, 1914), ch. 14. Arthur H. Armstrong, *Plotinus* (Cambridge, 1940; Cambridge, Mass., 1966-67), most recent Eng. study.

empirical and functional naturalist, like Aristotle, but rather a rationalistic and structural naturalist, like Spinoza. Spinoza, in fact, is the one philosopher among moderns with whom Plotinos can be most validly compared. Both Plotinos and Spinoza are rationalists with overtones of rational mysticism.

To be sure, Plotinos accepts the scale of values offered by Hellenistic experience, as expressed in the religious philosophies; he accepts them as facts of his world, as data to be reflected upon, as the subject matter to be understood by reason. He then tries to make this religious scale of values intelligible in terms of classic Greek thought, in terms of the distinctions of Plato and Aristotle. His is a genuine attempt to understand a kind of life in which the appeal of individual purity is a cardinal fact, a world in which thought is rated more highly than action. Plotinos thus offers as sincere and as rational an account of the facts of his cultural experience as, e.g., Santayana's combination of Platonism with Spencerian naturalism is of his own very different cultural experience. For Santayana, nineteenth-century science and its scale of values form a cardinal datum. Both Plotinos and Santayana are offering rational interpretations of their respective cultural and social experience, taken at its face value. Neither is a pioneer breaking fresh ground, neither is a reconstructor of the values he finds in his *Lebenswelt*.

The new in what was first in 1831 called "Neo"-Platonism— the term was invented by nineteenth-century German scholars —is not so much a new doctrine as a new emphasis. The ideas are all to be found in Plato and Aristotle: the "Platonism" Plato presents very sympathetically,[2] then comments on critically and ironically, and by his dramatic method places in

---

[2] See my *Plato: Dramatist of the Life of Reason* (New York, 1970), especially ch. 20, for the context in human experience of Plato's "Platonism." Gilbert Ryle finds this Platonism expounded only in the dialogues of Plato's "middle" period. See Ryle, *Plato's Progress* (Cambridge, 1966).

its context in human experience; the "Platonism" Aristotle began by sharing, then later almost but not quite wholly got over, by stating explicitly its natural context. It is the scale of values, not the ideas, that form the new element in the Neo-Platonism of Plotinos. And even that scale of values can be found, and was found by Plotinos, in certain parts of Plato and Aristotle. In both, to be sure, that subordinate scale is overshadowed by a much more humanistic scale of values that appeals much more strongly to most moderns than the minor strain that Plotinos emphasizes, because it corresponds to the experience of his own day.

This minor strain that Plotinos found made good sense to him he discovered most fully in the otherworldly atmosphere of the *Phaedo,* where, since Plato is portraying a great man dying, he naturally emphasizes that the most valuable things in human life are irrelevant to man's animal body. Plotinos found it most fully in Aristotle in those places where Aristotle's passion for knowing makes him emphasize *"Nous* nousing *Nous"* as the highest and most divine of all human activities, and leads him to embrace Anaxagoras' "greater" and "cosmic" *Nous.* So the new in Plotinos' "Neo"-Platonism is really a concentration on this subordinate scale of values to be found occasionally in Plato and Aristotle, a new emphasis and a new shading, which comes, of course, from the context of his Hellenistic experience.

But in singling out this strand of "Platonism" in Plato and Aristotle, Plotinos retains all that is Greek and Hellenic about it: the Greek love of beauty, the imaginative discernment of perfection in the suggestions given by imperfection, the Greek distinction between existence as sensed and Being as thought, *noēton.* This is in marked contrast to the Oriental, that is, the Persian distinction between body, *sōma,* which is evil, and spirit, *pneuma,* which is good, which had left its stamp on all the Oriental religious philosophies, derived ultimately from Persian dualism, of the first and second centuries of our era.

Plotinos, in fact, considering his birth in Lycopolis, or "Wolfville," halfway up the Nile from Cairo to Luxor, strikes the reader as remarkably Greek.[3] In view of the fact that he was born in this very Egyptian community, Plotinos seems very Hellenic. He is protesting strongly against all Oriental dualism, even when his own thinking is clearly colored by its scale of values. There is a certain irony in the fact that the thought of Plotinos the rationalist was used by his successors to rationalize all those very irrationalities to which Plotinos himself was most strongly opposed. His later followers, Jamblichus and even Proclus, succumbed to Persian dualism; and Plotinos, the greatest rationalist in Greek philosophy since Parmenides—in fact, the Greek Spinoza—became known and used as the theoretician of non-rational mysticism.

Modern scholars, notably the great authority on Hellenistic philosophy, Émile Bréhier, have urged a Hindu influence on Plotinos. This is based solely on the similarity of his thought to certain strains in the Hindus; there is no evidence of direct communication between the two.[4] Possibly, we may say, Plotinos seized on the most Hindu elements in Plato, which the latter had derived from the Pythagoreans. The assumption of a fresh Hindu influence is hardly necessary. For the reader

[3] Ancient Lycopolis is now the largest town in Upper Egypt, with some 60,000 inhabitants. Its modern Arabic name, Asyūt, comes from the ancient Egyptian "Syowt"; the Greek name, "Wolfville," derives from the shrine of the God Wep-Wawet, who was a Wolf of the desert. As seen from the French air-conditioned train, which takes five hours to get to it from Cairo, it seems to be in the very heart of Upper Egypt. It is a place of mud houses, palm trees, and files of camels; it seems to have changed little since the days of Plotinos, except that it is now surrounded by fields of cotton rather than, as in ancient times, of wheat.

[4] Father Paul Henry agrees that Bréhier went beyond the evidence in bringing in any direct contact between Plotinos and Hindu thinking.

is impressed that everything in Plotinos can be supported by some text in Plato himself, however different, and "neo," the tune.

Plotinos is, as we say, very academic: he lived with the theories, books, and even problems of previous thinkers; and he drew on the traditions of classic Greek philosophy to interpret the experience he observed about him, and perhaps even felt himself personally. Like all the Egyptians, Plotinos is clearly bowed down under the weight of past ideas, which he accepted literally, with little enough imagination, and little sense of Plato's own irony. This led to a process of interpreting and reconciling. He fled from his world to Plato and Aristotle, as a refugee, and made a system out of their suggestions. This process involved a keen analysis of Plato's poetry, and a skillful use of Aristotle's distinctions: Plotinos exhibits a much better logic than interested Plato, and a much more coherent system than Aristotle attempted.

Plotinos takes "Thought" as the primary fact of experience, "Thought" as a noun, as a finished logical system. He interprets existence in terms of such Thought and its structure. Our own scientific procedures and values make us prefer to take existence as primary, and to interpret thought in terms of existence. That is, Plotinos is making a logical analysis of the logical structure and conditions of existence; he is obviously not a natural scientist analyzing physical causes and consequences. This means that Plotinos is comparable to Russell in the *Principia Mathematica*, not to John Dewey in his *Experimental Logic* or his *Theory of Inquiry*. One can say, Plotinos pushed the logical side of Aristotle's analysis, not the physical or functional side.

Now, both are possible and true interpretations of the same world, the same subject matter. But the two analyses do not give the same results. The one analysis gives action, control, more and different existence; the other reveals insight, wisdom, more and different values. But what is the world we are living in, anyway? Is existence primary, and are thought, logical structure, value, something derivative from it? Or are thought, logical structure, value, primary, and existence somehow derivative from them? We must ask, "primary" for what? Which view we choose obviously depends on what we are trying to do: to act, manipulate, and control, or to understand, judge, and aspire. The danger, in either case, is that we may take an exclusive view: it is the danger of forgetting the world that is there, containing both existence, and thought and value. If we take Plotinos as offering a physics, then he does indeed furnish what Santayana called an "inverted physics." But equally, if we take natural science as itself an ethics, then does it not become an "inverted ethics"? All values, of course, derive their existence from imperfection, from matter. But Plotinos would say, all existence derives its value from perfection, from thought, from *Nous*.

Now, our own pluralistic and experimental temper makes us find things valuable in themselves, in what they do, individually, in their specific functions. It tends to distrust any such unified vision of perfection, by serving which particular things can alone become good. But we can observe the power, at least, of such an interpretation as that of Plotinos, the power of a unifying faith in a supreme Good, from which all value is derived, in Marxian Dialectical Materialism, the foremost present-day representative of Plotinos's single, unified, rational, and intelligible structure in the world—although a structure partly temporalized, in the fashion of Hegel. Indeed, "Diamat" itself claims—and rightly—to be, through Hegel, the direct heir of Plotinos. It is certainly the outstanding contemporary form of Neo-Platonism, with an added "Faustian" twist. It differs, just as Plotinos differs, from our scientific philosophies: it is a rationalistic monism, rather than an experimental pluralism.

It is worth pointing to these analogies. For it suggests that Plotinos is hardly to be dismissed as irrelevant to present-day concerns. He gives a rational interpretation of a form of experience, of a vision of the world, with many analogues in our own scene.

It is doubtful whether Plotinos is adequately understood by calling him a mystic—though many have so tried. This is especially the case if by mysticism we mean a strange and exotic flower. He is far closer, in fact, to ordinary experience, than the analytical empiricist. Plotinos' interest lies in a way of life, and in understanding the implications of that way for the world that sustains it; it does not seem to lie primarily in any final ecstasy at all. The important thing for Plotinos is the path you follow, the distinctions you make, rather than the ultimate goal. To be sure, the way is indicated, and the distinctions understood, only in the light of that goal: it is the necessary and essential point of reference. For the true mystic, ecstasy possesses cognitive value, it reveals Truth, it is noetic, as we say. But not for Plotinos: he must explain ecstasy and vision by thought, he must proceed rationally. For all exists to serve thought.

Hence Plotinos himself seems to illustrate, not so much the logic of mysticism, as many have put it, as the mysticism of logic, in the phrase of Bertrand Russell—the rational vision in which logic culminates, the vision of a completely intelligible universe. This is the vision inspired by Whitehead and Russell's *Principia Mathematica*. Significantly, Russell has been more enthusiastic about Plotinos than about any other Greek philosopher. And quite rightly, since the two are clearly kindred spirits—Russell in this phase of the *Principia* was also a systematizer of a unified Platonism. Both Russell and Plotinos are pure rationalists; and Russell has returned every so often to this Neo -Platonic mood.

Plato, in fact, can be taken as far more of a mystic than Plotinos. He is far more content to rest in vision, without, like Plotinos, attempting a logical analysis of that vision. In his own account of the supreme ecstasy and vision, Plotinos seems often to be trying to understand an experience that is rather alien to him. He often suggests the modern theologian seeking to use mysticism for his own primarily apologetic purposes. Plotinos, one suspects, is trying to understand the experience of Plato, or of some of his third-century contemporaries, not a first-hand experience of his own. It is significant that every one of his descriptions is couched in language borrowed from Plato's own metaphors. And this is not only because Plato is a gifted poet, whereas Plotinos is an analytic and dialectical thinker.

Porphyry reports that Plotinos himself thought that during Porphyry's stay with him Plotinos had managed to achieve final ecstasy perhaps four times. But the true mystic daily walks with God, and never loses the immediate sense of the Divine Presence. Hence it is very hard to sustain that claim that Plotinos is primarily a mystic. After Porphyry, the mystic experience, far from being basic for the Neo-Platonists, was regarded by the school as almost unattainable.

Moreover, we are also told by Porphyry that Plotinos was by no means a recluse, but shrewd and practical—that for him there was no retirement from action. He carried on his contemplation in the midst of active concerns: he was, Porphyry tells, made the guardian of many minors, and proved to be a skillful manager of their property, and trustee of their investments. The impression we get, in fact, from Porphyry's *Life* is of a kind of Gilbertian Lord Chancellor, and a much-sought-after referee in legal disputes. The whole picture of Plotinos presented by Porphyry almost suggests, indeed, that Plotinos developed his philosophy of contemplation just because he was a tired business man.

Be that as it may, Plotinos was no more, and no less, a mystic than that other supreme rationalist of modern times, Spinoza, with whom alone among moderns he is comparable as a systematic explorer of the implications of thought, of thought taken as an intelligible or rational structure rather than as a process of thinking. At least, we find no equal to Plotinos but Spinoza until Whitehead and Russell's *Principia Mathematica*.

It can be said, Plotinos is developing the First Philosophy or metaphysics implied in the Greek science of Plato and Aristotle, just as Spinoza is developing that implied in Cartesian mechanics. For both, their enterprise culminates in a vision, a *theōria,* of the logical structure of the world. The ultimate goal of thought is to see the part of your own human reason and mind in that structure—"to perceive the union that obtains between the human mind and the whole of Nature," as Spinzoa puts it.

In his analysis of the intelligible universe in which we find ourselves living, Plotinos starts from the cardinal fact of Greek philosophical experience: man is a dweller in two realms, that of the senses, and that of thought; and the latter is the real realm in which we alone find genuine knowledge. Plotinos proceeds to elaborate the necessary distinctions within the realm of thought. It is, of course, quite possible to translate Plotinos' Greek to make it mean modern philosophical idealism.[5] But this seems of doubtful validity. In his metaphysical ultimates there appears no Christian tradition of personality. The terms used should hence be as impersonal as those employed by Plato or by Aristotle. They indicate *archai,* not wills; truth, not thinking.

[5] Dean W. R. Inge follows this course. But it is hard to take Plotinos as resembling a Modernist Christian clergyman who had studied at Oxford in the old pre-linguistic days. Father Paul Henry, perhaps from a Christian bias, also finds personality in Plotinos' ultimates.

Thus the central realm, *Nous,* does not imply individual thinking or mind, any more than does Spinoza's "idea." It is an impersonal realm, the knowability of the world, the rationality of experience, intelligibility, logical structure; thought, not thinking, reason, not reasoning. Thinking and reasoning belong not to *Nous* but to Life, *Psyche. Nous* is the Platonic realm or domain of Ideas.

Within this domain of *Nous* are to be found three major distinctions. First, there are the elements, *ta noēta,* the Ideas or Intelligibles. Secondly is intelligible structure, *noēsis,* the logical relations between Intelligibles. And thirdly, there is the entire system itself, *Nous,* the whole realm or domain of Ideas, of truth. *Noēsis* is rather misleadingly translated "contemplation," or "beholding." It means primarily the presence or inclusion of *ta noēta* in the system of *Nous* or truth; it is like the logical relations of the propositions of a science to each other and to the whole science. The propositions in their logical relations constitute the science. Just so the *noēta,* related by *noēsis,* constitute and are the realm of *Nous.* This is a fact of logic, of intelligible structure, of implication, not a fact of psychology. There is nothing temporal about *Nous,* no functioning. *Nous, noēsis,* and *noēta* are all logical terms. *Nous* is the analogue of Santayana's "realm of essence," or of Whitehead's "realm of eternal objects." Plotinos calls this realm *theion* or divine, in the impersonal sense in which truth is the Divine.

This *Nous* is embodied in Nature, *Physis,* the scene of actions and events, as the world structure, the world process, as the world *Psyche,* the "life" of the universe, the *anima mundi* of the Latins; but not as the "world Soul," the conventional translation. The world *Psyche* does not mean what "soul" means to us, after centuries of Christianity; that is a very unGreek idea. It means the process of Nature, as a rational order embodied in events, the system of rational laws of

Nature. We may say, *Nous* is to *Psychē* as the structure of pure mathematics is to the structure of mathematical physics, realistically conceived.

The *Logos* Plotinos accepts as the actual rational ordering of the world, as the ordered events studied in experimental physics: this is Plotinos' recognition of the Stoic *Logos* as Rational Nature.

The "life" of man, or man's *psychē,* his "soul," is an instance of the life of nature, of the world life or world process, of the *anima mundi* or world "soul." It is life individualized and inhabiting a particular animal body. If a living body, says Plotinos, is a "particular organization of matter," its life or "soul" is its *archē* or principle of organization, i.e., that in terms of which its activities are to be understood. Men, that is, are parts of the world process, the world "Soul," not of *Nous* or truth. They are parts of the rational order that can organize materials. A man is an intelligible essence, or *ousia,* that can be realized in a body. As an essence, his life is still a part of the intelligible realm of *Nous.*

There are three levels of human life or soul: first there is reasoning, guiding action by intelligence, discovering truth: this is an instrumental and calculating process. Below reasoning there takes place life on the animal level: sensing, growth, maturation, nutrition, etc. These are the nonrational functions of life or the soul. Above reasoning, the human *nous* can participate in *Nous,* in the realm of truth: it can "behold" or "contemplate" the realm of Ideas, it can be present itself in that realm logically as a part of it.

So far we have distinguished two levels of thought, of truth. There is thought in itself, as *Nous,* the logical system of truth. And there is also thought embodied in Nature, in *physis,* as the structure of the world, as the Order of Nature. But Plotinos also finds a third level, a higher, underlying unity of *Nous,* which he calls "The One," *to Hen.*

Thought, truth, is a system of logically related elements: it displays the unity of a manifold, a harmony which makes it a system, and not isolated scraps, like Santayana's detached essences. This is the unified rationality of the world as a cosmos, a universe, the unity of the intelligible world as one single logical order. The logical implication of thought is that the world is one single unified system. Plato put it: there are sense-objects, light, and then the sun itself: this unity is the sun of the intelligible world.

Now, Plotinos asks, *why* is the world such a system? And he answers his question, there must be an *archē,* a principle of order, in the intelligible world. Being is not merely unified; there must be a reason why Being is unified. There must be an *archē* of Being itself. This *archē* must be logically prior to Being, as its logical source. The ultimate question is, why is Being a realm? Why does Being possess a unified intelligible structure? There must be a principle of structurability—and that is all we can say about it. It will be the ultimate *archē*: it will be not itself "a Being," but rather the "reason why" Being has a unified structure. This may well be the last reach of thought, of thought going beyond itself: the "reason why" truth is truth, good is good, and beauty is beauty. This ultimate reason why cannot be itself "true" or "good" or "beautiful": it lies beyond those attributes, as their logical source, their *archē.*

This is the ultimate potentiality of there being an intelligible universe: it makes *Nous,* the intelligible realm, itself an actualized potentiality. The argument for it runs: there is a unified, intelligible realm of Being, *Nous.* Therefore such a realm must be logically possible. If *Nous* is actual, as it is, it must also be possible. The possibility or potentiality of *Nous* is a necessary condition of its being, and of its being what it is.

This is obviously a question, and an answer, for those not content with the brute fact of the existence of order, and unable —or unwilling—to accept an answer in terms of an ultimate efficient cause, in terms of a creator of order: unwilling to agree that the reason for order in the cosmos is the will of its creator. The latter is the answer of the "Judaeo-Biblical mind," thinking, as is said, "historically," in terms of the Mesopotamian cosmogonies, in terms of efficient causes of order.

In actual fact, traditional Greek religion was very much like the Hebrew religion on this score, and any opposition set up between the two on these grounds seems to be unwarranted. Greek religion also explained the fact of order in historical terms, just as did the Hebrews, through gods who *created* order out of pre-existent chaos. The creation of order is actually one of the basic ideas of Greek religious thinking. In this, both Greek and Hebrew religious thought were probably reflecting the Babylonian cosmogonies.

The Greek philosophers, however, managed to get over this historical myth: they came to seek ultimate explanations, not in primitive cosmogonies, not in mythical efficient causes, like "creation" by a creator, but in ultimate rational principles, in ultimate formal causes, like the mathematical Idea of the Good of Plato, or the formal structure of ends, in Aristotle's Unmoved Mover. And biblical thought likewise eventually got over the historical myth of the creation of order by a creator. For the Fourth Gospel, the most philosophical of the Gospels, explicitly proclaims that order is uncreated and ultimate. The Prologue opens: "In the beginning was the Word [the *Logos*, Order], and the Word was with God, and the Word was God."[6] And the Council of Nicaea settled Christian orthodoxy

[6] John I, 1.

on this point in the doctrine of the Trinity: order is ultimate and uncreated, the Logos is coordinate with ultimate power, *homoousios* with the Father.[7]

So Plotinos, following Greek philosophy rather than Greek religion, asks for an ultimate *Archē,* or formal cause, of structure or order itself. He reads back the existent order of things into a logically prior structure, then generalizes the principle, and pushes it to apply to the very fact of structure, of intelligible order, itself.[8] That is, Plotinos' *Nous* implies a principle of structurability. That is all that can be said about it: it is a purely formal conception, an ultimate potentiality.

This ultimate potentiality seems at first sight to be in contrast with Aristotle's *Nous* as *noēsis,* which is an ultimate operation or actuality. But the two conceptions are not so opposed as they may seem. For this ultimate entelechy or "for what" of Aristotle, this ultimate final cause, loses all character of *kinēsis* or process, and becomes pure structure, pure intelligibility, just as does Plotinos' ultimate principle of structurability. When pushed to their logical limits, pure potentiality and pure actuality always turn out to be identical; and both agree also in being inconceivable to the human mind. In other words, the limits of systematic thought meet; and in the metaphysical tradition there is the long story of the ultimate identity of oppo-

---

[7] There is, to be sure, an opposition between Hebrew religious thought and Greek philosophy, and likewise one between Greek religion and Christian theology. But on this point there is no opposition between the Greek and the Hebrew religious thinkers; both resorted freely to historical myths. And there is no opposition between Greek philosophy and Christian theology—if the Gospel of Saint John and the Doctrine of the Trinity adequately represent Christian theology. Both had been able to outgrow the earlier historical myths.

[8] This is the issue, of course, between the logical "realists"—the structural realists, like Whitehead or Morris R. Cohen—and the functional realists, like John Dewey. Has the world a "logical" structure, or has it rather what Dewey called a "logiscible" structure of Being?

sites, most fully explored, perhaps, by Cusanus and Schelling.

Now all this is Plotinos' detailed analysis of the structure of the intelligible universe in which we find ourselves. It is all implied for him in the fact of the complete intelligibility of the world, just as Spinoza's analysis is all implied in the fact that *homo cogitat,* "man thinks." And it can all be taken as a valid analysis: it is true—if one asks such questions, and understands what their context is, what the answer means. It is all as true as any system of natural science; though its truth obviously has a different function from that of the truth of natural science. Plotinos' truth will never lead to triumphs of technology.[9]

This analysis also furnishes Plotinos with a scale of values; in his own language, with a scale of Being. The logical source, the *Archē* of Being, the One, is perfection, descending through truth and life to matter and nothingness. And this scale of Being implies a way of life, of aspiration to truth and perfect Being. All value, all reality, all Being, is an "emanation" from perfection. This process of emanation is not a process of the physical creation of existence, for all these levels have always existed. It is rather a *derivation of value and intelligibility.* It means, not that perfection has created anything, or brought anything into existence, but rather that perfection is the goal of all aspiration, the reason for all that exists. The One is not the physical efficient cause of anything, it does not make any events to happen. Plotinos is not much interested in efficient causes, but he does not make the mistake of thinking he has worked out a system of physics, "inverted" or otherwise. Perfection does not cause the existence of the world, in any sense of efficient causation. It rather generates values, it makes the

9 Or to H-bombs.

world rational and intelligible. It is the source of all the "reality," of all the "Being" in things.

"Being" or "reality" for Plotinos means value and intelligibility, not existence. The only cause of anything existent is some other existence. Matter, the world process, truth or intelligibility, the unity of the cosmos—all the levels of Being—are all equally existent: they have all always existed and always will exist. Yet understanding comes through seeing the lower level in terms of the higher, in terms of its end and reason why. The order between the levels is logical, not temporal or physical; it is an order of logical dependence, a logic of ends and functions. Hence the *Enneads* can be called the *Principia Mathematica,* in the Whitehead and Russell sense, of Athenian science: or rather, to put it more precisely, and to indicate the basic principles of that science, it is the *Principia Teleologica* of the Athenian scheme of understanding the world. The theory of emanation is a theory of intelligibility, not a theory of physical action; the higher is the reason for the lower, but not its cause. In just this way, the law of gravitation is the reason for planetary motions, not their cause; and the field theory is the reason for the law of gravitation, but not its cause.

This logical scale is *ipso facto* a scale of value. Value, what is real. Being, is what gives understanding: because Plotinos in his whole analysis starts from the experience of *knowing* as the basic good. He shares the religion of the Knower, for whom perfection, the highest Good, is the source of truth. Hence he affords the highest expression, the most consistent illustration of the Greek devotion to the life of *theōria.* Perfection thus generates a whole scale of values, just as, says Plotinos, the beloved gives value to her surroundings, to the rose she wears, the ground she treads upon, etc. There is an overflowing of value or Being from its central source, like, to use Plotinos' most famous figure, a fountain of light. The

Archē of value is thus "dynamic," it spreads itself abroad in all directions. It is the sun from whence all Being flows.

For man, the way is hence: "Flee to our dear Fatherland!" Achieve "life," which is real, has Being, only as it possesses value. The lover really lives only in the presence of his beloved, and he lives most truly in closest union with her. The philosopher lives only as he finds truth, the artist lives only as he achieves beauty.

The practical life is for Plotinos definitely a lower stage. It is essentially a way of purification. Through moral action, through embodying intelligence in one's decisions, one learns to follow *nous*, one gets an intellectual training in order and harmony. One thus gains freedom from the passions of the body, from the seduction of the senses, through practice in turning to reason and thought.

"But," says Plotinos, "it is not enough to be sinless; one must be positively good, perfect, and divine." And so he sketches the Platonic way. Starting with the beauties of the sense-world —there is no Oriental contempt for beauty in Plotinos, he is thoroughly Greek—starting from the senses, one can pass through the love of higher and higher goods, through the life of "the lover, the artist, and the philosopher." One can go through mathematics to dialectic, the science of the distinctions of Being and value. Love and thought can bring an eventual identity with their objects, and one can even hope in the end to become perfect: one can find complete union with the One and the Source. The musician becomes one with all music, the lover one with his true love, the philosopher one with truth, that is, one with the Divine Source, in the ecstasy of the final vision of perfection. In all this, Plotinos is of course closely following what Plato had taught him in the *Symposium*.

All this analysis and sketching of a way of life is thoroughly consistent and true, in the only sense in which a philosophy can be called true: it offers a rational interpretation of man's experience in his world, and a harmonious discrimination of values. Plotinos is to be criticised, not for what he maintains, or for what he positively counsels, but only for what he leaves out or minimizes, for the inadequacies of his vision and for his imperfect sympathy for the entire wealth of human experience. He does not deal with physics, which we moderns cherish, perhaps too highly; or with the problems of the practical life of men and cities, which all men need to take into account. In these inadequacies, if we may so call them, Plotinos once more resembles his modern counterpart, Spinoza, who likewise in his passion for rational truth subordinated all other goods to the intellectual love of God.

IX THE MAKING OF THE CHRISTIAN SYNTHESIS

It has often appeared a problem, why the Christian scheme of things was the final outcome of the ancient world. Men have asked, Was this all the harvest? Did Plato and Aristotle have to be forgotten? If it had to be a religious system, could not men have continued something of the naturalistic religious schemes of the Epicureans, or at least of the Stoics? Was Christianity indeed a strange new Oriental obscurantism?

Men have asked, with Nietzsche, would it not have been better had Persia conquered? There would then have been at least an emphasis on truth, and a clear distinction between good and evil. Since the time of Lessing, in the eighteenth century, it has often suited the prejudices of moderns to say, Judaism would have been a far better religion for the ancient world to transmit to the West: it possesses a sane moral scheme for this world, it has few aberrations of asceticism, it has always proved to be intellectually open-minded.

For almost a thousand years, Islam showed itself more progressive and more assimilative of the best Greek values and intellectual achievements. Western Europe was, in fact, the immediate heir of Islamic civilization and culture, certainly in its thinking. That culture preserved the accomplishments of the Greeks for centuries when Western Christians no longer cared. Even much of our modern moral scheme, our values of democracy and of human brotherhood, were rather stronger in some Islamic societies than in medieval Western Europe, or than in the Byzantine Empire. Islam has always displayed a minimum of race prejudice, and on this score clearly has had a better record than the Christians. Islam, in fact, except for the Turks, proved fairly wise and tolerant, until the Christians began attacking it. And even with those fanatics, after the initial Ottoman conquest the aggression was usually on the Christian side.

It is possible to view Christianity with some objectivity today, because few educated moderns can be said to believe in it any longer, in the traditional, literal-minded sense. Our great metropolitan centers today—London, Paris, New York, and the rest—are hardly to be called "Christian" cities. Most of their inhabitants are no longer even irritated by Christianity, and are rather amused at the heat of refugees from the less pleasant features of the more Christian provinces. Moderns may believe in the Gospel of Jesus; if they are sophisticated, they may believe in the Demonic, in Kairos, and in the Unconditioned. They may even believe in the persistence of sin in the lives of the redeemed. But they scarcely believe literally in what has traditionally been recognized as Christianity.

Now, if we really understand what the Christian system of

ideas was, its final "victory" in the Roman world no longer appears a problem. The victory of Swinburne's pale Galilaean would of course have presented a genuine one. And so would the victory of the teachings of Jesus, and of the Sermon on the Mount, often proclaimed to be the essence of Christianity by liberal Protestants.

There was never the slightest danger of such victories. It is clear that if the outcome of Hellenistic civilization had not been something that could be called "Christianity," but had been something else—"Mithraism," perhaps—there would have been little actual difference. There would have been a slightly different set of religious symbols: we should employ the Sun with its rays rather than the Cross, and the Blood of the Bull rather than the Blood of the Lamb. But there would have been the same organization of a universal and comprehensive religious system, the same incorporation of all the varied streams of Mediterranean culture. And even the religious symbols would have expressed very much the same attitudes and values, for they would have grown out of the same social and religious experience. In other words, the outcome was not a victory but a synthesis. It was not even the conquest of Greece by the Orient. For Greece, if it ever meant more than a handful of intelligent and thoughtful men, had vanished five hundred years before.

The building of the Christian synthesis was one assimilation after another of all the strands of Hellenistic experience by what started as a rather minor sect. Ever since disintegration of this system set in at the Reformation, and even before, among the Pre-Reformers, this process has often been viewed as a kind of corruption of an original purity, which men have felt ought somehow to be regained. But to the historian, there is little doubt, if the teachings of Jesus, or if the simple religious life of the Primitive Church, had remained pure, they

would never have been heard of by later generations. They
certainly would never have been taken over by our Western
European ancestors. They were rather accidentally incorporated in the final synthesis of Hellenistic experience. From
time to time, they have been rediscovered by individuals, or
by small groups, whose insistence on them has always produced a great shock to Christians. But they have never been
taken very seriously by the Church, or by Christianity—at
least, not by any church that has ever been taken very seriously.
Only minor sects, like the Friends or Quakers, have ever made
them very central. The other churches have been, not followers of Jesus, but "Christian"—which has historically always
been quite another thing. And again and again it has been
authoritatively proclaimed by Christian thinkers—by many
Christian realists in our century—that to attempt to follow the
teachings of Jesus literally is heresy—the heresy of perfec-
tionism.

No, the making of the Christian synthesis was hardly a
corruption, a dilution, but rather an enriching. It meant the
building of an entire culture, of a whole round of activities,
feelings, and beliefs. Naturally the greater the success of this
synthesis in incorporating and expressing the needs of one
type of social experience, the more there was present that had
to be reconstructed when Christianity was used to organize
and express another and alien social experience: when it was
employed for that purpose, for instance, by the barbarian
peoples of Western Europe. And again and again, since that
culture gave way to its many successors, it has happened once
more. Each elaborate adaptation has in turn demanded further
extensive revision.

This Christian synthesis was the work of generation after
generation of modernists, who succeeded in bringing in new
values and new ideals in the face of the traditionalists. All the

great theologians, prophets, and statesmen of the Church have been essentially assimilators of novelty into the Christian tradition. In Hellenistic times they succeeded in building up a tremendous system, the final synthesis of ancient culture, drawing on Egypt, Syria, Persia, as well as on Palestine, Greece, and Rome.

This synthesis was remarkably inclusive. Almost everything was drawn into it, from Greek rationalism to values and ideas of the Egyptian and Babylonian priests that were already old long before the Greeks discovered Greece. Every philosophy seems to be there, even if only as a heresy: that means it was near enough to the truth to be mistaken for it. The synthesis has room for every type of ideal and of life.

Hence it seems difficult to maintain that there is any discoverable single Christian ideal, or any one type of Christian civilization. Since the eighteenth century, men have often complained, "Christianity has never been practiced." One can only counter, how could it possibly have been? Has there ever been any one single Christian ideal that *could* be practiced? Rather, there has been a comprehensive storehouse of rich experiences and warring ideals, a great group of very human philosophies and ways of life, one of the most complex to which any culture has ever given birth. Perhaps we can say, this Christian synthesis has had the deepest roots in human experience—at least, in the experience of a pre-industrial and pre-technological age. It is proposed to treat it here in such terms. But it is possible to understand what Christianity has been in our tradition, only if we forget most of what passes for Christianity today, what we may have learned in childhood, or what we hear in the church from the average pulpit.

What values that we today cherish failed to get included in the Christian synthesis? What values were excluded? There are two elements notoriously missing in the shrunken Christianity of our own day: the faith in science, and an ethic of social control. Many are trying their best to bring them in. But we are apt to forget that both were present and indeed central when Christianity was a genuinely comprehensive religion.

Though not present at the outset, in the Gospels, or in the Primitive Church, up until the Reformation and the Council of Trent Christianity was able to assimilate the best knowledge and the prevailing intellectual systems of ideas. It successfully incorporated, first, the Platonic science of the Hellenistic world, then the Aristotelian science of the Middle Ages. In the eighteenth and nineteenth centuries, the Protestants tried valiantly to embody the new modern science of Newton; but they were hardly really successful. Most Christianity today "accepts" our burgeoning science, but can scarcely be said really to have made it a part of its body of ideas.

The second element missing today, an ethic of social control, was lacking in Roman Christianity, and has been largely lost by Protestantism. But such an ethic was developed by the medieval Church. It is almost impossible for it to survive in a sect; and in the modern world Protestantism, Catholicism, and Judaism have been able to exist only as sects. There has in modern times been no inclusive Church, save in the national churches of England and Scandinavia, in which nationalism rather than any Christian social ideal has been predominant, the factor making for cohesion.

There is, to be sure, a third element lacking in the original Christian synthesis, and never developed in the later tradition: the experimental attitude we are often told is demanded by our own civilization. But this element is found in almost no past religion or philosophy. Should it ever become widespread on a large scale, it would be something wholly novel and unprecedented.

This Christian synthesis has normally been highly unstable, since it has been held together, not by any one single consistent body of thought, but rather by the comprehensive types of experience embodied. And no man—not even the manifold genius of Augustine—could possibly enjoy all these different types of experience. "Christianity" has over the centuries embraced contradictory systems of thought, conflicting types of experience. Since the break-up of its synthesis at the Reformation, there has been the demand for intellectual consistency and uniformity. Consider Calvin's consistent working-out of one single major intellectual strand of the tradition, and one single religious attitude. This demand leads inevitably to what we call sects, that is, to groups of small numbers united under peculiar conditions. Since the Council of Trent even Catholicism has been in this sense a sect. The only true Churches have been the national Churches, Anglican and Lutheran. Since they have been able to subordinate Christian religious feeling to national loyalties and attitudes, they have been able to carry on the older Christian tradition that the "Church" must embrace a variety of religious experience.

This instability has led Christianity to constant change and reinterpretation, to the absorption of the ever-new elements of a progressive and growing culture. For a long time the Church was thus able to assimilate the new: it remained alive, we say. It was relatively immutable only during those times when men ceased to think, from the sixth to the twelfth centuries, in the West. Then the discovery of Greek thought started a new process of assimilation and consequent disintegration that has continued ever since, and has led to one new reconstruction after another.

Here we are interested in the intellectual elements in the synthesis, in the development of Christian thought, not primarily in the institutional and social side, which may well be ultimately more important. The most inclusive formulation of Christian thought in the ancient world is that of St. Augustine —though even Augustine leaves out a great deal that was transmitted through other strands of the tradition—the whole body of ideas, for example, that came down to the West from Dionysius the Areopagite.

How did this synthesis of Christian thought take form?[1] Let us try to enumerate the major stages in its making. It is well to remember that there is no single line of development, especially at the outset: the lines are many that happened to come together and fuse. The synthesis really began centuries before the life of Jesus. And the roots of the Christian system are to be found, not only in Judaism: they are located equally in Persian dualism, in Syrian mystery cults, in Stoic ethics, in Platonistic thought. It was mainly the accident of the inclusion of the Hebrew Scriptures in the Christian Canon, and hence in the synthesis, that has led to an undue emphasis on the Jewish background of Christianity, though Jesus himself was

[1] The clearest account in Eng. is Arthur C. McGiffert, *History of Christian Thought*, 2 vols., based on his famous lectures down to the Reformation (New York, 1932-33). The classic work is Adolf von Harnack, *History of Dogma*, Ger. version, 4 vols. (Freiburg, 1886-90; 6th ed., 1922); Eng. tr., 7 vols. (Boston, 1894-99). Harnack was a liberal Protestant and he perhaps overemphasized the influence of Greek philosophy, as did E. Hatch, *The Influence of Greek Ideas on Christianity* (London, 1888; new ed., F. C. Grant, New York, 1957). H. B. Workman, *Christian Thought to the Reformation* (New York, 1911), a brief manual. A. G. V. Allen, *The Continuity of Christian Thought* (Boston, 1884), classic interpretation by a Modernist in sympathy with the Greek but not the Latin Fathers. Best older Church histories: W. Möller (Protestant; Freiburg, 1889-94; Eng. tr., London, 1892-93) and J. B. Alzog (Catholic; Mainz, 1841). See also F. Loofs, *Dogmengeschichte* (Halle 1889; 5th ed., 1950); R. Seeberg, *Dogmengeschichte*, 2 vols. (Graz, 1895-98; 3d ed., in 4 vols., 1918-23), Eng. tr. (Philadelphia, 1904); J. Tixeront (Catholic), *Histoire des Dogmes*, 3 vols. (Paris, 1905ff.; Eng. tr., St. Lous, 1910ff.). E. Troeltsch, *Social Teachings of the Christian Churches* (Tübingen, 1912; 3d ed., 1923; Eng. tr., New York, 1932), illuminating classic.

of course a Jew. After these earlier roots have been explored, there are:

1. The Jewish religion of Righteousness, transformed in Jesus and the Gospels into purity of heart; that is, into what moderns have often called prophetic monotheism.

2. There ensues a double line of growth. On the one hand, Christianity first appears as a kind of universalized Judaism, as a moral law and a promise of immortality. At the same time, Paul started conceiving of Christianity, and furnished its first theological formulation, as a mystery religion, an interpretation pushed in the second century by the Gnostics. This conception, minor at first, made Christianity the Jewish way of personal deliverance and salvation.

3. There follows the rationalization of Christianity in terms of the common Hellenistic Platonic religious philosophies. There was, first, the necessity of providing an intellectual justification in the Hellenistic world: this was undertaken by those thinkers we know as the Apologists. There then developed, secondly, genuinely philosophical interests in the great Neo-Platonic Alexandrian theologians and doctors, the first systematizers of a Christian rational theology, who were defending and extending Greek conceptions and values against the Syrian ascetics and dualists of the School of Antioch. Thirdly, there followed the determination of what was to remain Christian orthodoxy in the great councils, especially those of Nicaea and of Chalcedon. In themselves these involved many political compromises, much like those familiar in recent experience among the determinations of "correct" doctrine among the Russian Marxian-Leninists.

4. Next came the incorporation of much of the Stoic ethics, so popular in the West, at the hands of the Latin Fathers, especially Ambrose, who wrote the classic document of Christian Stoicism, *De officiis ministrorum*.

5. The chief achievement of the Latin Fathers was to work out the intellectual formulation of the cardinal Roman experiences of sin and salvation and deliverance; here Ambrose and Augustine are the chief thinkers.

6. The doctrine of the Church as an administrative system was elaborated especially by Cyprian and Augustine, and consummated by Vincent of Lerins.

7. Almost a millennium later, in the Middle Ages, Christianity absorbed Aristotelian science, at the hands of the Schoolmen, following its earlier appropriation by the Moslems Avicenna and Averroes, and the Jewish Maimonides.

8. The Church managed to organize medieval society, with the aid of Roman law and Greek political philosophy.

9. The disintegration, and concentration on certain selected strands of the Christian synthesis began with the Pre-Reformers and the mystics, long before the rush came with the Protestant Reformation or Revolt.

10. In modern times there have followed a series of radical reinterpretations, adding quite contradictory elements. This process includes the Humanists of the Renaissance as well as the Reformers, and the long line of Humanists down to the present day; the Humanitarians, who came to the fore in the eighteenth century; and the Liberals and Modernists from the nineteenth century on, including the three great Romantic reinterpretations of Hegel, of Kant, Fichte, and Ritschl, and of Schleiermacher.[2]

[2] For this later post-Augustinian history of the Christian synthesis, see my *Career of Philosophy in Modern Times*: Vol. I, *From the Middle Ages to the Enlightenment* (New York, 1962); Vol. II, *From the German Enlightenment to the Age of Darwin* (New York, 1965); and Volume III, *The Hundred Years Since Darwin* (in preparation).

X THE GOSPEL OF JESUS AND
THE MYSTERY CULT OF PAUL

Jesus of Nazareth appears in the three synoptic gospels as a fairly typical Hebrew prophet. But there has never yet been agreement on just what he taught. The tradition has remained split, and since the birth of critical scholarship in the eighteenth century (going back, indeed, to Spinoza), there has been unending discussion and argument on this issue. The precise definition of the message of Jesus remains still a task for interpretation in the light of one's own ideals and religious commitments, even more than for historical scholarship. If we ask, however, not what Jesus intended, but what the Christian tradition has found there, the answer is clear: it has found many and diverse lights. For all these conflicting views, the Gospels seem to furnish some authority.

For some two centuries biblical scholars have been trying to get behind the present text of the Gospels to discover "what Jesus really taught." The higher criticism of texts has reached many illuminating conclusions; it is clearly one of the most fruitful intellectual instruments of the mind of man. It is also a fascinating game. If the teachings of Socrates, or the life of Plato, crumble away under such critical investigation, one can easily imagine what has happened where so many religious hopes and fears are involved. Ultimately, a few critics were led to the inevitable question, did Jesus ever actually live? or is he as mythical a figure as the other Saviors and Lords of the various mystery cults of that time? Critics have thrown doubts on all the positive evidence for his existence, and the Gospel stories and teachings are certainly paralleled by many other contemporary myths and documents.

Of course, this is an unacceptable conclusion. But it is significant that neither Paul, nor the Apologists, nor the Alexandrian theologians, nor even Augustine, seem to have cared much about the historical Jesus; and the Church has rarely made his precepts central. Many Christians would certainly have an easier conscience, if it could be shown that Jesus is a typical mystery Savior myth. There is, however, general agreement among the scholars, though it seems to rest on animal—or rather, on spiritual—faith than on any evidence, that Jesus of Nazareth did live on earth, and that we know almost nothing with certainty about his life or teachings—about what was distorted or added by the Evangelists, about what was lost in translation from his tongue, the Aramaic, into Greek, about what came from the use of the "form" of the Gospel. This lack of certainty, however, has not prevented scholars from elaborating a host of theories and versions of both his life and his teachings.[1]

[1] A. von Harnack, *Das Wesen des Christentums* (Berlin, 1900; Eng. tr., New York, 1901, as *What Is Christianity?*), by a liberal Protestant; A. Loisy, *L'Évangile et l'Église* (Paris, 1902; Eng. tr., New York, 1903), answer by a Catholic Modernist: Felix Adler, *Ethical Philosophy of Life* (New York, 1918), ch. 4, by a non-Christian. Social interpretations in Vladimir Simkhovitch, *Towards an Understanding of Jesus* (New York, 1916); Charles Elwood, *Reconstruction in Religion* (New York, 1925); Walter Rauschenbusch, *Christianity and the Social Crisis* (New York, 1907), and *Christianizing the Social Order* (New York, 1912); Harry F. Ward, *The Ancient Lowly* (New York, 1924); all classics of the early twentieth-century Social Gospel. See also Robert T. Handy, *The Social Gospel in America, 1870–1920* (New York, 1966).

Surveys of the state of New Testament scholarship: older, F. C. Conybeare, *Myth, Magic, and Morals* (London, 1909; rev., 1958); A. von Harnack, *History of Dogma* (Eng. tr., Boston, 1904, 1905; 2d ed., 1908), Vols. I and II; David S. Muzzey, *Rise of the New Testament* (New York, 1900). James Moffatt, *Introduction to the New Testament* (New York, 1925); P. Wernle, *The Sources of Knowledge of the Life of Jesus* (Tübingen, 1906; Eng. tr., London, 1907); E. F. Scott, *The Gospel and Its Tributaries* (Edinburgh, 1928), *The Ethical Teachings of Jesus* (New York, 1924), and *The*

The early Jewish Christians remained Jews, with no thought of embracing a new religion; they were merely convinced that Jesus was the "Messiah" or the "Christ," and they regarded his Messiahship as much more important than any new moral message he might be bringing. That is, they believed *in* Jesus, rather than *that* what Jesus taught was true—an attitude that remained characteristic of most Christian thought until the nineteenth century. This conviction involved certain intellectual beliefs or expectations: notably, that only righteous, Law-observing Jews who accepted Jesus as the Messiah would share in the Kingdom he would set up on his second coming. But their faith in Jesus was primarily a commitment *to* Jesus: it was practical rather than intellectual.

Much the same holds true of Paul, though his conception of the nature of the work of Christ was quite different. For him, this was not to found the Kingdom, but to transform human nature from flesh to spirit, and thus to save individual souls from bondage to sin and death. By accepting and believing in the Christ, men are united to him in a mystical union, die with him to the old Adam, put off the flesh with

Fourth Gospel (Edinburgh, 1906; 4th ed., 1926). See also Albert Schweitzer, *Von Raimarus zu Wrede* (Tübingen, 1906; 2d ed., 1913), Eng. tr., *The Quest of the Historical Jesus* (New York, 1910). Rudolf Bultmann, *Kerygma and Myth* (London, 1953), *Form Criticism* (New York, 1934), and *Die Geschichte der synoptischen Tradition* (2d ed., Göttingen, 1931; 3d ed., 1957; Eng. tr., New York, 1963); M. Dibelius, *From Tradition to Gospel* (New York, 1935). J. M. Robertson, *Pagan Christs* (2d ed., London, 1911), an older radical view.

Classic lives of Jesus by D. F. Strauss (1835-36), tr. by George Eliot, (London, 1848; 4th ed., 1902); Ernest Renan (Paris, 1863; Eng. tr., New York, 1864). Shirley J. Case (Chicago, 1927; liberal Protestant); J. Klausner, *Life of Jesus* (Hebrew, 1924; Eng. tr., New York, 1925; Jewish); Nathaniel Schmidt, *The Prophet of Nazareth* (New York, 1905). M. Dibelius, *Jesus* (Philadelphia, 1949); Günther Bornkamm, *Jesus of Nazareth* (New York, 1960). G. Stanley Hall, *Jesus the Christ in the Light of Psychology* (New York, 1917).

him, and rise with him, completely transformed in their nature, to live a new and divine life, a life "in Christ." This is all for Paul an intensely personal and practical religious experience. Believing in Christ is no mere intellectual assent, and acceptance; it is utter absorption.

Hence neither the early Jewish Christians nor Paul made central what Jesus taught.

Taken at their face value, against the background of what we know of the situation of the Jews at the time, the synoptic gospels show Jesus a prophet of nonresistance to Roman imperialism,[2] a figure somewhat resembling Gandhi in our own day, though without, of course, Gandhi's asceticism or his Hindu pantheism. Jesus taught confidence in the Jewish personal God of love and kindness: all men are His children. Yet He exacts in His Law—the Torah—which Jesus accepted, a high and stern ethical standard. The message of Jesus, as reported in the synoptics, seems to run: "The Kingdom of God is at hand."

What did Jesus mean by this? "The Kingdom of God" was a common and vague phrase, with several different meanings. Did Jesus himself intend a Zionistic kingdom under the "Son of David"? Did he mean an apocalyptic "end of the world," and the establishment of a new social order? Which sense did Jesus have in mind? Or did he have some new sense, not already familiar? Did Jesus expect a speedy end of the world, or only the reign of love and justice among men? Or did he intend a present reality, attainable by any man who repented? We do not really know what he meant—the scholars merely argue. It is obvious that in any social sense—in all but the most personal meaning—the "Kingdom of God" was *not* at hand, and it hardly seems imminent today.

[2] See Simkhovitch, *Towards an Understanding of Jesus*.

But the way of life Jesus taught seems fairly clear. Like all the prophets, he was appealing from the letter of the Hebrew Law to its spirit—to "righteousness" or "justice" as respect for that Holy Thing in every man; and to a vigorous protest at the injustice of its violation. He was appealing to the prophetic ethic of nonviolation and mercy. In this he is closest to those noble figures, Micah and the Second Isaiah.

In Jesus, the nonresistant facing insuperable injustice—the tramp of the Roman legions—the "righteousness" of the prophets was transmuted into something more inward, we say, into purity of heart, righteousness of motive. Meet triumphant evil, he counseled men, by casting it out of your own heart: meet prejudice by tolerance, arrogance by humility, hatred by love. Jesus urged "love," *agapē,* practical kindness, active benevolence toward all men, as children of the same Father, as human brothers. This inwardness, this emphasis on active love, was of course not unique in Jesus—fortunately. It can be paralleled in the very Pharisee tradition he so bitterly assailed, in the great rabbis, as Klausner and others have made clear. The same spiritual problem generated the same religious response. In the rabbinical tradition, to be sure, this appears as isolated sayings, and does not possess the same central emphasis as in the Gospels.

It is noteworthy that Jesus displays almost no asceticism, and little sense of sin, little sense of moral struggle; and certainly no sense of the need of any special supernatural power to do right. In this, Jesus does not seem to be expressing the more profound moral experience of his age, or its deeper plumbings of the ethical life. He seems, indeed, to have regarded righteousness and purity of heart as a natural human achievement, rather than as a supernatural gift from on high. Jesus seems to have had a rather high estimate of man's natural moral powers, much higher than the distinctly lower opinion entertained by the long line of Christian theologians from Paul to our own day.[3]

Jesus seems to have thought that men are free to change their attitude. In continually exhorting them to "repent," he used what appears in the Greek Gospels as the verb *"metanoiein,"* which means literally, change your mind, change your attitude.[4]

Like all the Hellenistic ways of life, the ethic of Jesus appears as an ethic of bearing evil. It is hardly an ethic of achievement; that is, it is an ethic of motive, not an ethic of mastery. There is in Jesus' words little insistent sense that good will needs enlightenment and intelligence. Christians have always found it hard to derive from them a facing of the problem, how can we use prosperity aright? To what end? Rather, there appears in Jesus' words the repeated strain, "take no thought for the morrow."

Thus the ethic of Jesus is perhaps adequate for the simple peasant society in which he lived, for a society of face-to-face personal relationships. This ethic is especially appropriate if the eschatological interpretation of the message of Jesus is correct, if he actually expected the speedy end of the world, as the primitive religious community that set down his precepts certainly did. It is appropriate if Jesus was consciously proclaiming an *Interimsethik,* an ethic for "the meanwhile."[5]

But the ethic of Jesus clearly breaks down in the face of the

[3] In the reported words of Jesus, there is little trace of the pessimism, the cynicism— however tamed— the realistic facing of the facts—so-called— about human nature, common today to conservatives and radicals alike. Jesus, indeed, seems never to have read or even heard of Kierkegaard, or Marx, or Freud.

[4] It is this strain in the Gospels that supports the interpretation of the religious liberals. It may well be merely that liberal biblical scholars have painted his portrait in their own image.

[5] As Albert Schweitzer vigorously maintained in his influential *The Quest of the Historical Jesus.*

moral problems of a complex civilization. It gives no guidance for the proper ordering of group relations, for instance, or for controlling riches and technology. These are just our own major difficulties. Hence the ethic of Jesus has always required supplementation when, as in the Middle Ages, it faced the organization of a whole complex society.[6] Without such development and supplementation, any Christian ethics that confined itself to the precepts of Jesus alone would doubtless prove inadequate to the needs of our technological civilization, with its intricate organization into conflicting and competing social groups.

The second stage of the making of the Christian synthesis[7] occurred when Christianity became a Graeco-Oriental religious cult, offering individual salvation, with a Lord, a *Kyrios,* who had died and then risen again. By magic union with him, the initiates or baptized might also rise with him. "Lord" meant a Divine Savior: the "Kingdom of God" was identified with the sacramental cult or "church"; the Hebrew Scriptures were turned into a Christian allegory. Jesus of Nazareth as a per-

---

[6] The efforts of several generations of liberal Protestants to look to the teachings of Jesus for a final moral ideal for modern culture have hence probably been misguided. Indeed, the way in which such religious liberals long took those teachings as an ultimate authority in moral matters was a major obstacle holding back the frank and realistic confronting of the most pressing problems of moral reconstructon facing our world. Fortunately, our best theologians have been trying to make this clear for a generation.

[7] The Rise of Christianity: Kirsopp Lake, *Landmarks in the History of Early Christianity* (London, 1920): ed. *The Apostolic Fathers,* 2 vols., (Loeb, 1912); A. C. McGiffert, *History of Christian Thought* (New York, 1932), Bk. I; and *The Apostolic Age* (New York, 1897).

Social Interpretations: S. J. Case, *The Social Origins of Christianity* (Chicago, 1927), and *The Social Triumph of the Ancient Church* (New York, 1933). Marxian: Karl Kautsky, *Foundations of Christianity* (Stuttgart, 1908; Eng. tr., New York, 1925, 1953); M. Beer, *Social Struggles in Antiquity* (London, 1922).

sonal moral prophet and teacher was largely forgotten, and Christianity was spread by men who had never seen him, and cared little about his personality. They preached "Christ crucified," not the Sermon on the Mount.

It was Saul of Tarsus—known to posterity as Paul[8]—who was the formulator of the whole Christian system of salvation from sin. His conception of the nature of Christianity, however, had very little influence among Christians for at least a hundred years. Paul suffered an intense personal experience of moral struggle and sin: the seventh chapter of Romans is probably autobiographical. Paul was unable to keep the Jewish Law: his besetting sin, it seems, was that he could not help getting angry. Generalizing from his own personal experience, he felt that man is by nature evil and wicked, because of the desires of the Flesh, which persist despite all man's efforts to struggle against them. Hence derives Man's bitter need of release from the Flesh, that is, from his natural desires, his need for a transformation of his very nature that can only be supernatural and magical.

Such a form of experience was common in that Hellenistic

[8] Irwin Edman, *The Mind of Paul* (New York, 1935). H. A. A. Kennedy, *St. Paul and the Mystery Religions* (London, 1913); Alfred Loisy, *Les Mystères Païens et le Mystère Chrétien* (Paris, 1914). S. Angus, *The Mystery-Religions and Christianity* (London, 1925), and *The Religious Quests of the Graeco-Roman World: A Study in the Historical Background of Early Christianity* (London, 1930). C. A. A. Scott, *Christianity according to St. Paul* (London, 1927), minimizes Hellenistic influence. T. R. Glover, *Paul of Tarsus* (New York, 1925). Albert Schweitzer, *Die Mystik des Apostels Paulus* (Tübingen, 1930; Eng. tr., New York, 1931). F. J. Foakes-Jackson, *The Life of St. Paul* (London, 1933). Kirsopp Lake, *Paul: His Heritage and Legacy* (New York, 1934).

See also Ernest Renan, *Saint Paul* (Paris, 1869); Mathew Arnold, *St. Paul and Protestantism* (London, 1883); A. Deissmann, *Paulus: eine kultur und religionsgeschichtliche Skizze* (Tübingen, 1911; Eng. tr., London, 1912; 2d ed., 1926). Albert Schweitzer, *Geschichte der paulinischen Forschung* (Tübingen, 1911); Eng. tr., *Paul and His Interpreters,* (New York, 1912).

world, and was stamped on Christianity by Paul. For Paul himself, it was an intensely personal and practical moral experience. Paul doubtless exaggerated it and made it central in the moral life. The exaggeration is clearly an aberration, and, according to our modern lights, perhaps even pathological. But it was probably inevitable in any Hellenistic religion that could hope to become widespread and popular. Then, the vision of the Risen Christ or the Living Christ on the road to Damascus *did* transform the nature of Paul himself. This was a fact of his experience, however we may try to explain it, psychologically or otherwise.

Now, Paul was a Hellenized Jew who had to understand what he believed. And he understood his experience and its fruits in terms familiar to one with a Hellenistic upbringing. The whole framework of the redemptive system in terms of which he proceeded to interpret the salvation he had won on the road to Damascus, is paralleled in, if not actually borrowed from, the many mystery cults of the time, with their widespread myth of a dying and rising Savior or Lord. But above all Paul had to construe his own experience in terms that would seem intelligible to him. Why? How? Why could he not keep the Hebrew Law? Who and what was the "Living and Divine Christ" who had saved him? What was the character of his supernatural "life in Christ" and "in the Spirit" after he had "risen with Christ"? To answer these questions he had to work out a whole theology. To the many inquiries of his fellow-Christians he was never at a loss for an answer. "God forbid!" he reiterates.

The vision of the Living Christ on the road to Damascus meant to Paul: Christ is the Messiah, a Divine Spirit, who put on the Flesh, then died, and was released from the Flesh. That is, Christ was a Mystery Lord, a *Kyrios.* By accepting and believing in the Christ, man can be identified with him in a mystic union, man can die to the Flesh with him, and rise with him, completely transformed in his own nature. He can rise to a new and divine life "in the Spirit" or "in Christ." The work of Christ is hence not to found the Kingdom, but to save individual souls.

Christianity, at the hands of Paul, became a mystical system of redemption, much like the cult of Isis, and the other sacramental or mystery religions of the day. Salvation is not forgiveness of sins, as it is for Jesus himself, but a transformation of human nature from the Flesh to the Spirit, from human to divine: it is literally a process of deification. The life of the Christian is literally supernatural, a life "in Christ." And it is a present reality, freeing the saved from sin. It carries with it a future life for the saved; but for Paul resurrection is essentially a spiritual thing. Men "rise with Christ" in this human life, they rise when they accept Christ. When he is so saved in Christ, the Christian leads a divine life. He is freed literally from the need to obey any Law, freed from the moral or Mosaic Law as well as from the ceremonial Law of the Jews. The Law, both ceremonial and moral, Paul held, was given to the Jews only to convince men that they are quite unable to keep it by their own efforts alone: they need a transformation of their human nature in order not to sin. The Law is hence a "schoolmaster" teaching men that they need Christ. The Christian is literally a supernatural being, who needs no law to tell him what is right, or to compel him to do it, for he *can* do no wrong. Paul is thus a complete antinomian, freed from any legalistic conception of the moral life. Naturally he was sadly puzzled by the goings-on of the not completely sinless Christians in the churches he had organized.

Paul's scheme differed from those of the other mystery cults, save that of Mithras, in his moral emphasis, which derives from his Jewish background: the salvation gained through accepting and rising with Christ is a *moral* freedom to love and serve one's fellows. Hence Paul adopted much of the ethical teaching of the Gospels. Ever since the eighteenth century Paul has been much disliked by liberal Christians, who differ with him on their estimate of the powers of human nature, and the need for a supernatural transformation of it. But such liberals have at the same time welcomed Paul's strong social emphasis: like the body and its members, Christians are all one in Christ, and should therefore serve each other. This is of course Stoic teaching, absorbed from the Hellenistic culture of the day, even to the figure Paul employs, a familiar Stoic image.

Paul differs from the other mystery cults also in the means of salvation he has discovered and is counseling. Salvation for him does not come primarily through a magic rite, through Baptism and the Eucharist; they are there in his thought, but are for Paul himself distinctly secondary. The means of salvation for Paul is a personal, mystical "union in faith." Faith is not for him something intellectual, it is not belief, as the later orthodox interpretation became, emphasizing belief in the creeds; but rather something mystical, very much like the Platonic love. Believing in Christ is much more than a commitment, it is for Paul complete union with the Christ; and faith is no mere intellectual assent and acceptance, but rather utter absorption. This subordination of the sacraments, and reliance instead on "faith" in his mystical sense, made Paul much later the great inspiration of the Reformers, and the Father of Protestantism.

Paul's whole theology is the attempt to answer the questions raised directly by what had happened to him in his own religious experience. Paul was doubtless mistaken in trying to universalize his individual travail and rebirth. But he himself never mistook the theology that for him explained his living experience for itself a way of salvation, nor did he ever set its acceptance as a condition of redemption. The later Church did so treat some of Paul's ideas; and with the Protestant Reformers his whole theology was made essential for salvation—and for church membership. Was it not to be found in the Scriptures, in the very Word of God? What Paul preached was "Christ crucified," and the promise of release from bondage to sin and death through union with the Christ. He had little interest in Jesus of Nazareth as a human personality, or in his moral teachings. Paul accordingly wrote no gospel account of the human life of Jesus. These were not the things that had saved him, but rather the Living and Risen Christ. Is it any wonder that his intellectual questions, and his answers, were about the Living Christ, not about the teachings of Jesus the moral prophet?

Christianity left Paul's hands a supernatural religion of redemption, a mystery cult, not too much unlike many others at its time, offering a kind of salvation few educated men today can be persuaded they need, by a means a modern thinker finds it difficult, without psychological interpretation, to credit. But Paul's religion of redemption has worked over the centuries for untold millions. Hence Paul's system of theology presents an ever-fascinating problem. How is its enormous effectiveness to be intellectually explained?

For a century Pauline Christianity, Paul's interpretation of the Christian scheme of salvation, had little influence, save on a few thinkers. It never became popular in the Eastern Church, and had to await the Latin Fathers to be made central. One of the most important first-century thinkers who hearkened to Paul is the author of the Fourth Gospel—conventionally known as "John the Evangelist."

The Fourth Gospel shares Paul's conception of Christianity as a redemptive system, as a transformation of human nature into a divine life. But "John" has interests that are much more intellectual and philosophical than those of Paul, much more Hellenic: Paul was essentially an activist rather than a philosophical thinker. And "John" was definitely trying to appeal to Hellenistic minds, consciously attempting to explain redemption to the Greek world. John's is the first attempt to bring Greek thought to the interpretation of the Christian scheme of things, the first of the Christian Apologists. In his Prologue about the Word, the *Logos,* he is adopting Philo Judaeus' earlier Platonization of the Hebraic tradition.[9]

For John the Evangelist, salvation is to *know* God. The transformation of human nature effected by union with the Christ is an *intellectual* illumination, the change from dwelling in a "realm of darkness" to entering upon a "realm of light." Perhaps, if evidence from the Dead Sea scrolls may be believed, it is a continuation of the teachings of the Hellenized Hebraic sect of the Essenes. For John, Jesus is primarily a teacher, who came to *show* God to man: "This is Life Eternal, that they shall know Thee the only true God." Hence John was led to write a Gospel, an enterprise in which Paul for all his activity was characteristically not interested. John wrote his Gospel to make clear to all men Jesus' vision of God as Love, *agapē.*

For John, the union with the Christ comes through faith, which he takes much more *intellectually* than Paul, as "belief." Hence John has to supplement such "faith" with "love," the mystical element and bond. In Paul, faith and love are fused together into one, which is his "faith." For Paul, faith is a mystical activity; for John, it is much more Greek: the

[9] Reinhold Niebuhr likes to emphasize this Apologetic concern of the Fourth Gospel as introducing the alien elements of Greek philosophy and Platonism into biblical thought. Unlike Paul Tillich, who is saturated in Greek philosophy, Niebuhr has tried to restrict Christianity, even in its early days, to the Hebraic tradition.

spirit of receptivity toward the vision shown by the Christ. Thus with the Fourth Gospel, a higher form of knowledge, the true revelation of God in Christ as being essentially Love, becomes central in Christianity.

One other figure, Ignatius of Antioch, one of the Apostolic Fathers, also took Christianity as a mystery cult. For Ignatius, salvation is the achievement of physical immortality: it is essentially the resurrection of the flesh, of the human body. This would have of course been abhorrent to Paul, for whom salvation was *release* from the Flesh. But the view of Ignatius became the orthodox doctrine of the Resurrection, and of the Christian future life. This makes the Platonic doctrine of the immortality of the soul strictly a heresy when it enters into the Christian system of thought. There has ever since been a dialectical tension in Christian thought between Ignatius' future life of a resurrected body, and the Platonic immortality of the soul, to which the body is itself quite irrelevant.[10]

[10] See my *Plato: Dramatist of the Life of Reason* (New York, 1970), chapter 16, "Platonic Immortality."

XI GNOSTICS, MORAL CHRISTIANS, AND APOLOGISTS

In the second century, the outstanding representatives of Christianity as a mystical redemptive system were the Gnostics.[1] The Gnostics were originally not Christian, but they welcomed

[1] See Arthur C. McGiffert, *History of Christian Thought*, 2 vols. (New York, 1932-1933); A. G. V. Allen, *The Continuity of Christian Thought* (Boston, 1884). Tertullian, *Against Marcion;* in *Ante-Nicene Fathers* (Edinburgh, 1867-1872; Buffalo, 1885-1896; reprinted, Grand Rapids, 1956), Tertullian, Vol. I (Edinburgh, 1868). T. R. Glover, *Conflict of Religions in*

Paul's interpretation of Christianity. Many, like Marcion, were professed followers of Paul. They provoked a reaction; and were condemned as heretics. The first Christian creed, the Apostles' Creed, was designed to be a shibboleth against Gnostic beliefs. And the Christian philosophy of the Alexandrian doctors was rather consciously built up in opposition to their thought and its extreme dualism. Clement's true or Christian Gnostic was definitely outlined in opposition to the false or Pauline Gnosticism.

There were at first many Gnostic sects, all with redeemers, with a God who became man to bring the *gnōsis* or knowledge that will make men Gods. Such a redeemer was called "Savior," that is, "Christos" or anointed, the "Son of Man."

Valentinus (c.160 A.D.) is a typical Christian or Pauline Gnostic. He was a dualist, with a strong ethical sense; the Gnostics were the heirs of Persian dualism and asceticism. He saw an eternal world conflict between God, who is good, and matter, which is evil. God simply could not have created our present world: Valentinus recites the evils of existence, and concludes, "God I dare not affirm to be the author of all this!" Again, "I will say anything rather than admit that God's Providence is wicked."

How is this conflict to be explained? The Gnostic read the conflict of religions as a philosophy of history. God, the Eternal Silence, the Non-Existent, produces pairs of Aeons who get worse and worse, as they emanate further and further from Him, and come nearer and nearer to evil matter. They are given Greek names: Nous, Logos, Phronesis, Sophia, Dynamis, powers and principalities: God produced a succession of thirty Aeons in all. The last and worst, the Demiurge, created the

---

the Early Roman Empire (New York, 1909), ch. X, "Tertullian." Hans Jonas, *The Gnostic Religion* (Boston, 1958). Robert M. Grant, *Gnosticism and Early Christianity* (New York, 1959).

world we know by uniting spirit to matter. This was a terrible blunder. And these anti-Semitic Christians believed the Demiurge, the Creator of the world, was Yahweh, the Hebrew God of the Jewish Scriptures. He had either no mind, or was else the Devil himself. Valentinus engages in a keen criticism of the cruel, barbarous Lord God of Battles of the early Hebrew Scriptures, and of the narrow and exclusive vengeance morality there expressed. He makes very clear why, without the purely allegorical interpretation introduced by the Alexandrian scholars, notably Origen, following Philo Judaeus, the Hebrew Scriptures would have been rejected by the Christians. It was Origen primarily who learned from Philo the way out, and the way to answer the Gnostic criticisms of Hebrew morality.

There is eternal warfare between Yahweh the Creator, and God, between Matter or Body and Spirit. There are Heavenly hosts on both sides: Valentinus counts 365 Heavens of angelic troops. Christ, an Aeon, a Spirit, allied himself with God in fighting Yahweh. He now reigns as co-God. He joined the man Jesus in baptism, and by magic rites we can ourselves join him, become ourselves divine, and thus be saved from Yahweh, from matter or evil. We can finally hope to take part in undoing the blunder of creation itself. The way of salvation is through a higher knowledge or *gnosis,* which is a secret mystic revelation; through asceticism; and through the magic sacraments.

This Gnostic vision of life in the world is exciting and exhilarating. It makes evil intelligible and good pure, with no blurred lines between the two. It emphasizes the moral responsibility of man: for the final victory over evil depends on us humans. But it is exclusive and aristocratic: only the intellectual élite that can understand the Gnosis can hope to be saved. Above all, Gnosticism is cursed by its strong dualism, with its attendant ascetic flight from life; and the Gnostic hatred of the evil body soon expressed itself in all kinds of excesses. Some Gnostics hated the Jews so much they counseled positively disobeying the Jewish Law, the Ten Commandments, and urged men to lie, steal, and commit adultery to show their contempt for Yahweh. Some became libertines, in order to wear out the body the sooner, and free man's spirit from it: in our wisdom we would today call them masochists.

The Gnostics repelled most of the Christians by their extreme dualism, by their bitter anti-Judaism, by their denial of Providence and of the Incarnation. The Gnostics thus provoked a strong reaction against the whole mystery cult conception of Christianity, and against the system and theology of Paul, from whom they professed to derive their ideas. The Gnostics were thus responsible for the imposition of the first Christian creed, the so-called Apostles' Creed. This was formulated in Rome around 150 A.D.; candidates for baptism were required to declare their intellectual disagreement with the Gnostics, especially with Paul's follower Marcion, and to proclaim their adherence to the teachings of the Apostles. Doctrinal standards, intellectual beliefs, were thus for the first time made a necessary condition of salvation for Christians. The Gnostics were also responsible for a more intellectual answer to their aberrations: they provoked the Christian philosophy of the Alexandrian theologians. Christian Platonism thus arose as the rational rather than merely credal answer to the errors of the Gnostic teaching, and to the pushing to extremes of Pauline denial that reason is sufficient to save man.

This *mystical* interpretation took Christianity as a redemptive system for the complete transformation of human nature. In the first century it appealed to only a few Christians, but seemed to be gaining adherents rapidly in the second, until it was discredited by the Gnostic excesses. But side by side with it there prevailed a quite different conception of the nature of Christianity, a *moral* interpretation. This view was at the outset far more popular, especially among the Jewish and the Roman Christians. It took Christianity to be a kind of universalized Judaism, to be a revealed law of conduct accompanied by a promise of immortality: as an ethical code prescribing a way of life, with a religious sanction. In it there was no need or promise of magic redemption. This view was Jewish and Stoic, and the very antithesis of Paul's conception: its emphasis was moral, not mystical. This universalized moral law appealed to many of the popular Stoic preachers or "philosophers," who on their conversion to Christianity not unnaturally viewed their new faith as the true philosophy. Christianity offers, they held, correct knowledge of the True God and His commands; this knowledge is the essence of philosophy, and Christianity possesses it. These men, all "philosophers" or liberal preachers by profession, and converted now to the true philosophy, undertook to explain the meaning of Christianity to the Hellenistic world. They became the first rationalizers, the first intellectual justifiers to the Greeks, of the Christian revelation.

Such men constitute the group of the Apologists of the second century.[2] Justin Martyr is typical of these ex-Stoic Apologists. He sounds to our ears very much like the much

---

[2] See *The Apostolic Fathers*, Kirsopp Lake, ed. (Loeb, 1912, 1913). The most important of these Apologists are Justin and Irenaeus, who brought the various strains of Christian thought together in his *Against Christian Heresies*. Amongst the Latins are Lactantius and Tertullian. The principal writings of these Fathers are translated in the *Ante-Nicene Fathers*.

Best survey, Kirsopp Lake, *Landmarks in the History of Early Christianity* (London, 1920); also A. C. McGiffert, *The Apostolic Age* (New York, 1897), and *History of Christian Thought*; and A. G. V. Allen. Harnack, *History of Dogma; Expansion of Christianity* (Ger. version, Leipzig, 1902; Eng. tr., Boston, 1904, 1905; 2d ed., 1908). W. Windelband, *Gesch. der abendländischen Philosophie im Alterum*, A. Goedeckemeyer, ed. (4th ed.; Munich, 1923), gives an excellent treatment of the Apologists.

later eighteenth-century Deists. He emphasizes what they took to be the three tenets of their rational religion: there is an omnipotent God; He has commanded a law of righteousness; and He will reward and punish men in a future life. Man is a free being, but he is stupid and forgetful: he needs to be reminded of these truths, which he could reach by his natural reason. Christ, a second God, came, not to bring men magic grace, not to give them any essentially new teaching, but to remind men that God means what He has said. Christ merely reaffirmed the true philosophy of Heraclitus, Socrates, and Plato. These Greek philosophers were all really Christians, because they were right, and the Logos was inspiring them.

The Logos, the supreme Reason, who inspires men with all their human reason and truth, inspired the prophets, and became incarnate in Christ, who as a teacher made things a little clearer and more certain, and thus renewed the revelation of the Eternal Divine Law. But his teachings contain nothing uniquely original. His teachings we know to be true, because he fulfilled earlier Jewish prophecy.[3]

What man needs is light, not power. There is no original sin, no war of the flesh against the spirit. Sin is due to ignorance: Justin is very much opposed to Paul. Men forget Hell, and so they naturally disobey the moral law. Men know what they ought to do, but they need religious threats to make them do it.

Other Apologists lost all sense of anything distinctive in Christianity: it was merely the true philosophy and rational religion. "All Christianity is to be found in the first six chapters of Genesis." Theophilus, for example, never mentions Christ at all; yet he is typical of the majority of second-century Christians. For the Apologists, the Christian revelation is

---

[3] See Justin Martyr, *Dialogue with the Jew Trypho* (in *Ante-Nicene Fathers*).

knowledge, and knowledge is identified completely with secular philosophy.

These two strains, the magic-mystical and the moral, were united to form what can henceforth be called "Catholicism" by Irenaeus, an Eastern Greek who became Bishop of Lyons in Gaul, around 175 A.D. Irenaeus undertook a pretty conscious and deliberate synthesis of the two conceptions of the nature of Christianity as the basis for an organized Church, and thus succeeded in accomplishing what may well be a more important task than either Origen or Augustine. The Fall of man (the Pauline conception) was in Irenaeus for the first time given a fundamental place in the thought of the Western Church. It never became central in the Eastern or Greek Church. That is, human nature is corrupt, lies in bondage to sin, and is doomed to death. Hence men need release from the power of sin, and a transformation of their nature, a deification, to become immortal spirits (these are all Pauline ideas). Men need *also* positive righteousness, obedience to the moral law (this is the legalism of the moral interpretation and of the Apologists).

The birth and death of the Christ-Logos secures release from sin, and bestows divinity and immortality on men (Pauline); and *also* gives the freedom to follow the natural moral law, found in the Decalogue, and in the hearts of men, and reproclaimed by Jesus: Love to God and to man (moral strain). Man gains salvation by sacraments uniting him to God in Christ, releasing him from sin, and deifying him—by Baptism and the Eucharist. Man *also* needs for his salvation right conduct, obedience to the natural moral law of Christ, made possible by mystic union in Christ. Irenaeus interprets Paul's "justification by faith" as meaning justification by obedience to the natural moral law.

Both are hence necessary: grace and works, mysticism and

righteousness. This combination of sacramental mysticism and ethical legalism constitutes the essence of "Catholicism." Irenaeus inextricably weaves the two strains together: men are saved by taking the sacraments *and* by being righteous, by uniting with Christ *and* by obeying the moral law.

XII THE CHRISTIAN PHILOSOPHY OF THE GREEK FATHERS

CLEMENT, ORIGEN, AND ATHANASIUS

Two major intellectual developments took place in the ancient Church. With real philosophical interests, the Alexandrian Neo-Platonic theologians. Clement of Alexandria, Origen, and Athanasius, worked out the doctrines of the Trinity and of the Person of Christ, defending Greek values and conceptions against the Syrian ascetics and dualists of the School of Antioch, led finally by Arius of Alexandria. Orthodox doctrine was determined in the ecumenical Councils, especially those of Nicaea and of Chalcedon. The decisions, there taken, though in fact political compromises, like those among the Dialectical Materialists in Russia during the nineteen thirties, forever enshrined Platonism and the Platonistic philosophy at the intellectual heart of the Christian tradition. The other great doctrinal achievement of the ancient Church was the intellectual formulation of the cardinal Roman experience of sin, and salvation by grace through the Church, worked out by the great Latin Fathers Cyprian, Ambrose, and Augustine. The two bodies of ideas were brought together in the thought of Augustine, who was philosophically half-Greek and half-

Roman; together they were transmitted to the West through his comprehensive writings.

The doctrines of the Trinity and of the Incarnation were developed in the Eastern or Greek Church. They are the first great instance, in the Christian tradition, of the identification of Christian truth with rational knowledge, the first rational or natural theology, the first systematic interpretation of the Christian religious symbols and beliefs in terms of a speculative and philosophical theology. In contrast to the theology of Paul, which was the effort to understand a personal living experience, they are the attempt to come to terms with a well-worked-out and established philosophical system, the Neo-Platonic philosophy. In the Latin Church, the Trinity has normally been taken as a "mystery" of faith, not intelligible to human reason. It was in the Western Empire accepted first on the authority of the Nicene Council, not because it was understood, or because it seemed to explain any problem, but as a sign of submission to the authority of the Church. Later attempts to "explain" the Trinity in terms of other philosophies have been apt to lead to heresies, like Hegel's in the early nineteenth century. Hence in the West the tradition soon grew up that the Trinity is not to be explained. For the Greeks, in contrast, the Trinity was originally not a mystery—though it became one later in the Eastern Church also—but a rational and philosophical explanation of puzzling questions.

This difference is characteristic of the great contrast in developed Christian philosophy between the Eastern and the Western Churches in ancient times. The Latin Church was interested in a way of life, in moral problems. Its concerns were the practical conditions of the moral life: sin, salvation, grace, and the Church. For the Romans, life was serious, a pretty solemn affair. It was so hard to do right! They were pessimists, and they welcomed Oriental or Persian thought with its dualism: it well expressed their own values. They loved authority in both Empire and Church; they were enthusiastic for the needed magic transformation of human nature, for dualism and asceticism. They had a Puritan conscience: they were natural-born deacons and moral reformers. They were uninterested in theoretical and speculative thinking. They hated Greek naturalism and reasonableness. They built their theology accordingly upon Paul and his Oriental dualism and magic, and upon his rigorous moralism.

In contrast, the ancient Greek Church was intellectual, and interested in speculative problems. Its thinkers felt the need to understand the universe, to live rationally and naturally. They could not accept any religious or theological doctrine they did not understand, and they passed on naturally to philosophical inquiry for its own sake, even if its bearings on the conditions of salvation were not immediately apparent. Christianity presented the Greek theologians with *intellectual* problems. They had to solve them in the world of Greek philosophy, and to express them in its language: just so, we moderns have to express and solve our intellectual problems in the world and language of evolutionary and experimental science, and hence cannot take literally the symbols of what for us has become an outgrown mythology, of a God "up there."

The Roman theologians hated science and culture: they were Fundamentalists. The Greeks were not Fundamentalists; they were something that is perhaps rather more restricting, they were intellectuals. Fortunately, Augustine himself was half Greek in his thought, or he would have transmitted to the Western tradition far less in the way of intellectual materials. Perhaps we may say, if Ambrose and Augustine had not also handed on the religious and philosophical heritage of the ancient Greek Church, some other Western thinker would have had to perform that necessary function. One trembles to think of the consequences for the Western intellectual tradition, had its heritage been limited to what Tertullian expressed, had Tertullian and Arnobius been the great Latin Fathers.

The Alexandrian Platonic theologians in particular were typical religious liberals.[1] They were intelligent, cultivated men, opposed to Oriental irrationalism and pessimism. They were broad-minded, tolerant, eclectic, imaginative and not literal-minded. They were rationalistic and even naturalistic in their devotion to typically Greek values. They worked out a rounded philosophical theology and Christology, in the language of the prevalent Hellenistic religious philosophies, that expressed their interpretation of the Christian insight in terms of those values and attitudes. The terms of the Trinitarian doctrine—the "Father," the "Logos" or "Word," the "Holy Spirit"—were originally traditional Christian symbols, embodied in the ancient baptismal formula. But the signification given them, and the relations established between them, by the Alexandrian theologians, were essentially philosophical. For the Alexandrians, the Trinity and the long discussions leading up to its formulation were far from an incomprehensible "mystery"

---

[1] On the Christian Platonism of Alexandria, see: A. C. McGiffert, *History of Christian Thought* (New York, 1932-1933) Bk. II; A. G. V. Allen, *Continuity of Chrstian Thought* (Boston, 1884), ch. I, classic defense by a liberal Protestant. See Adolf von Harnack, *History of Dogma; Expansion of Christianity* (Ger. version, Leipzig, 1902; Eng. tr., Boston, 1904, 1905; 2d ed., 1908); H. B. Workman, *Christian Thought to the Reformation* (New York, 1911); W. Windelband, *Gesch. der abendländischen Philosophie im Altertum*, A. Goedeckemeyer, ed. (4th ed., Munich, 1923). Charles Bigg, *The Christian Platonists of Alexandria* (Oxford, 1886; 2d ed., 1913). Harry A. Wolfson, *Philosophy of the Church Fathers* (Cambridge, Mass., 1956). E. F. Osborn, *The Philosophy of Clement of Alexandria* (Cambridge, 1957).

Texts in Eng.: in *Ante-Nicene Fathers* (Edinburgh, 1867-1872; Buffalo, 1885-1896; reprinted, Grand Rapids, 1956); J. E. L. Oulton and H. Chadwick, *Alexandrian Christianity* (Philadelphia, 1954), selections from Clement of Alexandria and Origen.

of faith. They were an intelligible answer to intellectual problems, a philosophical solution, not a perplexing enigma.[2]

Alexandrian thought is indeed very hard for us moderns to understand, for it is couched in terms of the Platonic philosophy of "substances" and their relations. Our own all-embracing scientific order of Nature, and the general philosophic monism as to substance prevailing since the end of the eighteenth century, make us moderns think in terms, not of the relations between different substances, but rather between *different functions* within the same "substance"—we think in terms of activities, behaviors, means, ends, and values. The Platonists thought and spoke of distinctions and relations between separate "substances." For moderns, there is only one Nature, one reality, one "substance"; we make our own distinctions within that single Nature, in terms of different operations and values. The Platonists, in other words, talked in terms of nouns and adjectives, while moderns prefer to use

[2] Of course, the Alexandrian Christian Platonists, being typical religious liberals, failed to achieve complete philosophical clarity in their interpretations of the traditional scriptural symbols. Above all, they did not aim to state explicitly just what they were rejecting: wise religious liberals never do attempt that disruptive procedure. Like all mediators, they emphasized the positive values and attitudes they felt to be important. They would doubtless have been hard put to it themselves to define precisely the negative implications of their thought. And it is still a much-debated question, how far the Platonic language they were employing must itself be taken as a symbolic rendering of human experience. But Clement of Alexandria, in defending the true "Christian gnostic" against the false Oriental Gnostic, as represented by Marción or Valentinus, for instance, is clear enough about the values he is himself supporting. And so is Origen, though his language and the terms he uses for his principles are definitely personal and Catholic.

In the following interpretation of the doctrine of the Trinity as a rational theology, the emphasis is placed on these human values expressed, not on the extent to which either the traditional scriptural language or that of philosophical Platonism was itself recognized by the Alexandrians to be not literal but symbolic, as we moderns should of course take both of them.

verbs and adverbs. To understand, therefore, what the Trinity actually meant to those trained in Platonism, we must never forget these two quite different philosophical languages.

Take, for example, the question of the relation between God, conceived as one "substance," and the world, another "substance." This problem is for us today an intensely vital one: in our own language, the issue is, "Can we hope to realize our ideals, to attain our highest ends? How far can we expect to achieve the values we are working and struggling for?" This is the issue between optimism and pessimism, between a hope in possible progress and a conviction of decay and degeneration and of the "sickness" of our society and its culture. It is the issue between meliorism and cynicism, between a pragmatic attitude and the absolutism of a totalitarian faith, which prides itself on its "correctness."

Or take the "Logos," which involved for the Greek Platonists the whole problem of knowledge and science. The Platonists asked, "Is there a 'rational Substance,' a 'Reason' or 'Logos,' in the universe? Is this rational Substance identical with the highest Substance, or does the highest Substance lie above it, and remain inaccessible to it, so that Reality transcends and eludes the intellectual grasp of knowledge, and to find it we must fall back on a nonrational revelation?" In our own different fashion, we moderns ask the same question: "How far can we hope to achieve genuine knowledge? Do the most important truths of all transcend all human knowledge? How ultimate is our science? How far is it 'mere science'?"

Or take the "Holy Spirit" or *Pneuma*, which as a "substance" meant man's natural and human moral power and good will. Is that moral power adequate to meet our problems of living, or do we need a supernatural grace to transform man's "substance," before we can hope to live well?

The relation between the Logos and the Holy Spirit is thus the relation between human intelligence and human moral power. Are they ultimately identical, or are they wholly disparate? This is the issue between a religious liberalism which trusts to man's intelligence to deal with his practical problems, and a revolutionary radicalism which trusts only the development of the economic process, and in the end has to fall back upon sheer force and violent revolution.

Consider the issue of the "divinity" of Christ. The Platonists conceived it in terms of the attributes of His "substance"; moderns construe it in terms of what He did and taught and stood for. The Platonists ask about the nature of the "substance" of Christ; moderns ask the value of His example and teachings, or of what He symbolized. The Platonists put their answer, "Christ's 'substance' is Divine"; moderns, to give the same Christian answer, would say, "Christ's life and moral precepts are of supreme value—the ideal of Love symbolized in the Christ is divine." For the Platonists the Virgin Birth is hence a natural myth or symbol; for the present-day thinker, for the evolutionary naturalist, it is something highly inappropriate or meaningless, and honest modern theologians often prefer to reject it entirely.[3]

Moderns find it very hard even to understand the idea of God as "Being"—theists seem often confused on that point, and fail to comprehend a thinker like Paul Tillich, who is employing that very traditional language. What the Platonists

[3] Thus, if a secular analogy may be pardoned, the Platonist might well ask, in his tongue, "Was the United Nations 'born of a virgin?'" and might well go on then naturally to the "immaculate conception" of Franklin Roosevelt. Moderns would of course put the inquiry, "How great is the value of the United Nations? What good can it hope to accomplish?" We are not much interested in Roosevelt's "substance" and the expression is very alien: we should like to "demythologize" the Virgin Birth.

call *theios*, divine, we call our highest ideals, our "ultimate concern"—but we mean pretty much the same thing.

Consider the problems faced by the Alexandrians in their struggle with the Oriental thinkers of the School of Antioch. Is man corrupt and fallen in "substance," or is he free and made in God's image? This is the issue between Arius, who on these values was followed by Augustine and the Latin Fathers, on the one hand, and Clement and Origen and the Greeks on the other. It means, concretely, "Is the Good Life to be a thing of restrictions and repressions, or is it to be a natural development of man's powers, guided by his intelligence?" The view of the School of Antioch, and of Augustine and the Roman Church, leads to such measures as the Eighteenth Amendment and the censorship of the stage (though it did not suggest these particular measures to Augustine himself, fortunately for the later tradition). The view of Clement and Origen leads rather to the practice of temperance and moderation, and to a free stage.

Again, is God "transcendent" or "immanent," far-off from man, or indwelling the world and human nature? This is the issue between the Arians and Tertullian, and Clement, Origen, and Athanasius. It means, "Is the Good Life impossibly beyond man's powers, or is it within his capacities?" Is it something externally imposed, or is it the wise use of natural impulses? Are science, art, civilization, culture—as Tillich puts it—bad, and to be rejected, or are they good, to be furthered, as the concrete embodiment of man's "ultimate concern"? Is man to be viewed as hopelessly full of the old Adam, or as with toil and patience potentially divine? Is it all a bad business, or can we hope and work for a better world, where even wars may in the end cease from troubling—and annihilating—us?

These issues are all summed up in the doctrine of the

Trinity.[4] Is the Christ-Logos "very God of very God, begotten not made, of one substance with the Father"? The formula probably means nothing in our own lives, and is apt to be as devoid of intellectual import to the man reciting it in church as it is irrelevant to those who have never heard of it. Is the Logos of the "same substance" with the Father, or only "of like substance," is it *homoousios* or only *homoiousios*? The difference, being a single iota, is always good for a laugh today: H. G. Wells, being not too philosophically sophisticated, could make great sport of it.

But to the Christian Platonist the issue was not silly or trivial. The Trinity, in its doctrine of the relation between "substances," summed up the fundamental contention of his whole religious philosophy. Its adoption, if seen as more than a mere political victory for one party, meant the triumph of Greek rationalism and humanism over Oriental asceticism and irrational faith. It meant that the Good Life, founded on knowledge and on the practice of intelligence, and sustained by the natural moral power of the Christian brotherhood and community, is both possible and attainable. Natural reason or knowledge in the world, the principle of Christ, of the Logos, the inspiration of all human science and wisdom, is the highest Good, the only valid human ideal. It is not in the end subordinated to anything else: there is nothing above it, forever eluding its intellectual grasp. It is equal with the supreme "substance." And the natural moral power of man, the *Pneuma* or Holy Spirit, indwelling them, and especially in-

[4] On the doctrine of the Trinity: McGiffert, *History of Christian Thought*, Bk. II; and *The Idea of God* (New York, 1924). Harnack, Workman, Allen, Wolfson.

Athanasius: *Incarnation of the Word, First Discourse against the Arians*, Eng. tr. in *Nicene and Post-Nicene Fathers* (1st ed.; Edinburgh, Series I, 1886-90, Series II, 1890-1900); *Athanasius*, A. Robertson, ed. and tr., Series II, Vol. IV.

dwelling the Christian community of the early Church—before, we must remember, the Church had been taken over by the Empire and had embraced the world—is sufficient for man's needs. There is no necessity of magic or miracle, of a supernatural transformation of human nature.

And the doctrine of the Incarnation meant for the Platonist that Jesus of Nazareth, in his character, acts, and teaching love for God and for one's neighbor as oneself, is the highest moral excellence, or fully *theios*, divine. Moreover, for the Alexandrians the Incarnation of the Logos in Jesus was not taken to be a wholly unique miracle, but rather a particular and accentuated instance of the Incarnation of the Logos in all mankind. It was a revelation of man's essential nature, of man's moral and intellectual possibilities, of his potential divinity. This was the explicit view of Athanasius, the great protagonist of the Trinity. The Greek Platonists said, "God is incarnate in humanity." To express these same values—values which to our twentieth-century experience, to be sure, seem rather unduly optimistic—a modern would put it, "Human nature, enlightened by reason and intelligence, and filled with adequate good will, is 'divine'—man can hope to achieve the Good Life, and can even today measurably live it, with no need of asceticism or magic rites." To Clement, Origen, and Athanasius, the doctrines of the Trinity and the Incarnation expressed their Greek naturalism and humanism; while the denial of the Trinity, Arianism, the subordination of the Logos to the Father, meant the denial of natural reason, natural moral power, and the natural life of man.[5]

[5] Hence in modern terms, since the decisions of the Councils of Nicaea and Chalcedon have always determined Christian orthodoxy, there is reason to suspect that the views of the so-called Neo-Orthodox may contain some taint of heresy. It is doubtful whether the Neo-Orthodox accept either the Trinity or the Incarnation in their original meanings.

Arius of Alexandria was an apostle of the Oriental thought and values of the School of Antioch; he was a disciple of Lucian of Antioch. He stressed the immense gulf between the human and the Divine, between man and the highest. He emphasized the arbitrary power and authority of God, and extreme asceticism. For Arius, the Logos is a Demiurge, an ambassador of God sent to man, revealing the impassable chasm between God and Man, proclaiming the Divine Judgment on Man, and exacting unquestioning obedience to the Divine Master.[6] Arius hated the rationalism and humanism of the Greek Fathers, their doctrine of the immanence of God; and he firmly resolved to unite the Oriental bishops against it —all those who looked to the School of Antioch for leadership.

Athanasius, in contrast, was Greek in his thought and values. He grew up in the tradition of Alexandrian thinking, for which God was not remote and inaccessible, but fills the world and mankind with His presence. The divine in mankind, man's reason and moral will, the Logos and the Pneuma, are of "the same substance" with the Father, with the highest, *homoousios*. Of course, the view that one substance or *ousia* could reside wholly in each person of the Trinity, as well as in humanity, and in one man, Jesus of Nazareth, was a commonplace of the universally accepted Platonic logical realism, just as the view that the whole essence of humanity could reside in Adam, and in each particular man. This ontological doctrine was no mystery to the Platonists, as it has come to be to later nominalists.

Of course, the values which the Greek philosophical theologians expressed in their doctrine of the Trinity did not long continue to be what that doctrine came to symbolize in the

[6] Hence Karl Barth, in his earlier phase at least, has been almost literally an Arian.

Christian tradition, especially in the Latin Church, which understood neither those values nor the Platonic philosophy in which they were formulated.[7] But without a knowledge of the original meaning of the doctrine of the Trinity, it is impossible to understand how again and again Christian Platonists, like Augustine, and the long line of Augustinians, Bonaventura, Cusanus, Malebranche, and Hegel, to name only certain of the outstanding Platonists in the Christian tradition, could find in the doctrine of the Trinity an admirable formulation of those humanistic and naturalistic ideals their own experience had led them to come to share.

Clement of Alexandria[8] was not a systematic thinker; but he is the sanest and most reasonable of the Greek Fathers. He was Dean of the Alexandria Theological Seminary, just across the street from the great Museum in the City of Alexandria. Clement was a religious liberal, with all the strength, and also all the weakness, of present-day religious liberalism or modernism. That is, he was not involved in intellectual paradoxes, requiring subtle dialectical solutions. But he was also serenely untroubled by the deeper moral problems a profound religious faith has to meet and somehow deal with. Clement was appealed to by the nineteenth-century religious liberals, who found in him patristic authority for their philosophy of divine

[7] It has already been pointed out that the Greek philosophical theologians themselves used a supernaturalistic language to express their rational and humanistic values, without bothering to go into how far that Platonic language was itself symbolic in character. A modern might well feel like doing a little "demythologizing" on the language of the Trinity itself; in fact, many present-day modern theologians do feel that to be necessary.

[8] Clement of Alexandria, *Stromata*, in *Ante-Nicene Fathers*; Clement tr. by W. Wilson. *Protrepticus*, G. W. Butterworth, ed. (Loeb, 1919).

E. de Faye, *Clément d'Alexandrie* (Paris, 1898; 2d ed., 1906); J. Patrick, *Clement of Alexandria* (London, 1914); R. B. Tollinton, *Clement of Alexandria: A Study in Christian Liberalism,* 2 vols. (London, 1914); E. F. Osborn, *Philosophy of Clement of Alexandria* (Cambridge, 1957).

immanence, which they had learned from German philosophical Idealism.

Clement was a philosopher seeking truth; and he found it in Christianity taken as a philosophical system, interpreted as Philo had already interpreted Judaism, using the same allegorical method. But Clement made Christian love central; he was, in fact, converted because he found such love, *agapē*, actually present in the Christian communities.

For Clement, the great thing is faith. Faith means for him, not belief in the creeds, and not something mystical, as it means for Paul. Faith means for Clement the receptive spirit, open-mindedness, trust in reason, the search for truth. He who has faith in this sense is already saved: the knowledge that is eternal life will come in due time. All genuine seekers, all receptive minds, will be saved. In this, Clement exhibits what we sometimes like to call the modern spirit. All knowledge is founded on an initial faith in the axioms and presuppositions, the *archai*. Believe in them, and you will find the fruits good.

Teaching is reliable when faith on the part of those who hear, being, so to speak, a sort of natural art, contributes to the process of learning. . . . For there is no good of the very best instruction, without the exercise of the receptive faculty on the part of the learner, not even of prophecy, when there is the absence of docility on the part of those who hear. . . . Hope, too, is based on faith. . . . Hope is the expectation of the possession of good. . . . Faith is the voluntary supposition and anticipation of pre-comprehension (*proleipsis*).[9]

For Clement, God is the transcendent source of Being, the source of the intelligible world. He is reached by Platonic abstraction: He is the Platonic "One." For Clement, He must be stripped of all anthropomorphism: He is the Unknown

[9] Clement of Alexandria, *Stromata or Miscellanies*, in *Ante-Nicene Fathers*, tr. W. Wilson, (edition, N.Y., 1913). Vol. II, ch. vi, "The Excellence and Utility of Faith," pp. 353-54.

Source. Yet God is also revealed in the world as the Logos, the indwelling rationality of things, the immanent power and reason of God Himself. And this Divine Reason or Logos is very near at hand: it taught all the prophets, poets, and philosophers of the past. The Logos is clearest in Christ, who is the most adequate revelation of the permanent rationality of man, the revelation of the possibilities of human nature. Christ reveals that Divinity is not merely good, but is good will, or rational love. The Logos is the Savior and Teacher of men, He is God's love for man. This is the specifically Christian element in Clement, not in Philo at all, to whom otherwise Clement's thought is very close.

Man is made in the divine image, rational and free. Man never fell; he suffers no insuperable guilt, he can solve his problems by reason. Man is free, but he stands in need of knowledge. Sin and evil come from man's ignorance. Man is saved by reason, by the same reason perfectly embodied in Christ. Salvation is a progressive being educated by reason; it is a natural way of life, with nothing magical about it, no transforming grace. The sacraments are merely symbols. The eucharist supper is in fact celebrated in every Christian household.

The Christian life is the search for knowledge and truth and virtue, the endeavor to resemble the Logos by knowing the truth, and so becoming divine; and by loving one's fellows, doing good for its own sake, especially by teaching other men.

Clement's Platonism differed from the other Platonisms, even that of Philo, in emphasizing the divine immanence, that there is no gulf between man and the ideal; and in what Clement took to be the specifically Christian truth, the importance of love. He found this love, or was so convinced, in the Christian community. And he is suffused by it.

Origen is unquestionably the greatest mind among the

Alexandrian Christians. He worked out a philosophical system,[10] and set the theological problems to be settled at Nicaea and Chalcedon. But Origen is harder, more dogmatic, more exclusive, than Clement; he is definitely Catholic, as Clement is ecumenical.

For Origen, faith is not mere seeking, as for Clement, but is the acceptance of the creeds. We can then, if we will, go on to philosophical knowledge, though this is not necessary for salvation, and is confined to those who have an intellectual interest. Origen's substances are more personal, though they indicate the same facts of human experience as do Clement's. That is, Origen uses more readily the language of mythology.

For Origen, God is not just "The Unknown"; God is definitely Spirit, *Pneuma*. Spirit is dynamic force in the universe, a good force that Origen identifies with "love." Force is immanent in the world, sustaining it as power, not as substance. Spirit in itself is simple; but because it is ultimately force, it is eternally generating the Logos, the creative force that sustains the world.

The Logos is the divine power in the world, uncreated but dependent on the primal force of Spirit. The Logos is a second God, necessary for the world and its existence, and hence in a sense subordinate to God the Father. The Logos is personal, and of "the same substance, *homoousios*, as the Father." But the Logos is "begotten"; that is, for Origen force is primary, and the order of Nature secondary, dependent on its source in force. Later, in 325 A.D., in view of the problems that had only

10 Origen, *De Principiis*, esp. Bks. 1 and 2, in *Ante-Nicene Fathers*, tr. F. Crombie; tr. G. W. Butterworth (London, 1936). *Contra Celsum*, H. Chadwick, tr. (Cambridge, 1953).

M. J. Denis, *La Philosophie d'Origène* (Paris, 1884); W. Fairweather, *Origen* (New York, 1901); E. de Faye, *Origène* (Paris, 1923-28; Eng. tr., London, 1926); J. Daniélou, Origène (Paris, 1948; Eng. tr., New York, 1955); H. Crouzel, *Origène et la Philosophie* (Paris, 1962).

emerged by then, this dependence of the Logos on the Father was condemned at Nicaea as heretical, in the light of the equation of the two in the Trinity.

The Holy Spirit or Pneuma is for Origen a third principle: it is the eternal power inspiring all good men; it is Origen's recognition of the fact of the Christian community, as in Clement. God or force is enough for Himself. But for the world and men, there is need of a Trinity. Origen makes force immanent in the world as the Logos for the sake of the world. As the theologians put it, "The Son is functionally subordinate to the Father."

All this is of course a philosophical theory: there is no religious need for these philosophical conceptions. They are needed for understanding rather than for salvation. Origen left the problem of the precise relations between his three principles, especially the exact relation between the Logos and the Father. This issue was settled at Nicaea as identity.

Origen also held that spirits were created before time, rational and free: the Logos was in them. Those who chose the good became angels, those who chose evil became fallen angels or devils, those who chose a little good and a little evil became men. These latter, men, needed another chance. So our material world was created in time to give man an opportunity to achieve the salvation he had missed before. Salvation itself comes from reason, the Logos, and from the Holy Spirit: that is, from knowledge and from moral power. And Origen held that even the Devil can be taught, and saved, and in the end led back to God—Origen was a universalist. Human reason, illuminated by the light that is clearest in Christ, and strengthened by the power of the Holy Spirit in man, is sufficient. Salvation is the knowledge of God, and communion with Him.

The Alexandrian doctrines of the Trinity and the Incarnation of the Word illustrate admirably one of the characteristic roles of knowledge in the religious life. They are not, like the theology of Paul, the intellectual construing of a living experience—though the Alexandrians did share in the life of the primitive religious community of the early Church. They are not fundamental religious beliefs—beliefs which function in the practice of the religious arts, like communion or prayer or worship. They are frankly speculative and philosophical, the answer to problems that are primarily intellectual rather than religious. Indeed, Origen, who largely formulated the doctrine of the Trinity, intended them for theologians interested in philosophical understanding, not for Christians in general: he never considered adherence to them a necessary condition of salvation. For that, faith, *pistis*, is sufficient. It consists in the accepted teachings of the Church as embodied in the creeds. After accepting these articles of faith, the intellectual Christian, to be sure, will then go on to knowledge and understanding. He will try to understand his faith, since he shares that intellectual need for understanding.

In this fashion Greek philosophy—the Neo-Platonic system of the early Christian centuries—entered as a central strand into the emerging Christian synthesis. Ever since, for those who have felt the intellectual urge to understand, that synthesis has provided a philosophical interpretation of the meaning of the Christian symbols, in terms of the best available body of ideas. Such a central intellectual interest has distinguished the whole later Christian tradition. Christianity has been impelled to seek, not merely a way of life, or a path of deliverance. At the least, it has felt the compelling urge to come to terms with the best independent or secular way of understanding the world and human life. The result of this initial impact of Greek philosophy has been the long adventure of Christian thought.

It was the accident of the Arian controversy, in which the Alexandrian doctrines came to symbolize the fundamental religious and moral values of the Alexandrian Neo-Platonists, that led to their formulation as a shibboleth, in the Nicene Creed. And even then it was the smallest of the three main parties at the Council of Nicaea that won out: Hosius the Alexandrian rewrote the compromising creed of Eusebius in Trinitarian terms. And the later interpretation of that creed by the Church, worked out by the Cappodocian Fathers, Gregory of Nyssa and Gregory of Nazianzus, construed the Nicene formula in terms of what is called the "Semi-Arian" position: not Athanasius' "same Being in three forms," but rather, "one substance in three hypostases," or persons.

Yet the Trinity remains the greatest and most successful instance in the Christian tradition of a rational, and, in the later sense, of a natural theology. It is an intellectual interpretation of the meaning of symbols, which in their imaginative form are used in the concrete religious arts. It interprets them by means of the concepts of a philosophical system worked out to make intelligible the world as the scene of human experience. It uses the prevailing Greek philosophy to understand the meaning of the Christian symbols and symbolic beliefs, just as Philo Judaeus had used the same philosophy to understand the Hebrew symbols. The primary sense of the doctrine of the Trinity is logical, in the interest of intellectual consistency. But it is really more than that: like Philo's doctrine, it has a genuinely religious function, for those intellectuals who have understood their experience in the light of Neo-Platonism.

Christian intellectuals can, and have, used many other later schemes of understanding to construe the Christian symbols, down to Whitehead and Paul Tillich in our own day. The task once begun by the Greeks and embedded in the Christian synthesis, is doubtless without end, so long as our understanding of the world and human nature continues to grow. Rational or philosophical theology has an undying appeal, for it performs a function that is essential for intelligent men. But the experiments of history make clear that the scheme of understanding employed must be a scheme which genuinely illuminates man and his experience. The Trinity is the most successful of all Christian philosophical theologies because Platonism managed to do just that. The only other really successful Christian philosophical theology, that of Thomas Aquinas, is not so adequate as that of the Platonic Trinity, because the Aristotelian science Thomas employed in the thirteenth century was oriented more towards Nature than towards man, and because he utilized primarily the Aristotelian *Physics*.[11] Had Saint Thomas drawn more heavily for his theology on the *Ethics* and the *Politics*, the results might have been quite different. The rational theology which the Enlightenment thinkers of the later eighteenth century tried to elaborate and popularize failed quite miserably, because the Newtonian science they were using left the whole of human life unintelligible. The Trinity was so successful, in fact, that the doctrine and its terms could themselves be transformed into genuine religious symbols, and as such they have far outlasted their original meaning and significance as an intellectual solution to the specific philosophical problems of the third century of our era.

[11] The Unmoved Mover of Book Lambda of the *Metaphysics* really belongs at the end of the *Physics*: and it is best treated in Book VIII of those lectures.

XIII THE LATIN CHURCH

TERTULLIAN AND ARNOBIUS

The Latin Church exhibited the temper of the Romans: it showed little interest in philosophy or theology, but great concern with political organization. Its outstanding leaders have always been, not theoretical thinkers so much as statesmen—or politicians. The supreme intellectual achievement of the Western Church, Scholasticism, is the organization of knowledge rather than its pursuit and discovery. Scholasticism is the careful adjustment of beliefs to each other through intellectual statesmanship.

Arnobius (fl. 303 A.D.) is typical. He asks: "What business is it of yours to inquire into Nature, or into the origin of souls? Leave all knowledge and science to God. The salvation of souls is the only thing *you* are permitted to inquire about." In the ancient Church, all the heresies came from the questioning Greeks. In the West occurred rather *schisms*, political revolts against the authority of the Church.

In the West the great task seemed to be to build up a Church; and there was certainly created a marvelous institution. In contrast, the Greeks hardly developed an organized Church at all; this was typical of the Greek lack of interest in political organization. Hence in the East the different churches were soon dominated by the State, and under the Byzantine Empire became practically a branch of the civil service. In the West, the Church soon became politically supreme.

The old Roman religion, it must be remembered, had been formal and political. It was founded on fear: the gods were taken to be very far from man. It exhibited no trace of mysticism. Into this intellectual environment Roman Christianity

came as essentially a new law. Salvation was taken as coming
primarily from obedience to rightful authority. When the
Western Church achieved an independent philosophy of its
own in Augustine, authority was naturally made central. The
vital question was of man's disobedience to God and of his
obedience to the Church. The Good Life, the Romans tended
to think, is utterly unnatural and irrational. Without the fear
of Hell, the most rational course for a man would naturally
be to enjoy all his lusts. This was the explicit view of Lactantius and of Ambrose. Sin is not ignorance, as the unrealistic
Alexandrians held, but disobedience. What man needs is not
knowledge, but submision—submission to the divine authority
of the Church. The philosophy and doctrines worked out
thoughtfully in the Greek Church were accepted in the West
not as knowledge, not as the answer to intellectual and philosophical problems of understanding, but as signs of submission
to authority. For the Greeks, the Trinity and the Incarnation
were rational explanations of man's experience of the world.
For the Latins, they were taken as a "mystery" to which man
must submit, whether he understood them or no.

The Romans, when they did think, thought as lawyers, in
terms of concepts that were essentially legal. For them there
was no mysticism, no rational relations between "substances,"
in the language of the Platonistic philosophy; but rather the
relations between human wills, between legal personalities.
Such an attitude in the West naturally played havoc with the
Trinity there. In their philosophic concepts the Roman thinkers were all Stoics: Neo-Platonism reached the West only
in the fourth century, in Ambrose and in Augustine, when
all the problems had already been formulated in legal and
Stoic terms. When it did come, the introduction of Neo-
Platonism naturally led to combination of ideas that were very
divergent and even inconsistent.

Tertullian (155-222) is typical of the Latin Fathers before Ambrose. He was a lawyer: most of the theologians who have sacrificed sensitivity to experience to logical consistency have been lawyers. Tertullian was a good man, and a stern Fundamentalist, in the Pauline sense. He possessed tender human feeling, he shrank from all cruelty, he sacrificed his legal career to join the Christians, because he had to take his stand with those who were oppresed; and he preached a ruthless hell-fire gospel. He is a fascinating human being and character, and a recurrent paradox: a most attractive personality, and very dubious ideas.[1]

For Tertullian, God is a personal sovereign, stern and just. He is Himself good, but His hatred and wrath for the sinner are mighty. Above all, God is absolute power. "I would rather have a wicked God than a weak one!" he exclaims. God has decreed a law: man is God's subject, who owes Him fear and humility, and unquestioning obedience. There can be no morality without fear. We are wicked if we obey God's Law because we think it good: we must follow it because we know it is God's command. Obey, and believe what you are told. "To know nothing in opposition to the Rule of Faith is to

[1] On Tertullian: see *Tertulliani Opera*, 2 vols., in J. G. P. Borleffs, E. Dekkers, et al., eds., *Corpus Christianorum, Series Latina* (The Hague, 1953-54). *Tertullian: Apologetical Works*, R. Arbesman, E. J. Daly, and E. A. Quain, eds. (New York, 1950), Eng tr. Eng. tr. also in *Ante-Nicene Fathers*.

See T. R. Glover, *Conflict of Religions in the Early Roman Empire* (London, 1909), ch. 10, "Tertullian." C. de L. Short, *The Influence of Philosophy on the Mind of Tertullian* (London, 1933); J. Morgan, *The Importance of Tertullian in the Development of Christian Dogma* (London, 1928). C. Guignebert, *Tertullien* (Paris, 1901); J. Lortz, *Tertullian als Apologet*, 2 vols. (Münster, 1927-28).

On the Latin Church in general: see A. G. V. Allen, *The Continuity of Christian Thought* (Boston, 1884); A. C. McGiffert, *History of Christian Thought*, Vol. II (New York, 1933); and P. de Labriolle, *Histoire de la Littérature Latine Chrétienne* (Paris 1920; Eng. tr., New York, 1924).

know all things." "Remain in ignorance, lest you should know what you ought not to know."

Believe, because it is irrational and incredible, and *therefore* Divine. "It is certain, because it is impossible."[2] Away with philosophy and natural reason! What has Athens in common with Jerusalem? "We need no curiosity after Jesus, and no inquiry after the Gospel."

Yet Tertullian was philosophically a Stoic materialist, one of the few Christian theologians who have been complete materialists. Only body is real. Therefore, God is corporeal, so is the soul and reason. Grace is a bodily substance; sin is inherited physically from Adam. Tertullian shows what Christianity would be like without Platonism, or without Paul.

Believe, because of the authority of tradition. There is no other rational truth or falsity. Faith Tertullian accepts as the property of the Church, owned by right of "prescription." The questioner is a thief, a robber. "Faith is my property. Get off!" Never argue with a heretic: invoke the law. Tradition, possession, is the final test of truth. Such an attitude is of course preposterous to an intelligent man; yet it is an attitude with a great appeal to those in authority.

Sin is a wilful act, guilt, rebellion. The soul is physically inherited from Adam, and it inherits physically Adam's guilt as well. It also possesses responsibility and free will. Salvation is escape from Hell. Tertullian thinks of it in wholly legal terms. Salvation is "acquittal," being declared "just" at the Judgment Seat, after due repentance and obedience. Grace physically strengthens the will, but it effects no change of "substance" in human nature. There is for Tertullian no mystical becoming like God, becoming divine, as for Paul.

Morally, Tertullian was not unnaturally a Puritan. Revolted

[2] *De carne Christi*, ch. 5. The familiar phrase, *Credo quia absurdum*, does not occur literally in Tertullian's writings.

by the Roman Church's acceptance of the world, the flesh, and
the Devil, he gave up everything a second time. He joined the
rigorous Puritanical sect of the Montanists. That is, Tertullian
himself became a heretic. He stood for his principles, and was
in the end condemned by them. It was he who was now the
thief, the robber, and the rebel.

Augustine is the formulator of the philosophy of the Western Church. He had two great advantages. There was, first, his
own vivid experience: all these ideas had a vital meaning in
his own life and experience. And, secondly, he knew Greek
philosophy: hence he could not give up intelligence and reason,
and their expression in Neo-Platonism.

XIV THE MANIFOLD EXPERIENCE OF AUGUSTINE*

St. Augustine is the intellectual father of the Western Church
and of Western Christianity. He is the one Doctor through
whose writings the whole body of religious and philosophical
speculation of the ancient Church descended to the Middle
Ages in Western Europe. For a thousand years, his thought
was *the* philosophy of the Western tradition. Even when in
the twelfth century the rediscovery of Aristotle brought new
intellectual interests, and came to express a new set of values,
medieval rather than Hellenistic, this new Aristotelian thought
was fitted into the Augustinian framework, and Augustine
himself was not rejected but rather reinterpreted. If philosophies are to be judged by their power, their power to express

* This chapter appeared in unrevised form in *The American Scholar,*
XXXVIII (Winter, 1968-69), 127-34.

and organize and direct human experience, in our Western tradition no other thinker can touch the power of the thought of St. Augustine.

After the more humanistic values and naturalistic thought of Aristotelian Scholasticism—from the middle of the thirteenth to the middle of the fifteenth century—Augustine proved more alive than ever during the Renaissance and the Reformation—so alive, that he was able to drive back Greece for some two hundred years. Again, he overwhelmed the optimistic rationalism of the Enlightenment, in the great religious revivals of the late eighteenth and early nineteenth centuries. And in our own day, in our own boasted reaction against reason and intelligence and in favor of human "existence" and commitment, though we have largely lost Augustine's religious symbols, Augustine's essential spirit has, ever since 1914, been driving out what we now consider Victorian complacency and humanistic and humanitarian acceptance of the world of modern science and technology.

Time was, not so long since, when Augustine's theology was a battle cry. In the America of the 1890s, in which my father grew to maturity, one had to be either for it or against it. But there are today few left who can be said really to believe in it literally. The Protestants, who triumphed in the sixteenth century in the name of Augustine, have now largely forgotten him. Even the Catholics have since 1879 based their intellectual life on Thomas Aquinas, who expresses values that are essentially modern, not the outmoded values of medieval Augustinianism, or the equally medieval values of the Augustinian Reformers.[1]

---

[1] Despite the efforts of the theologians of the last generation to revive the so-called Reformation theology, it is doubtful whether they had much effect on the bulk of American Christians, so-called, who remained unmoved by the values for which Augustine, the Reformers, and those neo-orthodox

We moderns are living in a different intellectual world. The great system of Christian thought, carefully elaborated in the ancient world, which endured for fifteen hundred years, has in our century been visibly crumbling. We have even been told recently that Nietzsche was right: "God is dead!" But just because no man of intelligence is today tempted to believe literally in the traditional Christian body of ideas, because there are even few left among the educated who have to emancipate themselves from it any longer, as in the nineteenth century thoughtful men had to, we are at last free to rediscover Augustine and his essential insights, as men have done before, over and over again. Even the Jews can enjoy this freedom. I am tempted to say, "especially Jews," since they can still view him with greater objectivity than most Christians are able to do. Christians are still too emotionally involved in the aftermath of rejecting his thought, and traditional Christian ideas in general, to judge its significance impartially. But those who are not or are no longer "Christian" in the conventional and traditional sense are free to appreciate the human significance of Augustinian Christianity, which in the long history of our Western culture has been so tremendous. The "Christian Epic," as Augustine recounts it, is certainly, to say the least, a marvelous work of human intelligence and human art. It has given the Western tradition as rich a realm of the imagination in which to dwell, as great a wealth of suggestive religious symbols, as any culture has ever enjoyed. It has furnished an unrivaled opportunity for the artist, the poet, the painter, and the sculptor, as well as for the religious genius. It has supplied a world of symbols capable of

---

theologians stood. And today, Augustinian neo-orthodoxy seems pretty dead, in the fact of the secular city and the revival of a social gospel, even among the theologians themselves.

focusing and expressing almost every human interest and emotion.

If we are no longer concerned to claim that this Christian system is literally true, why was it able to last so long? Why did it have such deep roots? Because it expressed, not any mere theory, but human life itself. Pascal gave the first modern answer to our question: Augustinian Christianity was rooted in human nature; it answered to, and expressed, both man's greatness and his petty and deadly weakness. So Pascal cried out, in the words of the Psalmist, to the God of Augustine, "Thou hast made my heart for Thee, and it will rest content only in Thee!"

So let us leave aside all Augustine's allegories, all his scriptural authorities and his syllogisms, and consider rather Augustine's vision, of human greatness and of human weakness, through which countless millions have gained spiritual freedom and deliverance, and salvation, such as is granted to man to attain.

Philosophies, the wise recognize, are hardly to be judged by their literal truth: they are all to be taken "seriously but not literally," as our intelligent theologians today put it. No system of ideas can be said to be literally true—not even our boasted science, powerful as it is in certain directions. All such systems are interpretations, in symbolic language, of the world and human life as men have experienced them. They can be called true only in the sense that they manage to organize men's beliefs and activities in terms of men's fundamental interests and commitments, in terms of their organizing or ultimate concern.

Augustinian Christianity furnishes a symbolic language for expressing human experience. Like Socrates, Augustine turned his back on trees and stones and sought man. He found, not the whole man, above all, not the fearless, searching, self-reliant intelligence of the inquirer. But how little and how rarely after all do men possess it! How readily are they willing to forswear it for faith in an absolutely certain ideal! But Augustine found humanity, as no philosopher since has found it. In comparison, these later philosophies seem little personal visions, temporary concoctions of shifting ideas, things of a day, weak and anaemic. Augustinian Christianity is strong because it is rooted in man's weakness, in his needs, aspirations, yearnings, struggles, and in his inevitable failures and frustrations.

Augustinian Christianity is of course very terrible. Tender minds, weak souls, shrink from it. They shrank especially in the proud, boastful, complacent days before the First World War. Those were the days in which men dwelt in a secure world, and were content with a rather sentimental optimism; the days in which all prosperous Christians shared the spirit of the Greek and Alexandrian Fathers of the Church, and built up a liberal religion on that spirit, as it filtered down to them through the German Idealists and the optimistic evolutionary philosophers, with their faith in a fairly automatic "progress." They then created an American religion of sentimental hope and smug philosophy. The Jews were in the same boat: their ancient faith had in this country been well Americanized.

Against this liberal religion, Augustine enters an emphatic "No!" Men inevitably fail. They fall short of their goals. The vast majority are "lost," through no personal fault of their own. They live like beasts in the field—or in an affluent society —delighting in their lusts. They are insensitive clods who never will see God. Worst of all, little children, called into a brief existence through the selfish desire of their parents, who then die, are "lost" through all eternity.

We moderns were dreaming, at the turn of the century, of

attaining complete social justice, of peace and democracy, of One World, and of a Good Life for all, of all mankind united in one great sticky gush of brotherly love. Americans still so dream: it salves their consciences for acting like the Devil—as they have also convinced themselves they must.

But Nature—and human nature, alas!—continue to mock such foolish confidence. The facts of life *are* terrible. Men do not realize their ideals. Merit plays little part in the measure of success accorded them. The vast majority are most of the time beasts, with only a glimmer of finer things. Little children who die never do, in any intelligible sense, save their souls. The "Earthly City"—though many have recently preferred to call it the "capitalistic system," and today the phrase runs, "our sick society"—has crushed us and drained our life. And though that is gone now—what in the nineteenth century we used to call "capitalism" seems pretty completely dead, especially in America—the "Earthly City" that is succeeding it scarcely seems to be ushering in the millennium.

Whatever else Augustine may be, he is surely what we like today to call a realist, with just that salutary freedom from sentimentality that suits the temper of the times, just the realism that fills twentieth-century art and writing, on which we pride ourselves—that realism that does not blink the more disagreeable facts, but shuts its eyes only to the brighter ones.

So Augustine hardly shocks men any more, when he says, the will of man, even of the best of men, is not good, but corrupt—something that before 1914 seemed utterly perverse. To be sure, we flatter ourselves that now we understand something of the causes of that corruption, though we can hardly be said to have discovered the cure. Men have been turning to the Augustinian spirit once more, as men have turned to it so often in the past, after similar periods of self-reliance and confidence in the intelligence and good-will of men. When self-reliance fails, as sooner or later it has always done in the past, and as it has recently shown marked signs of doing again, men are led to rediscover Augustine's vision of man's estate, of what is today called the human condition. And perhaps they may even find once more his faith, in a redemption bestowed gratuitously by God—or by Nature—with no regard for human merit. Augustine's symbols, to be sure, are not likely to be ours today, and we talk, not of the "corruption of human nature," but of the "sickness of capitalist society"; and we are likely to put our newfound faith—if we have indeed found one, which is today, to be sure, not very likely—not in the Cross, but in the Hammer and Sickle.

On the whole, the spirit shared in America down to 1929 was that of the Greek Alexandrian Fathers, Clement, Origen, and Athanasius: a trust in the good will of man, if it only be enlightened by intelligence. But in Europe men were drawing near to Augustine once more after 1914. And since the 1930s even in America men have been forsaking self-reliance in droves.

There is first the pessimism, even cynicism, that has been felt so deeply since the 1930s, which certainly fills contemporary literature. To our wisdom it seems so much deeper and more realistic than Victorian complacency and faith in an almost automatic progress. The very idea of progress has for a generation been in disrepute. Before 1914, our social scientists used to say, "we now hold in our hands all the knowledge necessary for us to make of our future what we will," a knowledge to be applied in our gospels of education, and in the preaching of good will to all. That is the promise I myself heard in my own college days, which began before 1917. When facts puncture such facile dreams, such an attitude breeds despair.

We do indeed seem to be looking at the world once more

through the eyes of Augustine. And I mean not merely our theologians, who began forsaking the uncritical optimism of liberal religion, which in Europe died in 1914, and in America was on the defensive after 1929. I mean the realistic temper of radicals and conservatives alike, extending far beyond those theological circles still committed to expressing that temper in the symbols of traditional religious thinking. We too find the life of man a sordid, sorry business, a struggle for power against power, to the ultimate destruction of all. We too have felt only too keenly human weakness and impotence, in the face of the social and economic problems all our boasted social planning has been able to do so little to alleviate. The younger among us feel alienated, and call for a complete destruction of the system they are inheriting—anything would be better than the mess the older generation have brought upon them. We are struck by the powerlessness of all our theories, all our programs for a "Great Society," the inability of even our cherished science, with its gospel of computers and automation, to bring us salvation, or to do aught but magnify the power of our human passions. We too have been feeling ourselves at the mercy of great forces, utterly beyond our control: deep-seated and seemingly ineradicable racial prejudice, virulent nationalism, the so-called responsibilities of our newly acquired American military power. Again and again we have seen clearly whither we were inevitably drifting— or being hurried along—but we have felt ourselves powerless to alter the course of our uncontrollable destiny. The depression, the war, the cold war, its aftermath in violent change—the domestic revolution of black power, the international insanities of our foreign lack of policy—they have all bred the widespread conviction, we will not acquire the know-how, we will not display the will—or the imagination—to work out an intelligent and dynamic policy that will enable us to guide our collective destiny. The men who show signs of having it we shoot in alarm. We still seem content, the rest of us, to acquiesce in a course whose inevitable outcome we know. We have neither the brains, nor the will, to insist on a policy that makes more sense. We have come to feel that men have been able to learn nothing, to understand nothing—or at least, they have been able to do nothing to implement the understanding some of us have been slowly acquiring.

In the light of this seeming collapse of the intelligence we used to boast of, the intelligence the younger, alienated generation finds it so hard to credit us with, it is little wonder that for some years many of our most sensitive were tempted to turn to the miracle of grace, to something wholly outside ourselves. We could do nothing, we were sure, until it came: the end of the war, revolution, Communism, the final destruction of our obviously sick society, of the impenetrable liberal Establishment on which nothing could make a dent—some such great external event would bring us salvation and power. Some, indeed, even turned for a while to a living faith, where Augustine turned himself, and millions after him, and where he gained peace, and strength, and integrity of purpose, just as they too hoped to gain strength and purpose, as they watched the City of God—or the City of Moscow, or now the City of Peking—triumph over its foes.

Secondly, men have been coming to believe once more in Original Sin. We are convinced, we are ourselves responsible for the faults of others, and we are suffering for the "inherited corruption of human nature," of our social system and its short-sighted policies. The individualist revolts, for this is a social conception; but we are now all increasingly socially minded. Today it seems a true metaphor to us to say, "All men fell in Adam"—though latterly we have been putting it, "All men fell in Adam Smith." We *are* responsible for the goings-

on in the American South, and the still worse backlash in
Northern suburbs, though we were not ourselves born when
the seeds of that bitter harvest were planted. But we have
acquiesced in the guilty fruits: we did nothing about it. We
are responsible for World War II, for the horrors of Dresden
and Hiroshima; we are responsible for the fruits of our "defense of freedom" in Vietnam. We cannot hope to keep our
souls clean, even if we flee the world, and become conscientious
objectors—even if we burn our draft cards and resist induction. We are responsible for that demonic force, Nationalism,
and its poisonous fruits in our modern world, from the Near
East to Africa and Vietnam.

The Greek Fathers would say, of course, we cannot help it.
We ourselves did not do it. We are not personally responsible.
But "original sin" means that what we cannot help, and did
not do ourselves, is nevertheless wrong. We *must* help it, we
must do something about it. There is a compelling incentive to
radical transformation in the sense of a common responsibility
—of a common "sin." In his Augustinian emphasis on sin,
Reinhold Niebuhr has been at his best in insisting that it is
not just the sins of the other fellows that are to be condemned
—those sins are only too easy to see. It is our own sins—not
just the sins of the South, but the sins of complacent Northern
liberals, of our boasted Liberal Establishment. It is not just the
sins of the Kremlin, or of Peking, or of Cairo, or of Johannes-
burg, but the sins of America, of American policy—or lack of
policy—of the Pentagon and the C.I.A. and the Department
of State, that weigh, and should weigh, upon our souls.

Thirdly, our return to the spirit of Augustine has been
hastened by the popularity of Freudian psychology, that has
made dark inner conflicts seem quite normal to us. This is so,
even though Freud's own mythology is quite as picturesque as
Augustine's. Augustine appears to us today as a fairly typical

specimen of what Freud has made so familiar. He can be said, we realize, to have founded Christianity on Freudian insights. And we see grace as sublimation, concupiscence as the libido, and confession of sins as a Freudian therapy. No wonder the wise priest smiles, and adds a few modern techniques. And our sophisticated theologians, unwilling to be out of touch with the latest fashion, have been seeking wisdom in the neurotic pages of the most Freudian specimen in the long line of Christian theologians, Søren Kierkegaard.

The real trouble, we have come to feel, with Augustinian Christianity, inevitable in his own day, is, first, that because Augustine had no real place for the Incarnation in his thought, he omitted the revelation of God in Jesus; and consequently there is for him no imitation of Christ. Where the Incarnation has been taken as central in the West, that has been due, not to the influence of Augustine, but to some fresh impulse, as in Saint Francis of Assisi, or in the Quakers.

And secondly, Augustine made sin not something primarily social, but rather something sexual. This strikes us moderns as a terrible aberration. For the moral life, the sexual impulse is indeed fundamental; but the particular form sexual relations come to take is really of secondary importance. Like all other human relations, they can be ordered better or worse; and of course sex is not something purely private and individual, as the anarchistic revolutionary is apt to proclaim, but of wide public and social concern. But to make them central in all our moral efforts seems to us moderns preposterous. We are too aware of how differently different cultures have been able to order them with reasonable success. It is especially unfortunate to try to order them in such a way that the effort to conform to some prescribed sexual "morality" has so often resulted in far grosser social immoralities and sins: in so much aggression and hostility and hate. Traditional and conventional Christian ethics, concentrating on sexual conduct, and stemming from Augustine, has unquestionably been an enormous distortion of values. It has strained at a gnat, but it has often been willing to swallow whole flocks of camels. This is perhaps the saddest fact of Christian history; and it certainly deserves no place in our world.

And yet—when we contemplate our modern life, our books, our plays and anti-plays, our magazines and tabloids and movies and TV shows, our psychological theories, to say nothing of our actual shenanigans and goings-on—I wonder, are we really in any position to cast the first stone at Augustine for having made sex his primary moral concern?

Now Augustine was a man converted to Christianity, and hence his whole philosophy, like that of Saint Paul, is a philosophy of conversion. The other great living Christian philosophy, the Thomism of Thomas Aquinas, is that of a man exploring his familiar and natural environment. Christianity could not possibly mean the same thing to two men of such different experience. In the Middle Ages there were in Western Europe no converts. Hence the Augustinian philosophy was then taken, not as a philosophy of salvation and conversion, for that had become an irrelevant problem, but as a philosophy of logical mysticism—actually, as what Augustine had himself been converted from, Neo-Platonism, or Christian Platonism. It became in that period the Christian form that the great Platonic tradition took in the West, the Western form of the tradition of Neo-Platonism. It lasted as such until the Christian humanism and naturalism of the Aristotelian Schoolmen became dominant. Then men began to be converted back to Augustine again—the heretics, the Pre-Reformers, and the Reformers. The great nineteenth-century Romantic Christian philosophies, of Schleiermacher, Hegel,

Schelling, Kierkegaard, and Ritschl, came from men converted from Augustinian philosophy, in its Lutheran version,
to other views: to modern humanism, to Romantic *Weltschmerz*, to humanitarianism and social reform, to collec-
tivism.

Now, the convert is a man who feels deep needs, and has
found something that satisfies them. That something is naturally so important for him that it overshadows everything else;
it is inevitably set off by a sharp gulf from the rest of the
world. Ontological dualism is thus a natural rendering of the
experience of the convert: there is the precious thing he has
found, and then there is the rest of things. Supernaturalism
is thus a natural fact of experience for the convert, the finder.

Augustine was a man of deep needs, and of very diverse
needs: he felt man's weakness in so many ways. So he tested
many philosophies, looking in each for deliverance and
strength; and he found something in them all.

He was first a Manichaean, because he felt so keenly the
moral struggle between good and evil. Manichaeism was in
the fourth century the successor to second-century Gnosticism,
or a new Persian form of that Gnosticism. Both were expres-
sions of the strong ethical dualism of the Persian tradition.
This answered Augustine's need for moral and ethical salvation. And though he later broke consciously with the Manichaean tenets, he did retain their main conviction, of the eternal
gulf between good and evil, of the unalterable election of
the few to salvation and of the many to damnation. This is
Augustine's strand of *ethical dualism*.

Augustine was, secondly, a Neo-Platonist, because he felt
the need of the mystic to sink into the Supreme Being or
Reality. He was an intellectual and logical mystic, who saw
all knowledge as dependent on and leading to Supreme Truth,
Sapientia or Wisdom. He was an ethical mystic, who saw all

good as dependent upon and leading to absolute Goodness, the Supreme Being and Good. Anything independent of that Goodness is less real, and therefore relatively evil. Allegiance to Supreme Being is the only good, the only life. Turning away from it is evil, death and nothingness. Augustine's conception of knowledge, and his metaphysics of Being and Good, remained fundamentally Neo-Platonic. This is Augustine's strand of logical mysticism and his *metaphysical monism* —it is what the Middle Ages emphasized as the Augustinian philosophy.

Finally, Augustine was a skeptic: man by himself is nothing, he possesses no truth, no power, no life. He is only a mass of needs. Hence Augustine felt the appeal of authority, as the skeptic always does. This is the strand of Augustine the Churchman, the Sacramentarian, the Bishop—the very "Roman" Catholic.

Augustine was an empiricist, who tested all things in the fire of his own burning experience; he was a rationalist, with a Platonic view of truth all naked and alone; and he was an institutionalist, who fully realized the human craving for social authority. Augustine's final philosophy embodied answers to all these diverse experiences, and responded to all these needs. Hence it is a weaving together, with marvelous subtlety, of strains that are logically quite independent, and which in most men appear as psychologically incompatible. What was so clear in Augustine's own living experience has rarely come to other men with equal force. Thus Augustine's theory of knowledge, his Christian Platonism, and his theory of grace, his Pauline doctrine of salvation, have seldom appealed with deep conviction to the same men. Those seeking above all salvation and deliverance have felt the power of the latter: Augustine's theory of grace and salvation was the very breath of life to the Reformers, and to their many late medieval predecessors.

But such men remained blind to Augustine's Platonic vision of truth. The earlier Middle Ages felt no such need of deliverance and salvation: that came as the natural operation of the unquestioned Church. What they wanted was his vision of certain knowledge, and they found it in *their* Augustine, simple, clear, and certain as God Himself. So Augustine's Neo-Platonic vision of truth and Being became one of the three main streams of medieval thought.[2]

In saying this, it is not meant that there are necessarily inconsistencies in the thought of Augustine. But the connections are to be found in his rich and manifold experience, not in any unified dialectical system. Augustine did manage to formulate a philosophy that succeeded in making all his experience intelligible. In controversy, indeed, he was pushed further off from Platonism to a more dualistic, and even Manichaean and Oriental or Persian attitude. At the end he seems near Muhammad.[3]

Latin Christianity in the West has hence always been a precarious thing. For men feeling only one of the needs Augustine felt so abundantly have singled it out, and have pushed the others into the background. Yet they are all human needs. Men have normally come to Augustine in search of one or another of the various ways of salvation he so bountifully offers. The very logical independence of these ways of deliverance from each other has made it possible to select from his riches that particular vehicle of salvation that would satisfy one's own craving.

Augustine is the most interesting of the Church Fathers, because he is so rich and varied, because he draws on so mani-

[2] See my *Career of Philosophy in Modern Times*, Vol. I, *From the Middle Ages to the Enlightenment* (New York, 1962), Bk. I, ch. 3, "The Three Medieval Philosophical Traditions," pp. 23-43.

[3] See Augustine's writings in the anti-Pelagian controversy, which greatly influenced Calvin.

fold an experience. Hence he has served as the apostle of very divergent groups. He was the great inspiration of the early Protestants, who took his experience of moral struggle and of immediate contact with God, with little need of any mediator: he was the source of nearly all the heresies during the Middle Ages. Yet the Catholics still vigorously acclaim him, and have never been willing to give him up. For he is the great apostle of the organized Church, of institutionalism and authoritarianism. And the mystics of the Middle Ages found in him the great expression of mystical metaphysics and knowledge. For them, both the Church and moral struggle were pushed into the background. And finally, Augustinian Christian Platonism not only dominated the philosophy of the Schoolmen until well into the thirteenth century. Reinforced by mathematics, it became the background of Cartesian rationalism in the seventeenth century, and of all the further developments of that prevailing strand in what we call modern philosophy.

Augustine has been so influential, because he combines the two chief elements in Christianity, or, one is tempted to say, in any inclusive religion: elements always fused yet ultimately unfusable. They are often in contradiction, and always in dialectical tension with each other; yet neither can be given up—power and goodness, transcendence and immanence, personality and pantheism, dualism and monism. Augustine's ethics is dualistic, his metaphysics monistic.

In the development of Augustinian thought, there has often been a tendency for sin and salvation to become central, for power to overshadow goodness, as in Calvin. The monism has again and again been reinforced by fresh waves of Greek naturalism, as in Thomas Aquinas; as, following the decline of Calvinism, in eighteenth-century humanism; and as again in nineteenth-century humanitarianism. Indeed, the history of Christian thought in the West exhibits just such an alternation, between the temper of humanism, as expressed in the Alexandrian Doctors, and the temper of humility, as found in the Latin Fathers and above all in Augustine,[4] between self-reliance and self-abnegation. The recent swing, under Karl Barth and Neo-Orthodoxy, has been towards the dualistic pole. In the 1960s, the pendulum seems to be going back to monism and secularism and humanism once again.

[4] For this interpretation of the history of Christian thinking, see Étienne Gilson, *Les Moralistes Chrétiens: Saint Thomas d'Aquin* (Paris, 1925), especially Introduction.

XV THE AUGUSTINIAN THEORY OF BEING AND KNOWLEDGE

Augustine worked out and stated three great doctrines: a theory of Being and knowledge, a theory of sin and salvation, and a theory of the Church, society, and history.[1] All three

[1] Augustine and the System of Latin Christianity: Texts: Migne, *Patrologia Latina*, 16 vols. 32-47. Many works already published in *Corpus Scriptorum Ecclesiasticorum Latinorum* (Vienna). *Confessions*, W. Watts, tr. (1631), in Loeb (1912).

Translations: Whitney J. Oates, *Basic Writings of St. Augustine*, 2 vols. (New York, 1948), contains *Confessions*, 12 *Treatises, City of God, On the Trinity*. All but the Platonic treatises are to be found in *Nicene and Post-Nicene Fathers*, Series I, Vols. I-VII. *Confessions*, E. B. Pusey, tr. (1838). in Everyman (1907). *Encheiridion* or "Handbook," brief survey of Augustine's philosophy; in Oates. *On Nature and Grace*, for his doctrine of salvation. *The Correction of the Donatists*, for his doctrine of the Church. *The City of God*, tr. also by J. Healey (1610), in Everyman edition. Ernest Barker. *On the Trinity*, especially Bks. 9-13. *On the Freedom of the Will*, especially Bk. II, contains Augustine's Platonistic metaphysics; tr. in R. McKeon, *Selections from Medieval Philosophers*, Vol. 1 (New York, 1929). *Concerning the Teacher, On the Immortality of the Soul*, tr. G. G. Leckie (New

were elaborated in the light of his intense experience of conversion: at every point Augustine emphasizes the power of the God who had saved him.

Augustine's theory of knowledge and his metaphysics of Being are the basis of "Augustinianism," one of the three great strains of medieval thought. This theory continued through the Renaissance into the seventeenth century, and was then reformulated by Descartes as mathematical rationalism,[2] which has persisted in some form during the whole modern period,

---

York, 1938); in Oates. *Against the Academics*, M. P. Garvey, tr. (Milwaukee, 1942).

Lives: Best short introduction, H. I. Marrou, *Saint Augustin* (Paris, 1958). Lives also by Joseph McCabe (London, 1902), Rebecca West (New York, 1933), J. J. F. Poujoulat (Paris, 1852), L. Bertrand (Paris, 1913; rev., 1945). F. Loofs in *New Schaff-Herzog Encyclopedia*; B. Warfield in *Hastings Encyclopedia*; E. Portalié in *Catholic Encyclopedia*. T. R. Glover, *Life and Letters in the 4th Century* (Cambridge, 1901), pp. 194-215. G. Bonner, *St. Augustine—Life and Controversies*, 2 vols. (Philadelphia, 1963). Peter Brown, *Augustine of Hippo* (Berkeley, 1967).

Augustine's Philosophy, as distinguished from his theological views: Ueberweg-Geyer, Vol. II. Best account: É. Gilson, *Introduction a l'Étude de Saint Augustin* (Paris, 1929; Eng. tr. (New York, 1960). Fullest Catholic study: E. Portalié, in Vacant, *Dictionnaire de Théologie* (Paris, 1908ff.); separate Eng. tr. (Chicago, 1960). Protestant studies in A. C. McGiffert, *History of Christian Thought*, Vol. II, Bk. III; H. B. Workman, *Christian Thought to the Reformation* (New York, 1911); Adolf von Harnack, *History of Dogma,* German version (Freiburg, 1886-90; 6th ed., 1922); Eng. tr. (Boston, 1894-99). Jules Martin, *Saint Augustin* (Paris, 1900; 2d ed., 1923). C. Boyer, *Christianisme et Néoplatonisme dans la Formation de Saint Augustin* (Paris, 1920), good outline of early dialogues. P. Alfaric, *L'Évolution Intellectuelle de Saint Augustin:* Vol. I, *Du Manichéisme au Néoplatonisme* (Paris, 1918). H. I. Marrou, *Saint Augustin et la Fin de la Culture Classique* (Paris, 1938), completed by his *Retractatio* (Paris, 1949).

Social Thought: J. N. Figgis, *Political Aspects of Augustine's City of God* (London, 1921). Herbert A. Deane, *Political and Social Ideas of St. Augustine* (New York, 1963).

[2] See my *Career of Philosophy in Modern Times*, Vol. I, *From the Middle Ages to the Enlightenment* (New York, 1962), Bk. I, ch. 3, pp. 23-43; Bk. III, chs. 1-4, pp. 363-433.

and is flourishing as one of the vigorous philosophies of today. This has been one of the greatest scientific philosophies in Western thought. Ironically enough, it was first formulated by Augustine in terms of theological symbols. This is proof, if any be required in our day and generation, that theological language is able to express a profoundly human and scientific philosophy. The Augustinian doctrine of knowledge and Being is beautiful; there is in it no trace of the harsh dualism of Augustine's doctrine of sin and salvation. It is Greek and Platonic: it expresses his Neo-Platonism, not his Manichaeism. It is the form in which the great tradition of Platonism was transmitted to the West, the West's direct heritage of Christian Platonism—what modern scholars consider a form of "Neo"-Platonism.

For this doctrine, the object of knowledge is the soul and God. Augustine asks, *"Nihilne plus?"* and answers, *"Nihil omnino"* (Nothing more? Nothing whatever). God is for it identified with what Plotinos calls *Nous,* and what the Christian Platonists of Alexandria called the *Logos,* the intelligible realm of Platonic Ideas. We reach this God by turning "within the soul," by a careful examination and analysis of the fact of knowledge, as that knowledge is found present in the soul. Mathematics is taken as the great illustration of a knowledge that is unquestionably valid.

Man is a rational being, and the natural end of such a being is to know, to know the highest truth, which Augustine calls *Sapientia,* "Wisdom," and identifies with the Logos, or God Himself. The first step in Augustine's analysis is to refute the skepticism in which he had wandered for so long, to prove that man has the capacity to know the truth, that men can attain certain knowledge. Augustine's argument runs: Even when man is doubting that he can know the truth, he cannot doubt that he is doubting. *"Si enim fallor, sum"* (For if I am mistaken, I am). That is, there is "thinking," indubitably; and there is a "thinker." And in knowing he is a thinker, man possesses at least one certain truth. This suggests that the later Cartesian doubt is really an Augustinian doubt—though Descartes denied he had ever read Augustine's argument.

Augustine next undertakes an acute and subtle analysis of the fact of knowledge. He brings remarkable psychological penetration to bear on establishing his own distinctive version of the Platonistic theory of knowledge, which was the form in which the philosophy of Platonism was inherited by medieval and seventeenth-century Europe.

The most certain thing about man is that man thinks: he is a thinker, he is a rational soul governing and using a mortal and earthly body. Man is an *animus*. The highest part of this soul and of man is the *mens*, mind. Mind contains both *ratio, dianoia*, discursive reason or ratiocination, and *intelligentia*, or *intellectus, nous*, direct intellectual vision. By self-examination, we find three levels of knowledge in the soul: sense; the inner sense that perceives both sensation and itself; and a reason, *ratio*, which judges sensations, and pronounces, e.g., "That is a tree." Reason knows sense, the inner sense, and itself. This reason possesses *scientia*, "science," or the understanding of temporal things.

All such knowledge, including *scientia* or the understanding of temporal things, depends upon sensations. But sensations, though they cannot occur without the action of corporeal things on the bodily sense-organs, are not the mere imprint of things upon a purely passive mind. Augustine has a much subtler, and, to our modern way of thinking, psychologically much more accurate conception of experience, than the mechanical views of the Atomists, or the logical and biological view of Aristotle. Augustine, in fact, broke with the Greek "spectator theory" of sense experience (the term comes from

William James), in which sensing is a mere passive opening our eyes and seeing. For the mind is never passive but is essentially active, even in sensing, which is an *action* of the mind, in response to a passion of the bodily sense-organ. Sensing is an *act of attention* directed toward a bodily change: it is something internal to the mind, not something received from without. We perceive, to be sure, only bodily things; but perception is not itself a bodily process. It is indeed stimulated by a bodily organ, when that organ is acted upon from without; but sensing is itself essentially not bodily. It is an *action* of the mind on itself and within itself.

All the more is the mind active, when we turn from sensible to rational knowledge, in which the mind draws its ideas, not from without, but from within. Take teaching, for example. Does the teacher ever really teach ideas to others? Think how rarely the ideas the pupil gets are those the teacher intends! Augustine has plenty of ammunition for the modern semanticist. And even when communication is successful, the pupil is really learning, not from the master without, but from the "Master within." The pupil asks, e.g., "What is a sarabella?" The teacher replies, "A sarabella is a kind of turban." But the pupil understands this answer only if he already knows what a "turban" is, and what "kind" means: he must know the words and terms employed. The teacher can thus never teach any idea not already in the minds of his pupils, or whose elements are not already there. We can thus never learn from without: "learning is *like remembering*." This is Augustine's version of the slave-boy of the *Meno*. Signs and suggestions from without, in the words of the teacher, or in things, call forth ideas from within the mind, from the truth somehow already there.

But this truth is not there actually before the suggestion occurs. Teachers are of some use after all; though if they

merely transmitted their own personal ideas, they would hardly
be. What they do is to make us see a *common truth,* common
to all rational minds. Augustine rejects innate ideas, the literal
"reminiscence" of the Platonists. Rather, learning is like remembering *without* previous knowledge. The theory of the
Platonists breaks down over the fact that there is no such
remembering of sensed things: we must have sense experience
of them.

Truth is not literally remembered, nor can truth be produced by the human mind. How could a temporal and
changing mind ever produce eternal truth? No, the truth of
mathematics, for instance, is not an invention, it is not a
making, but it is rather a discovery, a finding—of a truth
common to teacher and pupil alike, indeed, common to all
rational minds. This discovery or finding of truth is a learning
from an intelligible Teacher or Master within the soul. It is,
Augustine calls it, a kind of "memory of the present," a kind
of recognition.

The human *intellectus* or *nous* is the highest level to be
found in men. There is only one level of Being higher in the
universe, this "Truth" or "Master Within," the intelligible
realm, or realm of Ideas, the realm of eternal and immutable
Truth. This realm of Truth is the *Sapientia,* the "Wisdom,"
the *Logos* or Word that is God himself. Augustine thus
identifies God with the realm of Ideas of the Platonic tradition. This is what Thomas Aquinas calls "that Truth which
is the origin of all truth." It is what modern philosophical
realists like Meinong have called the realm of logical and
mathematical "subsistence." Mathematics, the relations of number and figure, supply the clearest illustration of eternal truth.
But, as in Plato himself, mathematics is ultimately important
as leading the mind on to the "relations of perfection," or of
the ends of things—of eternal moral truths.

Augustine has thus managed to effect a complete harmony between religion and science, between the aspiration of the saint and the knowledge of the thinker. He did it for the Platonic science of the ancient world, just as Albert and Thomas did it for the Aristotelian science of the thirteenth century, and as Spinoza did it for the Cartesian science of the seventeenth century, by identifying the objects of the two inquiries. Though often tried since, this enterprise of identification of the objects of science with those of religion has never again been really successful—*pace* Hegel. This was the form in which was handed down the Greek conviction, that that which is most clearly understood, and is most intelligible, is divine—is *theios*. God is that which science most completely knows, not that which forever eludes scientific determination.

Naturally, therefore, for Augustine there is no need of proving the existence of God. For God is that rational structure of the universe which alone makes any proof possible. Every time we demonstrate anything, we are inevitably illustrating the existence of God: when we prove, e.g., that two plus two equals four. For God is the structure of all proof and demonstration, the structure of truth itself. It is just this structure, this intelligible order, that is divine, that is God. It is hence necessary only to analyze any truth to find God implied in its truth, to find the way to Him, its intelligible source.

Human reason is changing and fallible: the Divine Reason, Truth, is unchanging, eternal, and certain. And it is a common possession of all men. It is ever present in their minds as a standard for judging all human truths. At times Augustine holds, man's intellect is able to see the Divine Truth or Wisdom directly: it can participate in the Divine Mind, and thus become itself eternal, in the fashion of the *nous* of Plato. At times, that is, Augustine appears to be what is technically called an "ontologist," like Malebranche, for example, the great seventeenth-century Augustinian, for whom men see all truth "in God." More often, however, he holds that the God who is Truth is the "source" of human truth, the *Archē* of the intelligible realm, the principle of all intelligibility. This is a typically Neo-Platonic, hierarchical notion: God is one step above the realm in which the human mind participates. God is the "Light" of the intelligible world, that Light in which we see light: *"In Lumine Tuo videbimus Lumen."* God is the "Teacher" in the soul, the "Master Within." Augustine prefers metaphors: human truth is the "image" of the Truth that is God, the "image" in man's soul, the "seal," the "imprint," the "signature."

Knowledge is thus ultimately a divine illumination. God, the Light of the soul, is not the object seen, but the Agent making men see his image, and causing the "seminal reasons" in the human mind to sprout (Augustine adopts the Stoic notion and term). God is a logical structure, itself transcendent, working in the human mind—the structure of *Verstand,* of understanding, Kant[3] was to say in his Augustinianism. Just so, in the more individualistic and humanistic philosophy of Thomas Aquinas, it is the human "active intellect," conceived as a part of the individual soul, that "makes us know." The functions of the divine illumination for Augustine, and of the active intellect for Thomas, differ, however, because the two thinkers have very different conceptions of the soul, and hence of cognitive experience.[4]

What the divine illumination does for Augustine is not to

[3] It is easy to see why the Germans tend to regard Augustine as a *Vorkantianer.*

[4] For Thomas, the active intellect first "abstracts" intelligible forms from the sense images by which they have been brought into the soul from the outside world: it "abstracts" concepts or universals from particulars. Secondly, it then "actualizes" them in the passive intellect. For Augustine, the divine illumination does not need to "abstract" anything, for ideas are already in the soul; and they are there as universal, not as embedded in particulars. Hence there is no need to "actualize" them.

present ideas to the mind, to convey facts; it is rather to make us see the truth of the ideas there, to behold their certainty. The Augustinian theory of knowledge is thus a theory of truth and of judgment, not, like Thomas', a theory of the way universal concepts are formed. It is a theory of logic, not a theory of psychology. What we see in the Divine Light is the truth of our ideas, not their content; it furnishes a standard of judging, not a supply of information. This standard comes from outside man: it is ultimately not the rationality of man, but the intelligibility of the universe. Man by his own power is unable to judge the validity of his ideas. The human mind thus needs the Divine Light to decide what ideas are true, just as the human will needs the Divine Grace to choose what is good.

Augustine himself is not too clear. He prefers metaphors: God, the divine *Sapientia,* is one level higher than the truths the intellect perceives, which are a reflection of that *Sapientia.* But whether the Wisdom in the soul is God, the Logos, immediately present, or is directly dependent on Him, in either case God is inescapably there, the basic fact in all human knowing. The divine illumination of the human intellect is like the influence of Divine Grace on the human will: both are the immediate working of God in the soul. Without the presence of God thus working in men, no knowledge or righteousness would be possible for them. There is a complete parallel between the operation of the human intellect and that of the human will: in both cases, all their power comes from God.

There is, to be sure, one important difference. Illumination is a "natural revelation" bestowed on all men alike—all men can learn geometry. But grace is supernatural, and is reserved for the elect. And the God who so freely gives intellectual illumination to all seems curiously different from the God who so thriftily, parsimoniously, and economically bestows grace on the few.

These Augustinian notions of divine illumination, the reason and truth in men's souls directly accessible to human reason, the logical realism, the turning for knowledge not to the world but within, became the source and inspiration of all the mystical doctrines of the Middle Ages, and developed ultimately into the successful rival, in the seventeenth century, of Aristotelian scholasticism. They form also the background of modern exact science, which emerged in the Middle Ages in extremely close dependence on the Augustinian philosophy, which found in the seventeenth century its first great interpretation in Cartesianism, a philosophy almost purely Augustinian in character; and which achieved its most successful synthesis in Spinoza, through an insistence on certain essential parts of Augustinian thought. It can plausibly be argued that mathematical physics today, interpreted not as the sophisticated philosopher of science but as the average physicist interprets it, as the truth about the world, is in its essential outlines a restatement of Augustine's metaphysics and theory of knowledge.

Moreover, Augustine's insistence that we must begin with self-examination, with the structure of knowledge and its implications, as we find it in the mind, became, when Descartes turned to it, the starting-point of the main current of modern philosophy. In this sense, Augustine can well be called the first "modern" philosopher. Modern philosophy has ever since started where Augustine started, with the fact of knowledge, not where Aristotle started, with the world of things. It has sought always to get from ideas to things, not from things to ideas.

In science we call this the use of hypothesis, and reckon it the chief glory of the scientific enterprise. In philosophy we call it the "critical" philosophy, which embraces both idealism and empiricism. And the whole great stream of modern philosophy, the philosophy of experience, in Descartes, through Kant and the Germans, down to Whitehead and Russell, Cassirer and Husserl, to say nothing of Kierkegaard and Heidegger and Jaspers, is a further development of the Augustinian philosophy. Augustinianism is clearly the great tradition. It has been extended, criticized, and reconstructed, but never overthrown by any rival. It is the tradition in which even the empirical philosophies have their roots, through Ockham and Hobbes, Locke and Hume and Mill, down to the logical empiricists. Indeed, just that element in John Dewey which the Aristotelian finds most uncongenial is due ultimately to Augustine, and the tremendous hold of his thought.

XVI THE AUGUSTINIAN DOCTRINE OF SIN AND SALVATION

Augustine's doctrine of knowledge shows how the intellect finds itself and God; his doctrine of sin and salvation, how the will finds its true self and God. Augustine is convinced, it is the same God, the same *fruitio Dei,* the enjoyment of the supreme Good of intellect and will, that is *beatitudo,* blessedness.

Both doctrines of Augustine reflect and express his intense personal experience of seeking and conversion. Intellectually, he was converted to Neo-Platonism; morally, to the way of deliverance of Paul. Hence in his doctrine of salvation two quite different philosophies are fused. The economy of salvation is treated in the terms of Paul; the intellectual problems involved in understanding it, in terms of the Platonic philosophy. Thus through his treatment there runs an all-permeating double aspect.

Augustine's whole theory is rooted in the facts of his own moral experience. Man's estate, the human condition, is that man is a sinner. He dimly sees better things, what he ought to do; but he finds he cannot do it. Hence he needs, first, the clear knowledge of good and evil; and he needs, secondly, the power to direct his will toward the Good. His will is wholly aimed toward the only life, life in the supreme Reality, and only in that life can it rest content. But man finds himself cut off from that life, and cut off from the only right, which is following the law of Love. Man is thus doomed to death: he suffers from the *non posse non mori,* the inability not to die; and man is doomed to sin, he suffers from the *non posse non peccare,* the inability not to sin. His great needs are to possess the *posse non mori* and the *posse non peccare,* the power not to die and the power not to sin.

Augustine thus sees man under a double aspect: as living only in so far as he lives in God, and yet cut off from God; and as a distinct person, an individual will, bound to obey the commands of a sovereign God and yet quite unable to obey them.

The God whom man so sorely needs to live, and to live rightly, must therefore also have a double aspect, both metaphysical and ethical, reflecting both Platonic and Manichaean ideas. God is the only Being, the only Reality, the only source of life and good: this is His Neo-Platonic aspect. Hence, from this point of view, evil is *privatio boni,* privation of good, deficency of Reality, nothingness, death, non-Being. This is the negative aspect of evil. But God is at the same time a personal sovereign, a Holy Will, a power commanding righteousness. From this point of view, evil is sin, guilt of will, disobedience to God's commands. This is the positive aspect of evil. Thus

God is at once metaphysical Good and ethical Holiness, the only Reality and the all-controlling Will, immanent Substance and transcendent Personality, Neo-Platonic and Manichaean, Greek and Roman.

How render this experience of man's estate intelligible? This is the philosophic question. Augustine gives two quite different kinds of answer: through the history of mankind, and through Platonic philosophy.

The answer furnished by man's history is an explanation, not in terms of the timeless principles of Greek philosophic thought, but in terms of the dramatic historical myth of Jewish and Christian cosmogony. This is a typical myth of origin, explaining the character of the protagonist of history, man, through his manner of generation.

The Christian Epic Augustine sets forth is a picturesque, poetic, and wise mythology, as mythologies go: it is a dramatic version, a symbolic rendering of human nature. It makes God's power superior to his goodness, and imputes to God a rather damnable character. But the Nature that has created man *is,* by all the evidence, more powerful than it is good. And if we yield to the deep-seated human tendency to conceive it in the moral terms appropriate to human life, if we commit the pathetic fallacy, as religions do, and are yet at the same time honest enough to discount rumor and stick to evidence, we must, in all sincerity, assign to it a morally damnable character.

God created the angels, endowing them with free will. Some, alas, chose evil, and fell; and to remedy this defection of his creatures, and to recruit the depleted Heavenly ranks, God created the world as the scene of a new effort. He created man, with his will determined in Adam to the Good. But also, for the sake of probation, lest there occur a second rebellion of the disloyal in Heaven, man was endowed with the power to choose evil as well as good: God gave man the *posse peccare,* the power to sin.

But Adam, whose only life lay in God, deliberately, through pride and self-confidence, disobeyed God: he turned away from the supreme Good and turned to himself. His turning away, his disobedience, his sin, and guilt, lay in directing himself toward a lesser good, himself, rather than toward the Highest, God, the source of all his being and good. Adam's sin, pride, independence, self-sufficiency, expressed itself in ignorance, and in concupiscence or lust. Hence it propagated itself, and appears now in man as concupiscence and self-reliance, devotion to temporal goods, rather than to the Highest. Hence Adam and all his descendants lost life, the *posse non mori;* they lost God, the "second death"; and they lost the power not to sin, the *posse non peccare.* This is why men today find themselves in bondage to death and to sin.

Augustine was not content with this dramatic myth of the origin of sin and of man's present estate alone. He undertook a searching philosophical analysis, an investigation of the nature of evil, in Neo-Platonic terms. God is the supreme Good, the supreme Being, which are of course for the Platonist identical. But everything else in the universe has necessarily lesser Good and lesser Being. There is a great hierarchy of Good and Being stretching down through all the grades of Being, to sheer non-Being at the bottom, nothing at all, pure evil. Everything has been created by God *ex nihilo,* out of "nothing"; and all that is made out of "nothingness" must participate in both Being and Non-Being, in both good and evil. It has an element of imperfection, and is not eternal, but is subject to mutability and corruption. In so far as things "are," as they have Being, they are good; in so far as they "are not," and are imperfect, and not what they should be, they are evil.

Evil is thus a privation of Being, and of Good: it is a lack, a failure, a falling short, an imperfection. Evil is from this approach not something positive: it is essentially negative. It is the absence of Being, ultimately, nothing at all. Hence evil can reside only in what by nature, as being at all, is good. Evil is sinking lower in the scale of Being than a thing rightfully belongs, it is not realizing that thing's potentialities. The evil of the will, sin, lies in not choosing the best; though what the will does choose, in being at all, is to that extent good.

Hence God did not create evil: for evil, being nothing at all, cannot be created. Yet in any creation evil is inevitable, for what is created must be less perfect than its creator, and must hence be relatively evil: and being created *ex nihilo,* is necessarily mutable and corruptible.

Since God could not create a world without this element of imperfection and corruptibility, why did He create anything at all? Because every thing that "is," in being at all, is good; and the whole hierarchy and order of the universe is a beautiful spectacle. There is a certain perfection even in ceaseless change and corruption. Augustine falls back, as men always have, on an aesthetic theodicy.

Moral evil, sin, is due to man's will, not to God's. But why did God create human wills capable of choosing less than the Highest? Because the free choice of the Highest is itself the highest thing God could create; and such free choice necessarily involves the risk of the will's choosing the less high. This risk and danger is the necessary condition of the highest good conceivable to man, the free choice of beatitude.

Moderns can understand this free choice best when they translate it into social terms. Augustine is saying, freedom and democracy are of supreme importance. They necessarily involve the risk of electing less than the best candidate. But that is far better than *having* to vote for a *Politburo.*

But why did man choose sin, and fall short of what he might have chosen? Since God is the cause of everything, is not God the cause of Adam's sin? No! Adam's turning away from God was an absence of Being, that is, it was Non-Being, nothing at all. And God is not the cause of nothing. No intelligible cause is needed to explain a "lack," a "nothing." Augustine is here saved by his Neo-Platonism. This was a resource denied to Calvin, for instance.[1]

Yet men can find God again—some men. This is based on Augustine's own experience of receiving salvation through grace as a source of power. This experience was and is a fact, however we try to make it intelligible in terms of our psychologies. Salvation through grace is widespread, and true. The power of "grace" does bring life and the freedom to follow the good. Since Augustine's God is the only source of life, and the all-controlling Will, salvation must come wholly from Him; it cannot be due to man's exertions at any point. Hence Augustine holds to absolute predestination. Grace is a substance that transforms man's human nature, literally "recreating" it, creating it a second time, after it has been corrupted, giving it back the Being it had lost.

Grace is, for Augustine, first, a 'free gift" to those on whom God chooses to bestow it. God's choice is based on no human condition or effort on man's part; it is entirely undeserved. It is not given as the reward for any merit or righteousness in man, but is, on the contrary, the cause and necessary condition of all human merit. Secondly, grace is "prevenient": the beginning of the process must come from God, not from man

[1] To ascend for the moment from the ridiculous to the sublime, the author is clearly the cause of all the truth the reader is here learning, but he is not the cause of the truth the reader might be learning but is not, of his failure to learn all he might. That is the reader's insufficiency, his own Non-Being.

himself, even the desire to pray for God's grace. And thirdly, grace is "irresistible": no man will or can resist it, if he be truly of the elect.

God sends this saving grace only to some men: God chooses some men to salvation, but most to damnation. Why? God could give saving grace to all men, and then none would be damned. But He does not. The number of the elect is determined and foreknown by God, and it is unalterable. Why does God not elect all men? Why does he elect those particular individuals he does? It is due to no merit on their own part. Why does he "harden the hearts of the reprobate"? To this ultimate question, even Augustine has no answer. God's judgment is "inscrutable." It is a mystery. But at least we know it is just; because all men deserve damnation. The elect hence manifest God's mercy, the damned, his justice; and both alike make manifest God's glory.

Such is the logical outcome of conceiving the power of Nature in moral terms. Whatever it may do to God's character, it is at least a recognition of the facts of experience, without that fog of sentimental self-deception with which many liberal Christians infect their judgment. On any conceivable theory of "salvation," however that process be taken, it remains bitterly true, that "many are called but few are chosen." We honor Darwin for revealing this principle as the law of all life. And the gifts of natural endowment or economic privilege bestowed on children at birth are surely not the reward of merit but the cause. "Damnation," in any sense that Nature can be said to inflict it, is eternal. For Augustine, the eternal punishment of the damned, for those personally blameless, like the noble pagans who lived before Christ, or like unbaptized infants who have died, was never to see or enjoy God. As Dante puts their plight, "Without hope we live in desire."

Grace releases man from past guilt, from sin, both original and personally acquired; it transforms human nature, and strengthens man's will. Grace "justifies" man: it works gradually to make him "just." It bestows, first, faith, which is manifested in love to God, and this love is expressed in good works toward other men. Grace finally brings salvation, which comes as *beatitudo,* the *visio Dei* and the *fruitio Dei* in eternal life. Salvation is the *non posse mori* and the *non posse peccare,* the inability to die and to sin, which is perfect Freedom. And all comes from God: predestination, election, vocation, justification, love, good works, glorification—there is no human merit or desert at any point. Augustine reached this final position in his controversy with Pelagius, who made salvation depend on man's merit and efforts, and it is set forth in the treatises *On Nature and Grace.*

Yet Augustine insists, predestination and the absolute mastery of God are not incompatible with the free choice of man's will, the *liberum arbitrium.* Even after the Fall, man never lost the complete freedom to choose as he wants. Free choice, *liberum arbitrium,* is indeed the very essence of the human will. Of course, God foreknows just what free choices man will make. How are these two positions reconcilable?[2] The will is determined by motives, and it is God who determines the motives that will be presented to the will, and knows what choice the will will freely make. Men are always free to choose the most appealing motive; but God arranges which motives will appeal most strongly.

Hence, though the ability not to sin is preserved after the Fall, an adequate motive or incentive is not: that is provided only by God's grace. So the damned freely choose damnation

[2] I am here following the brilliant analysis of E. Portalié, the standard Catholic treatment, which first appeared in Vacant's *Dictionnaire de Théologie.* Now published separately in Eng. tr. (Chicago, 1960).

in Hell, God knows that they will, and refrains from sending his saving grace. Augustine constantly affirms the possibility of the elect falling, and of the reprobate saving themselves. Yet it is absolutely certain that in fact none ever will: they always *can,* but they will never *want* to.

There is thus for Augustine no conflict between "free will" and determinism. The will operates in a deterministic system of "free" choices; the will acts by freely choosing to follow the best motive. That is, stones and wills are equally "determined." But stones fall by reason of efficient causes, while wills act because of motives or final causes. Stones do not act from final causes, but wills are determined teleologically, not mechanically.

Indeed, for Augustine, perfect freedom is perfect determination, i.e., determination by the highest motive or end, the love of the highest Good. Such freedom is vastly more important, he holds, than the freedom of choice or *liberum arbitrium,* which the will possesses by definition. That is, men are free in the full sense, not just when they are doing what they want to do—they are ultimately always doing that. They are free when they want the Best, and have the power to do it. That comes, for Augustine, only with grace, which though determined and sent by God, adds to the will's freedom of choice the choice of the Best, and its realization, which is genuine freedom.

Freedom, Augustine holds, is the right use of choice, choosing the right things: "The confirmation of the will in the Good through grace." Freedom is the action of a free will orientated toward the Good. Freedom is not merely doing what you want, it is wanting to do what is Best, and being able to do it. Hence "Perfect freedom is perfect obedience to perfect law," and the "law of freedom" is the law of love for the Highest. Christian liberty is "that employment of all things which leads to the enjoyment of God."

This Augustinian conception of freedom as determination or rule by what is rationally best became the classic tradition of freedom in the West. Thomas Aquinas, Spinoza, Rousseau, Kant, Hegel, all followed it. "Rational freedom," or the "freedom of reason," has been at the basis of every anti-individualistic and collectivistic scheme and social program in the Western tradition, down to the Marxian present. For this conception of freedom, it is no sacrifice of freedom, but rather its only realization, to participate in a rationally organized social system; while the freedom to do anything one wants, the freedom of *laissez faire,* and of its advocates today, appears as a temporary and provincial aberration, and is thoroughly anti-Christian.

Augustine's theory of grace and salvation seemed novel and startling in the West itself, though it had forerunners, notably St. Ambrose. But it proved congenial to Roman authoritarianism. However, it is well to be clear that it was never accepted by the Church: Augustine's doctrine never became the official Catholic position. But it was taken over by Luther and Calvin, and pushed further by the Calvinists, who left out Augustine's Platonism. Hence they had no conception of evil and sin as negative, as privation of Being. So they were forced to make God the creator of evil as well as of good, and to teach a "double predestination": of the reprobate to Hell, as well as of the elect to Heaven. This emphasis was pushed by Théodore Béza to "supralapsarianism": God first decreed election and damnation, and then decreed the Fall, to justify his earlier decision. The doctrine was never pushed further: it could not be.

The Church, after condemning both Pelagianism and Augustine at the Council of Arles in 472, and the Council of Lyons in 475, adopted the compromise known as semi-Pelagianism: transforming grace is needed for salvation, but it is neither prevenient nor irresistible; men must ask for it and freely accept it. Finally, at the Second Council of Orange, in 529, the Church adopted its permanent medieval position, known as semi-Augustinianism. Man needs grace, prevenient grace. This is given in baptism. Man then has the power freely to accept or reject the "concomitant grace" necessary for salvation. The process of salvation was thus transformed from the living experience it was for Augustine into an automatic system.

XVII THE AUGUSTINIAN DOCTRINE OF THE CHURCH

So far, Augustine's thought is complete without Christ or the Church. He has no really thought-out theory of the work of Christ. Christ was really not very important for his scheme of salvation. His own experience was of immediate contact with God: he had no real need for any mediator.[1] Hence Augustine does not furnish any very consistent doctrine of Christ: he merely repeats a rather confused variety of traditional phrases and piety. Yet Augustine did have an intense need for a social institution. And so for him the major work of Christ is to serve as head of the Church, and to gain for the Church the all-important grace.

For Augustine, the Church is the sole ark of salvation, and the supreme authority. This view is in some conflict with his predestinarianism, which is based on his own experience of

---

[1] I am here following A. C. McGiffert, as set forth in his *History of Christian Thought* (New York, 1932), Vol. II; and in his magnificent lectures on one of his especial enthusiasms.

personal contact with God. Hence for most men there have always been really two Augustines: the independent mystic or Protestant, and the sacramentarian and Catholic. No man, he holds, can be sure of salvation through partaking of the sacraments alone: there is no "perseverance of the saints." But there can be no grace received without those sacraments.

Augustine was building his doctrine on the principles of Cyprian (d.258), the great earlier Latin theorist of the Church; and he is defining his own position in opposition to that of the Donatists, a schismatic sect in the Western Church, with a rather Protestant view of the sacraments. The Donatists claimed absolute freedom from all civil obligations: they regarded the State as so profane as to be positively diabolical.[2] In Augustine's day Donatism was already a hundred years old; and it was well established. In Hippo there were more Donatists than Catholics.

Augustine worked out his own doctrine of the Church on the suggestions of Cyprian, of the Church as a Divine institution and authority. For Cyprian, the Church is, first, the sole ark of salvation. Without the Church, no salvation is possible. "Only the man who has Mother Church can have the Father God." Secondly, the Church alone possesses Apostolic truth— heretics are lost—and saving grace—schismatics are lost. Only Bishops have these essentials. Hence "The Bishop is the Church": he is the only true priest, though he may delegate his authority to his subordinates. Grace thus descends from the Apostles to the Bishops to presbyters. Thirdly, the unity of the Church consists in the unity of the Bishops in council: this is the ultimate authority. Hence Church councils are not mere political expedients, they have a dogmatic basis.

Cyprian's theory was accepted by the Western Church, and

[2] Some will think the Donatists had hold of something in this view.

received further development. It was accepted completely by the Donatists: Cyprian himself took the Donatist position. Hence it was very hard to prove that the Donatists were mistaken.

In opposing the Donatists, Augustine himself built on the views of Optatus, Bishop of Milevis, who had attempted to refute the schismatic Donatists. Optatus held, first, that the Church is holy. Its sanctity depends not on the character of the priest administering the sacraments, but on the fact of the possession of the sacraments themselves, objectively—a position denied by the Donatists. Secondly, the Church is "catholic"—that is, it is universal, and hence cannot be identified with a sect. Thirdly, the Church is apostolic: it has a legal right to the episcopal succession.

These views Augustine pushed farther. On Augustine's theory, the true Church is first, one: the bonds of unity are faith (heretics are excluded) and love (schismatics are excluded). Secondly, the Church is holy, in possessing the sacraments. The character of the administrant is irrelevant, for the sacraments work *ex opere operato,* not *ex opere operantis.* They work, that is, of themselves; they work by magic, or supernaturally.

The sanctity of the Church proved to be the difficult point. For Augustine, its sanctity lies in its possession of the means of sanctification, the sacraments. Augustine was the first to draw the distinction between the "visible" and the "invisible" Church. For most later Protestants, the visible Church was the communion of the elect. For Augustine, the visible Church was the inclusive Church, comprehending also the human Roman Catholic institution. But for Augustine, both are true Churches. For the visible Church—the Pope's bailiwick—though clearly itself wicked, has nonetheless got the sacraments by rightful legal inheritance. Also, the visible Church—the *Civitas Dei,* or "City of God"—is the "Kingdom of God" referred to by Jesus. Hence all the scriptural passages about the "Kingdom of God" or the "Kingdom of Heaven" can be applied to the Catholic Church.[3]

Thirdly, the Church is apostolic: in its doctrines, and in the episcopal succession. Augustine's arguments are here directed against the Manichaeans. The Church has the writings, the doctrine, the descent from and the communion of the Apostles. The infallibility of the Church is based on its apostolicity. But Augustine fails to indicate any particular organ of infallibility within the Church; he left this problem to be solved.

Fourthly, the Church is the supreme authority. It is intellectually infallible. But Augustine was realistic enough to hold that even Bishops in council can err. The Church is morally supreme: it can declare the will of God, and bind and loose in penance. And it is politically infallible and supreme, for it is the earthly embodiment of the City of God.

Finally, on the problem Augustine left unresolved, Vincent of Lerins, in his *Commonitorium* of 434, determined the seat of intellectual authority in the Church, a doctrine which held throughout the Middle Ages. That authority is the Bible, as interpreted by tradition. The canons of tradition are: the decisions of the ecumenical Councils, and the writings of those Fathers in good standing, as judged by their universal reception, their antiquity, and their acceptance—*Quod ubique, semper, et ab omnibus receptum est.*

Thereafter, further Church councils to determine the faith were unnecessary. Only one such was held during the Middle Ages, the Fourth Lateran Council, in 1215, called to deal with the heresies verging on pantheism of Amalric of Béné and David of Dinant.

---

[3] Catholics have hence been apt to identify their human Church with the "Kingdom of God"; while Protestants have always been able to see a certain distinction; or, at most, have said, the "Kingdom of God" is the "Church Invisible."

XVIII THE AUGUSTINIAN DOCTRINE OF THE CITY OF GOD

CHRISTIAN SOCIETY AND THE PHILOSOPHY OF HISTORY

Augustine assumes that man is by nature social: he is no individualist. Because he was a skeptic, he was a strong institutionalist: he sorely needed the support of human ties. Hence human society in general, and Christian society in particular, form for him a central interest. His social philosophy remained one of his most influential doctrines. And since he took so seriously the dramatic historical myths of the Christian tradition, it led him to undertake a full-scale examination of the historical relations between human society and Christian society.

Now, the common love of men for the same object naturally generates a society, a *civitas* or "city," which is the dwelling place of a "people." A people is "an association of a multitude of reasonable beings, bound together by will and by the common possession of what they love." There are for men two great objects of love: temporal things, the pomp and power of this world; and eternal things, God. Hence man finds himself with two collective loves; and there are thus two peoples, two cities, the Earthly City and the City of God. These two cities are symbolized as Babylon and Jerusalem, those who love themselves to the contempt of God, and those who love God to the contempt of themselves. Both cities aim at peace, for the supreme aim of every society is peace. The condition of social peace is a functional order, in which each man serves the common end in his own way.

There are thus two social organizations, the one bent to

power, and the enjoyment of material things in peace; and though it is a false order and a false peace, in being order and peace at all, it is good. It is imperfect compared to the other city, which is bent to the enjoyment of the eternal peace of God. In one sense, there is only a single city, the City of God, for the Earthly City is no true "city," and has no true order or peace. But Augustine's realism compels him to insist, the Earthly City is a fact. The Roman people is an imperfect people, but it is still a people.

What relations obtain between the two cities? History records continual conflict between them, and Revelation shows that terrestrial history is only an episode in the conflict between the two cities since the creation of time. The Heavenly City began with the creation of the angels, the Earthly City with the fall of Lucifer. On earth, Cain built the first human city, while Abel, a member of the City of God, built none, but lived as a pilgrim toward eternal life.

On this basis, Augustine works out a philosophy of history, dealing with the meaning of "history" for all mankind. It is a view of the history of the entire human race, taken as a unity, which is to be understood as the progressive establishment of the Heavenly City in the midst of the Earthly City. In this Augustinian philosophy of history, the temporal and historical sense of the Hebrews is woven into the timeless concepts of Platonic thought.

These two cities are not distinct. The members of the City of God dwell on earth among the members of the Earthly City; but they are not of them. What is the *modus vivendi* between the two cities? Take property, for instance, which is created and established by the laws of the Earthly City. In the Heavenly City, he who misuses property, who treats it as a private possession and as an end in itself, has no right to it, only he who uses it for God. In another life, perfect justice will reign. But in the Earthly City, legal and civil rights must prevail. But the member of the City of God, the Christian, must use his property in the light of the divine end.

In general, the Earthly City has its own laws and its own order, and to attempt to apply there the perfect order of the Heavenly City is impossible, and would lead only to disaster. But the order of the Earthly City is a relative and an imperfect order. It aims, not at subordinating the temporal to the eternal, but at social peace. And it cannot achieve even that. Just so, Rome is far from a perfect order, but it must do what it can. Even if the whole system crashes, as when the Goths took Rome in 410 A.D.—the immediate occasion for writing the *City of God*—the members of the Heavenly City will continue to follow the laws of the Earthly City, as the necessary condition for attaining the City of God.

How, then, should the Christian act towards the State? "Render unto Caesar what is due unto Caesar, for the love of God; and refuse to render unto Caesar what is not due unto Caesar, for the love of God." Augustine is not interested in any particular form of earthly government: temporal laws change and are corrupted. In theory, the radical difference in ends between the two cities assures their complete independence: the one aims at social peace, the other at eternal salvation.

But Augustine was driven more and more to call on the civil authorities to support the religious. The Earthly City is not identical with the State, but is the society of the damned; while all the elect are members of the State also. The City of God is not identical with the Church, but is the communion of the saints, of all the elect, past, present, and future; while the Church clearly contains many of the damned. *"Perplexae quippe sunt istae duae Civitates in hoc saeculo, donec Ultimo Judicio dirimantur"*—the two Cities are mystic bodies. Hence

Augustine never stated the medieval theory of the supremacy of the Church over the State; but that theory was an inevitable development of his views.

This development was aided by Augustine's reluctant recourse to the State against heretics and schismatics. At first, with the Manichaeans, he refused to do more than argue, lest they become *"fictos Catholicos,"* pretended Catholics. But when he could not convince the Donatists, who themselves were using force freely, and when he saw the Imperial laws driving them into the Church, Augustine changed his mind—like many who start as "liberals." He wrote *Compelle entrare,* "Compel them to enter in." The penalty of the State will make men think, and will lead them to see the error of their ways: it will be educational. And it will be persuasion "for the good of the soul." Persecution is justified when it is the good who are using force to stamp out the bad.

Once enjoin the State to punish heresy, that is, to take orders from the Church in religious matters, the limits become very elastic; the outcome is apt to be religious tyranny. The medieval ecclesiastical theocracy did not scruple to identify the Church with the City of God and the Kingdom of Heaven.

But this was far from the only influence of Augustine's social theory. His contention, that human society, organizing itself without God, is unjust and immoral, and is to be bent to the services of a more perfect order and a more perfect justice, became the source of all the radical social movements of the Middle Ages and the Reformation. And the Augustinian philosophy of history, the story of the long struggle of the City of the Saints against the City of the Damned, will hardly sound strange to ears accustomed to hearing—in what is at bottom only another and more secularized version of that philosophy of history—of the long struggle of the "toiling masses" against the "oppressing classes."

XIX EPILOGUE: THE HERITAGE OF ANCIENT PHILOSOPHY

With Augustine, the intellectual development of the ancient world ended, in a completely worked-out and inclusive religious philosophy. Science, except for mathematics, had stopped short two hundred years before. Greek thought, which had discovered all its ideas and concepts several centuries earlier, persisted in Neo-Platonism, a philosophy that was itself growing more and more Oriental. Neo-Platonism was now just as irrational, just as much a rationalization of religious faith, as Christianity; and one far more remote from ordinary human experience. It had become a mixture of superstition and of an academic tradition. In Christendom it stopped short in 529 A.D.: the philosophers fled to Persia, driven out of the Empire by Christian fanaticism and intolerance. A thousand years of intellectual life were ended. But there was now no real change. That change had taken place at the death of Aristotle, at the death of Greece, when men had turned from the search for truth to the pursuit of deliverance and salvation. The way to be followed for another thousand years was now perfected.

But Greek thought was still left as a deposit: it was always there, as a mass of material to be used. But there was no further development. There was no further evolution, no continuity. When Greek thought was discovered again, it was by alien peoples, with an alien social experience and alien values and ideals. Greek ideas were never again fostered by men to whom *theōria,* the dramatic and aesthetic contemplation and vision of human life in a natural world, was an ultimate intellectual goal. That vision was never again beheld by *Nous*. *Nous*, though "deathless and eternal," was now dead! even though, as Hegel would put it, *Nous* was rather *"überwunden und aufgehoben."* That episode in the human journey was now over.

Greek ideas have furnished the basic materials for the intellectual life of the peoples of Western Europe: they have provided forms for expressing their moral ideals and values and organizing their social experience. They gave the concepts and methods that determined the channels of natural science, from the twelfth century to the nineteenth. Not until the present century can our science claim to have freed itself from dependence upon Greek ideas. And even today Greek ideas persist, as the classic tradition in Western thought, and remain strong wherever the new science is not yet taken seriously as an intellectual force, but only as a physical force—where its full impact has not yet been felt. But Greek thought was never in any real sense revived. It was never again shared. It was looted, pillaged, used for novel and alien purposes, to build wholly original intellectual structures.

Greek thought left three main strands, which had varying fortunes and appeals, and which were absorbed in a very different order from that in which they had been worked out by the Greeks. There was first Platonism, as a religious philosophy, and as an intellectual vision of a "realm" of logic and mathematics. This was the Platonism that is but one of the strains in the Platonic dialogues themselves: since the nineteenth-century scholars have distinguished it from the wealth of strains in the dialogues by calling it Neo-Platonism. Secondly, there was Aristotelianism, as a humanistic philosophy, and as a method of making the natural world intelligible.

And thirdly, there was Alexandrian mathematical and mechanical science, as a mystic faith and as a technique of analysis and control.

Only the last strand enjoyed any real continuity; and even with it there were periods of cessation, of forgetting and remembering. When resumed, this science was taken up once more pretty much where it had been left off: in the thirteenth and fourteenth centuries, and again from the seventeenth century to our own. Today, the mystic faith that originally attended it is gone, the technique has been transformed. But Platonism and Aristotelianism were never resumed. They were used—or rather, misused and manhandled.

The Arabs were the first to stumble on Greek thought: they were the first impressive heirs of Hellenistic civilization, the first of the looters. The Western Europeans found this Greek heritage in Islam, the highest culture in the world they knew, when they had themselves become civilized enough to appreciate it. They used it to express their own experience, to rationalize their own religious tradition, and to organize their society. The intellectual ancestry of Western Europe is thus to be traced, not in the backward peoples of the Christian Dark Ages, but in cultured Islam.

Three great peoples in succession discovered Greek thought: the Arabs, the Jews, and the Latin Western Europeans. Each used it at first to rationalize an Oriental religion; each went through the same intellectual stages, each saw the genesis of the same problems and the formation of the same intellectual parties around them, each reached the same philosophical conclusions and solutions. Out of the Christian appropriation of Greek thought developed modern Western culture. The Christians were the last of the three peoples to come upon Greek thought; hence they could build on the work of the earlier Arabs and Jews. They also possessed the richest structure of their own, the least stable and hence the most progressive, for one of the three major strands of Greek thought was already embodied in the Christian set of ideas, and in the synthesis of Augustine—Platonism—though it was hardly appreciated until it was found also in the culture of the Arabs and of the Jews.

INDEX

Academy, Platonic, 18, 20-22; and Skepticism, 62, 63; Middle Academy, 64, New Academy, 65, Old Academy, 68

Adams, Henry, 10

Adler, Felix, viii

Aenesidemus of Cnossus, 69

Aeons of Gnostics, 159

Aition, "cause," 88

Alexander of Aphrodisias, 20

Alexander the Great, 1, 3-5, 12

Alexandria, 1, 4, 13, 14

Alexandrian science, 14-18, 234

Allen, A. G. V., vii

Ambrose, 143, 144, 165, 167, 185

Anaxarchus, 61, 62

Andronikos of Rhodes, 20

Antigonids, 4

Antioch, 4, 15; school of, 165, 172, 175

Antiochus of Ascalon, 68, 69, 85, 86

Apollonios of Perga, 17

Apollonios of Tyana, 112

Apologists, Christian, 143, 162

Apostles' Creed, 159, 161

Arabs, 2n; and Greek thought, 234

Archimedes, 15, 17

Aristarchus of Samathrace, 16, 17

Aristobulus, 112

Aristotle, 1, 19, 20; way of life, 49; Aristotelianism, 233, 234

Arius of Alexandria, 165, 172, 175; Arianism, 174

Arkesilaos, 21, 62-64

Arnobius, 168, 184

Athanasius, 165, 172, 174, 175, 182

Athenian Age, intellectual traits, 7, 8

Athens, 1, 4, 13, 14, 18, 19

Atomism of Epicurus, 34-36; its problems, 34-35

Augustine, viii, 3, 4, 6, 165-67, 172, 188; realism of, 193, 194; morality as sexual, 198, 199; as convert, 199, 200, 205; his needs, 200; as Manichaean, 200, 202; as Neo-Platonist and mystic, 200, 201; as Skeptic, 201; diversity in thought of, 201-3

—— *theory of Being and knowledge:* 206-13; doubt, 206, 207; Wisdom, 206, 209; sensing, 207, 208; activity of mind, 207, 208; Truth, 209, 210; God, 210; Divine illumination, 211, 212; and grace, 212-14

—— *doctrine of sin and salvation:* 214-24; man's estate, 215; explanation through history, 216, 217; evil, 215; neo-Platonic theory of, 217-19; salvation, 219-21; theory of grace, 219-21; history of, 223, 224

—— *theory of Church,* 224-27

—— *philosophy of history,* 229

—— *social philosophy,* 228

—— *influence of:* 188, 189; twentieth-century abandonment, 189, 190; source of power, 191, 192; and liberal religion, 192-94; Augustinian Platonism, 199, 203, 205, 206,

—— influence of (Cont.)
213; and modern philosophy, 213, 214; social radicalism, 231

Bacon, Francis, 33
Balfour, A. J., 77
Barth, Karl, 175n, 204
Benevolence in Stoicism, 53, 54
Béza, Théodore, 223
Boyle, Robert, 56
Buchanan, Scott, 2
Bush, Wendell T., ix

Callimachus, 16
Calvin, John, 223
Cappodocian Fathers, 182
Carlyle, Thomas, on Seneca, 98
Carneades, 37, 60, 65-68; critique of reason, 65, 66; of theology, 66, 67; mission to Rome, 81
Cellini, Benvenuto, 28
Celsus, 16, 106
Chalcedon, Council of, 143, 165
Christ: divinity of, 171; work of, in Augustine, 224
Christian Epic, 190, 191, 216, 217
Christianity, "triumph" of, 2; a synthesis, 137-39; not a corruption, 137, 138; stages of synthesis, 142-44; as a mystery cult, 151, 152, 154, 156, 161; as a universalized Judaism, 162-64
Christian Platonism in Alexandria, 165, 166, 168, 169, 176, 181, 182, 185
Christians, liberal, viii
Christian thought, history of, vii
Chrysippus, 41
Cicero, 19-23, 53, 66, 68, 79; De Officiis, 84, 87-96; ethics, 84, 92; education, 88; translations from Greek, 88, 89; and science, 89;

wisdom, 89; nature, 90; mundus, 90; dialogues, 92; religion, 93
——social philosophy, 93-96; sociability, 89, 93, 94; commonwealth, 94; law, 94; law of nature, 94, 95; as standard, 95, 96; equality of men, 94, 95
City of God, 228, 229; relation to Earthly City, 229, 230
Claudius, 7
Cleanthes, 41
Clement of Alexandria, 159, 165, 172, 174, 176-78; on faith, 177; on agapē, 177, 178; on Logos, 178; on man's freedom, 178
Clitomachus of Carthage, 65
Conservatism and Skepticism, 77, 78
Corinth, 4, 18
Corruption vs. freedom of man, 172
Cosmopolitanism in Stoics, 53
Criterion of Truth, Skeptic critique of, 65, 66, 75
Cyprian, 144, 165, 225, 226

Democritus, 25, 35, 36; in Pyrrho, 61, 62
Dewey, John, 122
Didaskeleion, 15
Diocletian, 6
Diogenes Laertios, 27
Diophantos, 17
Divinity of Christ, 139, 141
Donatists, 225, 226
Dualism, moral, vs. philosophical monism, 117; in Augustine, 203
Duty, in Stoicism, 51

Eclecticism and syncretism, 57
Ectasy, in Plotinos, 124, 125, 134
Edelstein, Ludwig, 10
Emanation, in Plotinos, 132, 133
Epictetus, 41, 50, 54
Epicureans, naturalism of, 22; anti-

scientific, 23; uneducated, 23; quietism of, 25, 26; dogmatism of, 33; in Rome, 81, 82

Epicurus, 21, 22, 26, 27, 29-31, 52, 55; gospel of salvation, 24-26, 30, 31; and control of nature, 32, 33; letters to Pythocles and Herodotus, 34; and gods, 36

Epochē, in Stoicism, 43

Equality of men in Stoicism, 53

Erasistratus, 16

Eratosthenes, 16, 17

Ethics, Christian, viii

Euclid, 17

Experimental attitude, 59, 60, 66, 140

Failure of nerve, 100

Fideism and Skepticism, 60, 69, 70, 77-80; in Rome, 78, 79; in Christianity, 79, 80

Freedom, human, in Augustine, 221-23

Freudian psychology in Augustine, 197-99

Friendship, in Epicurus, 52; in Seneca, 52

Galen, 16

Garden, Epicurean, 18, 21

Glanvill, Joseph, 56

Gnostics, 143, 158-61; limitations of, 160, 161; and Christian Platonism, 161; and Manichaeism, 200

Grasping impressions, in Stoicism, 42, 43

Greek Church, ancient, 167, 184

Greek empires, Hellenistic, 3

Greek Fathers and sin, 197

Greek period, 1

Hadrian, 7, 19

Hedonism, varieties of, 28-30

Hellenism, revival of under Antonines, 3, 5, 6

Hellenistic age, 1; three stages, 3; intellectual traits, 8

Heraclitus, 46, 47

Heritage of Greek thought, 1, 2; of ancient philosophy, 232-34

Hermotimus of Lucian, 73-75

Hero of Alexandria, 17

Hierophilus, 16

Higher criticism of Scriptures, 145, 146

Hipparchus, 16, 17

History vs. reason, in Greek and Hebrew thought, 130, 131

Honestum, 91, 92, 97

Hoon, Paul W., x

Hosius of Alexandria, 182

Humanism and humility, 204

Hume, David, 65-67, 77

Hypatia, 17

Ignatius of Antioch, 158

Impersonality of Plotinos' terms, 126, 127

Incarnation, 174; in Augustine, 198

"Indifference" in Skepticism, 58, 78

Individualism, Hellenistic, 10-12

Irenaeus, vii, 164, 165; and Catholicism, 164, 165

Islam, 136

Jesus, message of, 145, 148; and sin, 149, 150; way of life, 149; limitations, 150, 151

Jewish colony in Alexandria, 14, 15, 18-22; 112, 113

John the Evangelist, 156, 157; love and faith, 157, 158

Judaism, 5, 135, 136, 143

Justinian, 3, 6, 19

Justin Martyr, 162, 163

Kant, Immanuel, viii

Kathēkon, "duty," 88, 89

Kemble, Edwin C., x
Kingdom of God, 148, 226, 227
Kristeller, Paul Oskar, x

Labor, dignity of, in Stoicism, 52, 53
Lactantius, 185
Latin Church, ancient, 166, 167, 184;
    and authority, 185; legal thinking,
    185; and Stoicism, 185; and Pla-
    tonism, 185
Lessing, G. E., 135
Library of Alexandria, 14
Life, *Psychē*, in Plotinos, 127, 128;
    life of man, 128
Literary science of Alexandria, 15, 16
Logos: Stoic, 43-45; as fire, 46, 47;
    in Philo of Alexandria, 113, 115,
    116; in Plotinos, 128; in Fourth
    Gospel, 157; in Justin Martyr, 163
"Lord" of mystery cults, 104
Love, *agapē*, 149, 157
Lucian of Samosata, 70-75; critique
    of religious myths, 70, 71; of Ori-
    ental faiths, 70, 71; of philosophers,
    71-75, 80
Lucretius, 21, 27, 29-31, 82, 83, 91;
    anticlericalism, 31, 32
Lyceum, Aristotelian, 18-20
Lycopolis, 121

Macedonia, 4
Marathon, 1, 2
Marcion, 159, 161
Marcus Aurelius, 7, 9, 19, 29, 30, 54,
    55; human situation, 48, 49; way
    of deliverance, 48; ethic of consola-
    tion, 50; and religious rites, 82
Marx, Karl, 37
Materialism as ethical philosophy, 36,
    37; Stoic, 45, 46
Maximus of Tyre, 106, 107
McCrea, Nelson Glenn, viii

McGiffert, Arthur Cushman, vii
McKeon, Richard P., viii
"Meaning," *lekton*, in Stoicism, 44,
    45
Mercy, in Seneca, 96, 99
Messiah, belief in, 147
Metrodorus, 27, 33
Minucius Felix, 79
Mithraism, 104-6
Monism in Augustine, 203
Montaigne, 77
Montanists, 188
Murray, Sir Gilbert, 8, 100
Museum of Alexandria, 15, 18
Mystery cults, 104

Nationalisms, Oriental, 5
Natural history at Alexandria, 16
Nature: follow, in Stoicism, 50, 51;
    Physis, in Plotinos, 127, 128
Nazareth, Prophet of, vii
Neo-Pythagoreanism, 111, 112, 116;
    number daimons, 111
Newtonian science, 183
Nicaea, Council of, vii, 143, 165, 166,
    179, 180, 182
Niebuhr, Reinhold, 157n, 197
Nietzsche, F., 135
Novelty of Hellenistic Period, 1, 2
Numa, religion of, 101
Numenios, 116

One, the, *to Hen*, in Plotinos, 129-31
Optatus of Milevis, 226
Orientalization of Greek culture, 2, 3,
    7, 12
Origen, vii, 165, 172, 174, 178-80;
    God as Spirit, 179; Logos, 179,
    180; faith and philosophy, 179-81;
    the Fall and universalism, 180;
    Holy Spirit, 180
Ousia, 89

Panaetius, 83, 84

Pappus, 17

Pascal, B., 191

Pater, Walter, 29; *Marius the Epicurean,* 73-75, 101

Paul, 143, 152-56; and Seneca, 99;
and mystery cults, 105; and Jesus,
147, 156; his experience, 152, 153;
his interpretation of it, 153, 154-56,
166; faith, 155; 181

Pauline version of Christianity, vii

Pelagianism, 221, 223

Peloponnesian War, 3

Pergamum, 1, 4, 15

Persecution in Augustine, 231

Person of Christ, 165, 166, 174

Persuasive, the, in Carneades, 67, 68

Pessimism, contemporary, 194; and
Augustinian temper, 196

Philip of Macedon, 3

Philodemos, 28, 33

Philo Judaeus of Alexandria, 15,
113-16, 182; and the Law, 113;
and Christian theology, 113, 116;
method, 113, 114; God and negative theology, 114; God's powers,
115; Logos, 115, 116; salvation,
116; two lives for man, 116

Philo of Larissa, 68

Philostratus, 112

Platonism, 119, 120, 233, 235; Middle Platonism, 106, 107

Plotinos, ix; as rationalist, 117-19,
121, 124; and Spinoza, 119-21,
126, 132, 135; scale of values, 119;
new emphasis, 119; and mysticism,
119, 121, 124, 125; and Oriental
dualism, 121; and traditionalism,
122; and practical action, 125, 134

Plutarch, 106-10; immortality, 103;
institutionalist, 108, 109; no fate,
109; gods and daimons, 110; and
superstition, 110

Porch, Stoic, 18, 21

Porphyry, 125

Poseidonios of Rhodes, 15, 46, 47, 84,
85

Preconceptions, Stoic, 43, 44

Proclus, 121

Protagoras in Pyrrho, 62

Ptolemies, 4

Ptolemy, Claudius, 16, 17

Ptolemy Philadelphus, 14, 17

Ptolemy Soter, 14

Pyrrho, 61, 62

Randall, Francis B., x

Reasonable, the, in Arkesilaos, 64

Reason in Stoic ethics, 51

Religion: Egyptian under Ptolemies,
102; pagan, revival of in Rome,
100-2

Religions, salvation, 102-4

Rhodes, 1, 4, 15

Righteousness of Hebrew prophets,
149

Romantic Christian philosophies, 199,
200, 203

Rome: conquest of Greece, 5; peace,
6, 7; law and Stoicism, 53; philosophy, 86, 87; culture, 90, 91;
religion, 184, 185

Russell, Bertrand, 37, 122, 126, 133

Salvation, pursuit of, 3, 9, 12; ways
of, 21

Santayana, George, 37, 119

Schmidt, Nathaniel, vii

Scholasticism, 184

Schools, philosophic, 13, 14, 18-22

Science, Hellenistic, 13-18; in Christian synthesis, 140

Scientific method and Skepticism, 60,
67, 76, 77

Seleucids, 4

Semi-Augustinianism, 224

Seneca, 52, 96-99; *Natural Questions,*
97; consolation, 97, 98; foresha-
dowing of faith, 99
Septuagint, 112
Sextus Empiricus, 69
Sin: and salvation by grace, doctrine
of, 165; original, return to, and
Augustinian temper, 196, 197
Skepticism, 21, 54-69, 75-79; varie-
ties of, 58-60
Social control, ethic of, 140
Socrates, 191
Spencer, Herbert, 22, 24, 37
Spinoza, 145
State, duty to, in Augustine, 230, 231
Stoicism in Rome, 82, 83, 86
Stoic system, 41, 42; logic, 42-44;
empiricism, 43, 44; physics, 45-47;
providence, 46, 47; cyclical view
of history, 46; ethics, 48-55; of
consolation, 50; of guidance, 50-52
Strabo, 16
Studium humanitatis ac litterarum,
90, 91
Substances, Platonic, 169; relations
between, God and world, 170;
Logos as substance, 170; Holy
Spirit, 170; relations to Logos, 171
Synoptic gospels and Jesus, 148
Syrcause, 15
Syria, 4

Tarsus, 15
Taylor, Henry Osborn, viii
Technology, lack of, 9, 10
Tertullian, 168, 172, 186-88; and
reason, 187; Stoic materialist, 187;
prescription, 187

Theocritus, 16
Theology, philosophical, 166, 168,
180-83
Theophilus, 163
Theophrastos, 19
Thomas Aquinas, 183, 199, 203;
theory of knowledge, 211, 212
Thought, *Nous,* in Plotinos, 122-24,
127, 128
Tillich, Paul, 157n, 171, 182
Timon of Phlius, 62, 64
Torquatus, *De Finibus,* 23, 24, 26
Transcendence vs. immanence of God,
172
Trinity, vii, 165, 166, 168, 170, 173,
174, 180-83, 185
Tropes, Skeptics', 69

Unification, political, of Greece, 3, 4
Unity of Greek culture, 4

Valentinus, 159, 160; critique of
Hebrew morality, 161
Values: scale of, in Plotinos, 132-34;
lacking in Christian synthesis, 139,
140
Vergil, 86, 87
"Victory" of Christianity, 137
Vincent of Lerins, 144, 227

Wallas, Graham, 9
Whitehead, Alfred North, 182
Wilson, J. Paul, x
Woodbridge, Frederick J. E., viii
Woodbridge, Frederick J., x

Zeno the Stoic, 21, 39-41; his gospel,
40, 41